C O N T E M P O R A R Y ' S

PRE-GED
MATHEMATICS

CONTEMPORARY
BOOKS

TRIBUNE NEW MEDIA/EDUCATION

Photo Credits

Cover photos: Panoramic Images; Interior photos: Tribune File Photos, 10, 44, 108, 148; John L. Wilkes/Phototake, 184; Bill Bachmann/Photographic Resources, 238

Series Developer

The Wheetley Company, Inc.

Published by Contemporary Books, Inc.
Two Prudential Plaza, Chicago, Illinois 60601-6790
Manufactured in the United States of America
International Standard Book Number: 0-8092-3490-4
10 9 8 7 6 5 4

Editorial Director	*Editorial Production Manager*	*Cover Design*
Mark Boone	Norma Underwood	Michael Kelly
Editorial	*Production Editor*	*Interior Design*
Gary von Euer	Thomas D. Scharf	Lucy Lesiak
Sandra Hazel		
Jody Levine	*Electronic Composition*	*Illustrations*
Eunice Hoshizaki	G & S Typesetters, Inc.	The Wheetley Company, Inc.

Contents

To the Student

Congratulations on your decision to use *Pre-GED Mathematics* to strengthen your mathematical and problem-solving skills! The skills you develop by using this book will help you in many ways in the classroom, your daily life, and on the job.

Pre-GED Mathematics presents the important math skills that everyone should have mastered. If you have not previously learned the skills presented in this book as well as you would have liked to, now is your chance. Or, if you would like more practice in order to build your confidence, here is your opportunity. Regardless of your background, you can use this book to learn and practice the mathematical and problem-solving skills that are most important.

Here is an overview of what you will find in this book, along with some tips for using the book.

Mathematics Pre-Test   The Mathematics Pre-Test, found on pages 1–9, will help you decide which skills you need to work on the most. It will give you an overall picture of your current mathematical ability in reference to topics presented in this book. It will direct you to the parts of the book you may want to spend the most time with. Before you start working through the chapters in this book, take the Mathematics Pre-Test that begins on page 1.

Chapter 1: Whole Number Review and Problem Solving   By working through Chapter 1, you will review whole numbers and basic computational skills. More importantly, you will learn and practice problem-solving strategies, mental math strategies, and estimation strategies. These strategies will help you to do much more with numbers than calculate.

Chapter 2: Decimals   In this chapter you will learn and practice all the necessary computational skills with decimals. Many word problems involve money and require calculations with decimal numbers, since our monetary system is based on decimals. This chapter will also prepare you well for working with percents, found in Chapter 5.

Chapter 3: Fractions and Mixed Numbers   This chapter teaches you to add, subtract, multiply, and divide fractions and mixed numbers. And, as with every other chapter in this book, you will have plenty of practice solving word problems. You will need to know how to do fractions for most other areas of mathematics, including ratios and proportions (Chapter 5) and probability (Chapter 6).

Chapter 4: Measurement and Geometry   In this chapter you will learn to use standard metric units of measurement. You will learn the basic definitions of geometry. You will learn how to find perimeter, circumference, area, and volume of basic geometric figures. You will need to understand these ideas completely in order to learn the geometry for GED math.

Chapter 5: Ratios, Proportions, and Percents   This chapter presents plenty of problem-solving practice with ratios, proportions, and percents. You will also see and use the important relationships among fractions, decimals, and percents. By working through this chapter, you will also strengthen your skills with decimal numbers and fractions.

Chapter 6: Data Analysis and Probability   The ideas presented in this chapter are commonly found in daily life but have not traditionally been emphasized in schools, so some of the ideas may be new to you altogether. This chapter includes concepts, such as mean, median, mode, range, bar graphs, line graphs, circle graphs, and probability. Complete Chapter 6 to gain skills and practice in this area. The probability sections will give you another chance to see the relationships among decimals, fractions, and percents.

Chapter 7: Basic Algebra Concepts   This chapter gives a solid introduction to algebra. You will study exponents, square roots, and order of operations. You will solve equations, use formulas, graph points on a coordinate plane, and find the slope of a line.

Pre-GED Practice   At the end of each chapter, a review of key concepts is provided. These reviews include many five-item multiple-choice questions that help you prepare for GED-level study.

Mathematics Post-Test   The Mathematics Post-Test, found on pages 277–289, will help you to see how well you have learned the mathematics and problem-solving skills presented in this book. The Mathematics Post-Test contains 56 five-item multiple-choice problems.

Answer Key   This feature provides answers and steps for solving all the problems. Use the answer key only after you have attempted a problem yourself. If your answer to a problem is incorrect, look at the steps given, and compare them to your own.

Glossary   Throughout the book, key terms that are important for you to know are printed in boldface and italic type and are defined in the glossary at the back of the book.

Good luck with your studies! Keep in mind that mathematics and problem-solving skills are worth learning for many reasons.

Pre-Test

The Mathematics Pre-Test that follows is a guide to using this book. You should take the Pre-Test before you begin working on any of the chapters. The test consists of 56 problems with seven different sections that correspond to the seven chapters in this book.

Read and work each problem as carefully as possible. Check your work. Do not look at the answers until you are finished with the test. If you find that a problem is too difficult, skip it and come back to the problem later. When you have completed the test, check your answers on pages 6–7.

Using the Evaluation Chart on pages 8–9, circle the number of each question that you missed. If you missed many of the problems that correspond to a certain mathematical skill, you will want to pay special attention to that skill as you work through the book.

If you do very well on the Pre-Test, congratulations! You can strengthen and broaden your skills, as well as gain confidence, by working through this book. More practice doing mathematics and solving problems will only help you.

CHAPTER 1: WHOLE NUMBERS AND PROBLEM SOLVING

Directions: Solve each problem.

1. Add: 68,145 + 9,828

2. Subtract: 90,627 − 19,544

3. Multiply: 174 × 28

4. Divide: 8,241 ÷ 3

5. Write as a whole number: three million, two hundred nine thousand, six hundred fifty-one

6. Round to the nearest dollar: $14.49

7. On January 10, 1911, in Rapid City, South Dakota, the temperature dropped from 55°F to 8°F in 15 minutes. How much was this drop in temperature?

8. Mario wants to buy jeans for $29.99 and a sweater for $19.99. Excluding sales tax, can Mario buy both items with a $50 bill?

CHAPTER 2: DECIMALS

Directions: Solve each problem.

9. Which is greater, 0.06 or 0.5?

10. Round 101.6549 to the nearest hundredth.

11. Add: 3.4 + 16.08 + 9.55

12. Subtract: $20 − $4.69

13. Multiply: $16.50 × 4

14. Divide: 1.246 ÷ 0.2

15. Paula has a twenty-dollar bill, three five-dollar bills, six one-dollar bills, five quarters, eight dimes, and four nickels in her purse. Find the value of the money in Paula's purse.

16. Frozen bread dough is priced at $3.39 for 3 loaves. Find the unit price (the price of one loaf).

CHAPTER 3: FRACTIONS AND MIXED NUMBERS

Directions: Solve each problem.

17. Rewrite 9.125 as a mixed number.

18. Rewrite $\frac{3}{5}$ as a decimal.

19. Which is greater, $\frac{3}{4}$ or $\frac{2}{3}$?

20. Add, and reduce to lowest

    terms: $\frac{7}{8} + \frac{3}{8}$

21. Subtract: $\frac{1}{2} - \frac{1}{3}$

22. Subtract: $3\frac{1}{2} - 1\frac{3}{4}$

23. Multiply, and reduce to lowest

    terms: $2\frac{2}{5} \times \frac{1}{4}$

24. Divide, and reduce to lowest

    terms: $\frac{1}{9} \div \frac{1}{3}$

CHAPTER 4: MEASUREMENT AND GEOMETRY

Directions: Solve each problem.

25. How many minutes are there in one day?

26. Change 68 centimeters to millimeters.

27. Is the statement true or false?
"Parallel lines form right angles."

28. Find the perimeter of the rectangle shown in Figure 1.

Figure 1

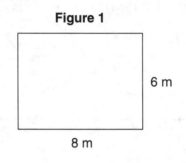

6 m

8 m

29. Find the area of the rectangle shown in Figure 1.

30. Find the circumference of the circle shown in Figure 2. (Use $\pi \approx 3.14$.)

Figure 2

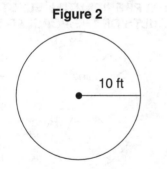

10 ft

31. Find the area of the circle shown in Figure 2. (Use $\pi \approx 3.14$.)

32. Find the volume of a cube whose side is 9 inches.

CHAPTER 5: RATIOS, PROPORTIONS, AND PERCENTS

Directions: Solve each problem.

33. There are 10 women and 15 men at a party. Write the ratio of women to men in lowest terms.

34. Solve the proportion: $\frac{2}{3} = \frac{h}{24}$

35. Change 28% to a decimal and a fraction in lowest terms.

36. Change 0.09 to a percent.

37. Change $\frac{4}{5}$ to a percent.

38. What is 80% of 9,000?

39. What percent of 40 is 8?

40. 25% of what number is 50?

CHAPTER 6: DATA ANALYSIS AND PROBABILITY

Directions: Solve each problem.

Table 1

High Temperatures for a Week

Day	Fahrenheit Temperature
Sunday	72
Monday	80
Tuesday	83
Wednesday	78
Thursday	70
Friday	74
Saturday	75

41. Refer to Table 1. Find the mean (average) high temperature for the week.

42. Refer to Table 1. Find the median high temperature for the week.

43. Refer to Table 1. Find the range of high temperatures for the week.

Figure 3

MEDALS WON BY CANADA, 1994 WINTER OLYMPICS

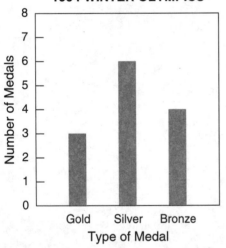

44. Refer to Figure 3. How many medals did Canada win in the 1994 Winter Olympics?

Figure 4

REVENUES FROM WIRELESS TECHNOLOGY
(in billions)

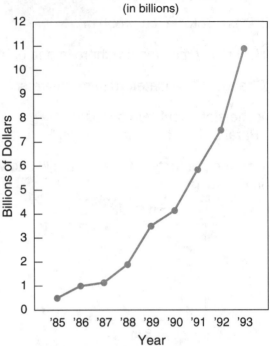

45. Refer to Figure 4. In what year were the revenues from wireless technology almost six billion dollars?

Figure 5

1992 PRESIDENTIAL ELECTION RESULTS OF THE POPULAR VOTE

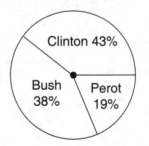

46. Refer to Figure 5. What percent of the popular vote did Clinton not get in the 1992 Presidential election?

47. When you roll two dice, what is the probability of getting doubles?

48. A hat contains 10 names, one of which is yours. A friend's name is drawn first, for first prize. What is the probability your name will be drawn next?

CHAPTER 7: BASIC ALGEBRA CONCEPTS

Directions: Solve each problem.

49. Find the value of $\sqrt{81}$.

50. Find the value of
$8 + 4 \times 6^2 - (3 + 7)$.

51. Solve: $x + 9 = 21$

52. Solve: $a - 8 = 12$

53. Solve: $4n = 120$

54. Solve: $\frac{y}{7} = 5$

55. If you invest $5,000 for a year and earn $400 interest, what is the annual interest rate? (Use the formula $i = prt$.)

Figure 6

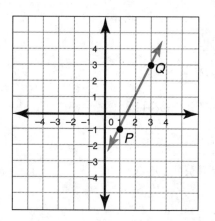

56. Find the slope of the line passing through points P and Q.

ANSWERS ARE ON PAGE 6.

Pre-Test Answer Key

CHAPTER 1

1. 77,973;
$$\begin{array}{r} 68,145 \\ + 9,828 \\ \hline 77,973 \end{array}$$

2. 71,083;
$$\begin{array}{r} 90,627 \\ - 19,544 \\ \hline 71,083 \end{array}$$

3. 4,872;
$$\begin{array}{r} 174 \\ \times\ 28 \\ \hline 1392 \\ 348 \\ \hline 4,872 \end{array}$$

4. 2,747;
$$\begin{array}{r} 2,747 \\ 3\overline{)8,241} \\ \underline{6} \\ 22 \\ \underline{21} \\ 14 \\ \underline{12} \\ 21 \\ \underline{21} \\ 0 \end{array}$$

5. 3,209,651
6. $14
7. 47°F; $55 - 8 = 47$
8. yes; $\$29.99 + \$19.99 \approx \$30 + \$20 = \$50$

CHAPTER 2

9. 0.5
10. 101.65
11. 29.03;
$$\begin{array}{r} 3.4 \\ 16.08 \\ + 9.55 \\ \hline 29.03 \end{array}$$

12. $15.31;
$$\begin{array}{r} \$20.00 \\ - 4.69 \\ \hline \$15.31 \end{array}$$

13. $66;
$$\begin{array}{r} \$16.50 \\ \times\ 4 \\ \hline \$66.00 \end{array}$$

14. 6.23;
$$\begin{array}{r} 6.23 \\ 0.2\overline{)1.246} \end{array}$$

15. $43.25; $20 + 3(5) + 6(1) + 5(.25) + 8(.10) + 4(.05) = 20 + 15 + 6 + 1.25 + .80 + .20 = 43.25$
16. $1.13; $\$3.39 \div 3 = \$1.13$

CHAPTER 3

17. $9\frac{1}{8}$; $9\frac{125}{1000} = 9\frac{1}{8}$

18. 0.6; $3.0 \div 5 = 0.6$

19. $\frac{3}{4}$; $\frac{3}{4} = \frac{9}{12}$; $\frac{2}{3} = \frac{8}{12}$; $\frac{9}{12} > \frac{8}{12}$

20. $1\frac{1}{4}$; $\frac{7}{8} + \frac{3}{8} = \frac{10}{8} = 1\frac{2}{8} = 1\frac{1}{4}$

21. $\frac{1}{6}$; $\frac{1}{2} - \frac{1}{3} = \frac{3}{6} - \frac{2}{6} = \frac{1}{6}$

22. $1\frac{3}{4}$; $3\frac{1}{2} - 1\frac{3}{4} = 3\frac{2}{4} - 1\frac{3}{4} = 2\frac{6}{4} - 1\frac{3}{4} = 1\frac{3}{4}$

23. $\frac{3}{5}$; $2\frac{2}{5} \times \frac{1}{4} = \frac{12}{5} \times \frac{1}{4} = \frac{12}{20} = \frac{3}{5}$

24. $\frac{1}{3}$; $\frac{1}{9} \div \frac{1}{3} = \frac{1}{9} \times \frac{3}{1} = \frac{3}{9} = \frac{1}{3}$

CHAPTER 4

25. **1,440 minutes;** 1 day × 24 hours/day × 60 minutes/hour = 1,440 minutes
26. **680 millimeters;** 68 cm × 10 = 680 mm
27. **False;** Parallel lines do not intersect, while perpendicular lines form right angles.
28. **28 m;** Perimeter = 8 + 6 + 8 + 6 = 28
29. **48 m², or 48 square meters;** Area = 8 × 6 = 48
30. **62.8 ft;** Circumference = $\pi \times 2 \times 10 \approx$ 3.14 × 2 × 10 = 62.8
31. **314 ft², or 314 square feet;** Area = $\pi \times 10 \times 10 \approx$ 3.14 × 10 × 10 = 314
32. **729 in.³, or 729 cubic inches;** Volume = 9 × 9 × 9 = 729

CHAPTER 5

33. **2 to 3, or 2 : 3, or $\frac{2}{3}$;** $\frac{\text{women}}{\text{men}} = \frac{10}{15} = \frac{2}{3}$

34. **16;** 2 × 24 ÷ 3 = 16

35. **0.28, $\frac{7}{25}$;** 28% = 0.28 = $\frac{28}{100} = \frac{7}{25}$

36. **9%**

37. **80%;** $\frac{4}{5} = \frac{4 \times 20}{5 \times 20} = \frac{80}{100} = 80\%$

38. **7,200;** 0.8 × 9,000 = 7,200

39. **20%;** $\frac{8}{40} = \frac{h}{100}$; 8 × 100 ÷ 40 = 20

40. **200;** $\frac{50}{h} = \frac{25}{100}$; 50 × 100 ÷ 25 = 200

CHAPTER 6

41. **76°F;** 72 + 80 + 83 + 78 + 70 + 74 + 75 = 532; 532 ÷ 7 = 76
42. **75°F;** in order: 70, 72, 74, <u>75</u>, 78, 80, 83
43. **13°F;** 83 – 70 = 13
44. **13 medals;** gold medals + silver medals + bronze medals = 3 + 6 + 4 = 13 medals
45. **1991**
46. **57%;** 38% + 19% = 57%

47. **$\frac{1}{6}$;** $\frac{\text{favorable outcomes}}{\text{possible outcomes}} = \frac{6}{36} = \frac{1}{6}$

48. **$\frac{1}{9}$;** $\frac{\text{favorable outcomes}}{\text{possible outcomes}} = \frac{1}{9}$

CHAPTER 7

49. **9;** 9 × 9 = 81, so $\sqrt{81} = 9$
50. **142;**   8 + 4 × 6² – (3 + 7) = 8 + 4 × 36 – 10 = 8 + 144 – 10 = 142

51. **$x = 12$;** $x + 9 = 21$; $x + 9 - 9 = 21 - 9$; $x = 12$

52. **$a = 20$;** $a - 8 = 12$; $a - 8 + 8 = 12 + 8$; $a = 20$

53. **$n = 30$;** $4n = 120$; $\frac{4n}{4} = \frac{120}{4}$; $n = 30$

54. **$y = 35$;** $\frac{y}{7} = 5$; $\frac{y}{7} \times 7 = 5 \times 7$; $y = 35$

55. **8%;** $i = prt$; $400 = 5{,}000 \times r \times 1$; $r = \frac{400}{5000} = 0.08 = 8\%$

56. **slope = 2;** $\frac{\text{vertical change}}{\text{horizontal change}} = \frac{4}{2} = 2$

Pre-Test Evaluation Chart

On the following chart, circle the number of any problem you got wrong. After each problem you will see the name of the section (or sections) where you can find the skills you need to solve the problem.

Problem	Section	Starting Page
1, 2, 3, 4 5 6 7 8	**Pre-Test 1** **Whole Numbers and Problem Solving** The Basic Operations Writing Whole Numbers Estimation Problem-Solving Strategies Multiple-Step Problems	 13 14 32 35 40
9 10 11, 12 13 14 15, 16	**Pre-Test 2** **Decimals** Comparing Decimals Rounding Decimals Adding and Subtracting Decimals Multiplying Decimals Dividing Decimals Solving Problems Involving Decimals	 47 50 53 57 61 64
17 18 19 20 21 22 23 24	**Pre-Test 3** **Fractions and Mixed Numbers** Changing Fractions to Mixed Numbers Changing Fractions to Decimals Comparing and Ordering Fractions Adding Fractions (Like Denominators) Subtracting Fractions (Unlike Denominators) Subtracting Mixed Numbers Multiplying Fractions and Mixed Numbers Dividing Fractions and Mixed Numbers	 70 76 81 84 88 95 98 101
25 26 27 28, 30 29, 31 32	**Pre-Test 4** **Measurement and Geometry** Standard Units Metric Units Geometric Definitions Perimeter and Circumference Area Volume	 109 113 117 123 128 134

Problem	Section	Starting Page
	Pre-Test 5 **Ratios, Proportions, and Percents**	
33	Ratios	149
34	Solving Proportions	158
35, 36, 37	Common Percents, Fractions, and Decimals	166
38	Percent of a Number	168
39, 40	Percent Problems and Proportions	175
	Pre-Test 6 **Data Analysis and Probability**	
41, 42, 43	Mean, Median, Mode, and Range	185
44	Bar Graphs	191
45	Line Graphs	200
46	Circle Graphs	210
47	Probability	219
48	Dependent Probability	227
	Pre-Test 7 **Basic Algebra Concepts**	
49	Exponents and Square Roots	239
50	Arithmetic Expressions	246
51, 52, 53, 54	Variables and Simple Equations	250
55	Formulas and Problem Solving	254
56	Slope of a Line	264

1 Whole Number Review and Problem Solving

PLACE VALUE

The **number system** used today is based on the **digits** 0 through 9 arranged in a particular pattern. The numbers beginning with 0, 1, 2, 3, and so on are the set of **whole numbers**.

The value, or amount, of a digit depends on its position in that number.

WHOLE NUMBER CHART

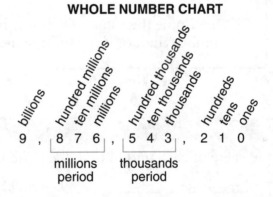

Starting from the ones position, commas are inserted to separate the numbers into groups of three or **periods**.

EXAMPLE 1   Find the value of the 2 in the number 23,476.

STEP 1   Write the digit and insert zeros for each position to the right of the number.

23,476 → 20,000

STEP 2   Determine the value of the 2. Use the chart, if necessary. The 2 is in the ten thousands position. The value of the 2 is 20,000.

EXAMPLE 2   Find the value of the 3 in 23,476.

STEP 1   Think of 23,476 as a 3 followed by three zeros, or 3,000.

STEP 2   The 3 is in the thousands position. The value of the 3 is 3,000.

EXAMPLE 3   What is the value of each digit in the number 98,015?

STEP 1   The 9 is in the ten thousands place. Its value is **9 ten thousands**, which is written 90,000.

STEP 2   The 8 is in the thousands place. The value of the 8 is **8 thousands**, or 8,000.

STEP 3   The 0 is in the hundreds place. Therefore, no hundreds are in the number 98,015.

STEP 4   The 1 is in the tens place. Its value is **1 ten** or 10.

STEP 5   The 5 is in the ones place. Its value is **5 ones** or 5.

Now review Examples 1–3 looking for a general method to find the value of a digit within a number. A summary is written in the box below.

PLACE VALUE SUMMARY

1) Write the digit and insert zeros for each position to the right of the number.

2) Determine the value of the new number by referring to the whole number chart or its position in terms of the periods.

EXERCISE 1

Directions: Write the value of each underlined digit. The first one is done for you.

1. 3<u>7</u>8   *7 tens or 70*   9. 4,8<u>2</u>9,156   _____

2. 1,42<u>9</u>,871,552   _____   10. <u>5</u>,829,003,524   _____

3. 9,26<u>5</u>   _____   11. <u>4</u>,002   _____

4. 697,<u>0</u>38   _____   12. 34,87<u>1</u>   _____

5. 7,<u>3</u>00,561,892   _____   13. 9<u>9</u>0,980   _____

6. 2,<u>8</u>76,913   _____   14. <u>6</u>00   _____

7. 21,<u>3</u>50   _____   15. <u>6</u>0   _____

8. <u>6</u>94,720,581   _____   16. <u>6</u>   _____

ANSWERS ARE ON PAGE 290.

EXERCISE 2

Directions: In each box write the sum of the row and column number.

1.

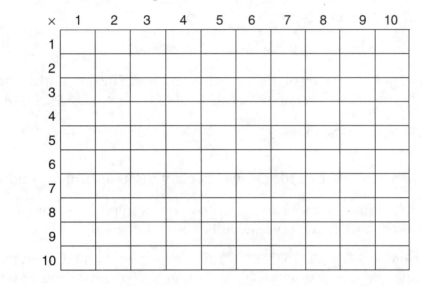

Directions: In each box write the product of the row and column number.

2.

Directions: Add, subtract, multiply, or divide.

3.   598
        + 769

6.   39,907
        −17,488

9.   83,592
        290,033
        + 7,366

12.   123,123
        − 87,654

4.   795
        × 13

7.   5,739
        × 20

10.   283,006
        − 79,658

13. 15,778 ÷ 7

5. 9)73,584

8. 25)$82.75

11.   357
            42
        + 5,028

14.   305
        × 17

ANSWERS ARE ON PAGE 290.

READING AND WRITING WHOLE NUMBERS

To read a whole number, you combine the values of its digits.

EXAMPLE 1   Read the number 28,304.

   STEP 1   Think of what periods are involved in 28,304.

   The 2 and 8 are part of the thousands period. The 3, 0, and 4 (the last three digits) are treated separately and are not considered to be a group.

   STEP 2   The number 28,304 means 28 **thousands**, 3 **hundreds**, 0 **tens**, and 4 **ones**.

   STEP 3   Read the number 28,304 as "twenty-eight thousand, three hundred four."

   To write a number, imagine positions and periods from the whole number chart. Remember the following points:

- Numbers from 21 to 99 are written with a hyphen between the tens and ones value. For example, 67 is written as *sixty-seven* and 83,000 is written as *eighty-three thousand*.

- The word *and* is not read or written as part of a whole number. For example, 5,728 is read as *five thousand, seven hundred twenty-eight*.

- A comma is placed after each period except for the last three digits.

EXAMPLE 2   Write *six million, two hundred ninety-one thousand, fifty* as a whole number.

STEP 1   *Six million* becomes 6,000,000.
Two hundred ninety-one thousand becomes 291,000.
Fifty becomes 50.

STEP 2   Combine the whole number parts.

6,000,000 + 291,000 + 50 = 6,291,050

TIP: Remember that zeros hold a position and should not be ignored. Write a zero for each position that is not expressed in words.

Now review Examples 1 and 2. A method for reading or writing whole numbers is given below.

READING AND WRITING WHOLE NUMBERS SUMMARY

To read whole numbers:

1) Concentrate on each period and the position of all digits.

2) Write whole numbers by thinking of the whole number chart.

3) Insert zeros as needed.

EXERCISE 3

Directions: Fill in the blanks with the correct digits.

1. 97 has _____ tens and _____ ones.

2. 8,502 has _____ thousands, _____ hundreds, _____ tens, and _____ ones.

3. 364 has _____ hundreds, _____ tens, and _____ ones.

4. 316,008 has _____ hundred thousands, _____ ten thousands, _____ thousands, _____ hundreds, _____ tens, and _____ ones.

5. 4,870,921 has _____ millions, _____ hundred thousands, _____ ten thousands, _____ thousands, _____ hundreds, _____ tens, and _____ ones.

6. 7,915,243,600 has _____ billions, _____ hundred millions, _____ ten millions, _____ millions, _____ hundred thousands, _____ ten thousands, _____ thousands, _____ hundreds, _____ tens, and _____ ones.

Directions: Write each of the following number phrases in symbols.

7. Two hundred fourteen _____

8. Sixty-nine thousand, four hundred thirty-six _____

9. Nine million, one hundred ninety thousand, six hundred forty-seven

_____

10. Four billion, eight hundred nine million, one hundred ninety thousand, two

_____

11. Seventy million, nine hundred thirty-three thousand, eighty-eight

_____

12. Fifty thousand, three hundred ten _____

Directions: Write the value of each digit for each number.

13. 532,907 _____

_____

_____

_____

_____

14. 4,605,873 _____

_____

_____

_____

_____

_____

_____

15. 39,901 _____

_____

_____

_____

_____

ANSWERS ARE ON PAGE 291.

ROUNDING

For some problems, an exact answer is not necessary. An **estimate** (an approximate or "about" answer) will be sufficient. It is also wise to estimate an answer first, solve the problem, and then check your solution by comparing the estimate to the exact answer.

One of the most common estimation strategies is **rounding**. Think of a number as being part of a hilly number line like the one below.

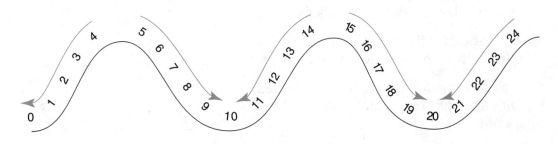

The numbers have a tendency to roll forward or backward to the closest valley. Numbers ending in 0, 1, 2, 3, and 4 will roll back to the nearest 0. Numbers ending in 5, 6, 7, 8, or 9 will roll ahead to the nearest 0.

EXAMPLE   Round each number to the nearest ten or nearest hundred: 53 and 227.

To the nearest ten, 53 rounds backward to 50.

To the nearest hundred, 53 rounds forward to 100.

To the nearest ten, 227 rounds forward to 230.

To the nearest hundred, 227 rounds backward to 200.

EXERCISE 4

Directions: Write each of the following amounts using a dollar sign and decimal point. Then round each amount to the nearest dollar.

1. Four dollars and fifteen cents _____

2. Twenty-eight dollars and sixty cents _____

3. Thirteen dollars and ninety-five cents _____

4. Two dollars and a quarter _____

5. A ten-dollar bill and eight nickels _____

6. A five-dollar bill, six one-dollar bills, four dimes, three nickels, and twelve pennies _____

7. Two twenty-dollar bills, three five-dollar bills, five quarters, a dime, and twelve pennies _____

ANSWERS ARE ON PAGE 291.

HOW TO SOLVE WORD PROBLEMS

Problem solving is an important part of your study of mathematics and everyday life.

The following five-step approach will help you solve problems of all types and will help you organize your thinking.

- STEP 1 After reading (and rereading) the problem carefully, decide what the problem asks you to find. In other words, **understand the question**.

- STEP 2 **Decide what information is needed** to solve the problem. Also determine what information is irrelevant to the question.

- STEP 3 **Choose the most appropriate operation** or operations (addition, subtraction, multiplication, or division) to solve the problem.

- STEP 4 **Solve the problem**. Make sure your solution answers the question asked.

- STEP 5 **Check your answer** by reading the question again to see if your answer makes sense.

EXAMPLE 1 Paul works from 4 P.M. to 7 P.M. Mondays through Fridays. How many hours does he work each week?

STEP 1 Reread the problem to understand the question.

The problem asks you to find the number of hours Paul works each week.

STEP 2 Decide what information is needed.

You know that Paul works three hours (from 4 P.M. to 7 P.M.) five days a week (Monday through Friday). You want to determine how many hours he works each week.

STEP 3 Choose the most appropriate operation.

You want to multiply the number of hours worked each day (3 hours) by the number of days worked each week (5 days).

STEP 4 Solve the problem.

3 hours per day × 5 days per week = 15 hours per week

STEP 5 Check your answer.

If Paul works three hours for five days a week, he works fifteen hours each week. The answer makes sense.

> **TIP:** Sometimes more information is given than you need to solve the problem asked. Be careful to ignore unnecessary information.
>
> Other times information is not provided directly in the problem. Necessary information could be found in a related list, chart, or drawing.

EXAMPLE 2 Marcella bought shampoo for $3.19, hair rinse for $2.38, and a brush for $1.99. She gave the clerk a ten-dollar bill. How much did the items cost altogether?

STEP 1 Understand the question.

The problem asks you to find the total cost of three items.

STEP 2 Find the necessary information.

You must know the cost of the three items: $3.19, $2.38, and $1.99.

STEP 3 Choose an arithmetic operation.

Decide whether you should add, subtract, multiply, or divide. Since you are finding a total, you must add.

STEP 4   Solve the problem. $3.19
                                    2.38
                                  + 1.99
                                  ────────
                                   $7.56

STEP 5   Check your answer.

          If you rounded the prices to the nearest dollar, the sum would be $7
          ($3 + $2 + $2) so an answer of $7.56 seems reasonable.

EXERCISE 5

Directions: For each problem below, circle the letter of each phrase that best describes what you are asked to find. Solve each problem, showing your work.

1. The Bodemer family watches about 25 hours of television each week. About how many hours of television do they watch per month?

   a. hours of television per day;

   b. hours of television per week;

   c. hours of television per month

2. Sixteen men and fourteen women were enrolled in Mr. Judd's class. If two students dropped the course, how many students finished the class?

   a. men in the class;

   b. women in the class;

   c. men and women finishing the class

3. When Julio receives his paycheck, $156.82 has been deducted for federal income tax, $78.14 for state income tax, and $10.83 for city income tax. How much tax is deducted each paycheck?

   a. city and state taxes;

   b. federal, state, and city taxes;

   c. federal and state taxes

4. In June, Mary Jane paid $438 rent, $98.52 for electricity, $152.75 for her car payment, $25 for cable television, and $64.39 for phone calls. If she cancels her cable, estimate her monthly expenses.

    a. rent, electricity, car, cable, and telephone expenses;

    b. rent, electricity, and telephone expenses;

    c. rent, electricity, car, and telephone expenses

Directions: Underline the numbers that are used to solve each problem. Then solve each problem.

5. George directly supervises three women and four men out of the 25 women and 32 men in his department. How many people does George directly supervise?

6. Nadia estimated that 350 people would attend the family reunion. She expected each person to use three napkins. Only 287 people actually attended the reunion. How many napkins did Nadia buy?

7. One Saturday Mrs. Wu stopped at her bank to get $200. Then she spent $52.49 at the grocery store, $23.50 at the dry cleaners, and $15 for gasoline. How much money did she spend that day?

8. When Helen calls her sister, she must remember that the time in California is two hours earlier than her time in Illinois. If she calls her brother in Georgia, the time is an hour later. If it is 6 P.M. in Georgia, what time is it in California?

Directions: Use the five-step problem solving method. Underline the necessary or key information, list the operation you will use, and then show any work you did to solve each problem.

9. Karen pays $425 a month for rent. How much rent does she pay in a year?

10. At a garage sale, Mark sold twelve albums for $1.25 each and a turntable for $10. How much money did he receive from his albums?

11. On October 1, 1992, the gas tax in Alaska was 8 cents per gallon. In Rhode Island, the gas tax was 26 cents per gallon. How much more tax would you pay per gallon to drive in Rhode Island than Alaska?

12. According to the National Association of Realtors, in 1983 the median-priced home was worth $70,300. By 1993, the median price had risen $35,800. What was the value of a median-priced home in 1993?

13. In 1992, the gross average weekly earnings for an employee of an iron and steel foundry was $525.46. If the employee worked 43 hours, find the hourly wage.

14. In 1900, over five million women were in the civilian work force. By 1990, the number of female employees was over 11 times the 1900 figure. Estimate the number of female employees in 1990.

ANSWERS ARE ON PAGE 291.

EXERCISE 6

Directions: Change each quantity to the unit indicated. Remember that to change larger units to smaller units, you multiply. To change smaller units to larger units, you divide.

1. 3 ft = _____ in.   **4.** 2 qt = _____ pt   **7.** 6 min = _____ sec

2. 2 lb = _____ oz   **5.** 3 gal = _____ qt   **8.** 64 oz = _____ lb

3. 72 in. = _____ yd   **6.** 3 T = _____ lb   **9.** 108 in. = _____ ft

Directions: Change each quantity to the unit indicated. Write each remainder as the number of smaller units left over.

10. 32 in. = _____ ft _____ in.   **13.** 9 qt = _____ gal _____ qt

11. 40 oz = _____ lb _____ oz   **14.** 38 ft = _____ yd _____ ft

12. 138 min = _____ hr _____ min   **15.** 100 hr = _____ da _____ hr

Directions: Fill in the blanks with the correct digits.

16. 5,308 has _____ thousands, _____ hundreds, _____ tens, and _____ ones.

17. 9,732,194 has _____ millions, _____ hundred thousands, _____ ten thousands, _____ thousands, _____ hundreds, _____ tens, and _____ ones.

18. 28,536 has _____ ten thousands, _____ thousands, _____ hundreds, _____ tens, and _____ ones.

Directions: Write the value of each underlined digit.

19. 4,329 _____   **21.** 9,007,261 _____

20. 80,746 _____   **22.** 927,441 _____

Directions: Add the following quantities and simplify each sum.

23.　　9 ft　3 in.
　　 + 3 ft 10 in.

27.　　2 hr 50 min
　　 + 5 hr 16 min

31.　　5 dollars 78 cents
　　 + 12 dollars 65 cents

24.　　3 yd 2 ft
　　 + 7 yd 2 ft

28.　　5 qt 1 pt
　　 + 8 qt 1 pt

32.　　3 yrs 7　mos
　　 + 12 yrs 10 mos

25.　　6 gal 3 qt
　　 + 2 gal 1 qt

29.　　13 min 18 sec
　　 + 19 min 45 sec

33.　　32 wks 1 d
　　 + 18 wks 6 d

26.　　2 lb 14 oz
　　 + 9 lb　7 oz

30.　　15 wks 4 d
　　 + 28 wks 6 d

34.　　23 min 48 sec
　　 + 29 min 12 sec

ANSWERS ARE ON PAGE 291.

CLUES IN CHOOSING AN OPERATION

Many times the hardest part about solving a problem is deciding whether to add, subtract, multiply, or divide.

One way to determine which operation will be used is to focus on key words. Noticing these words will often provide a clue to determining the appropriate operation. Some key words or phrases are listed below.

Addition	Subtraction	Multiplication	Division
sum	difference	product	quotient
total	more . . . than	times	split
altogether	less than	twice (× 2)	divided by
combined	minus	when finding several of a given amount	when given amount of many and finding one
increased by	decreased by		
when combining different amounts	farther than	when given part and finding the whole	when sharing, cutting, or splitting
	when comparing one amount to another		

Compare the relevant numbers in the problem to your solution to determine if you chose the correct operation.

Remember that adding the same number repeatedly is the same as multiplication, and subtracting the same number repeatedly is the same as division.

EXAMPLE 1   David rode his bicycle for 17 miles on Saturday. On Sunday he rode it 25 more miles. How many miles did David ride altogether?

STEP 1   Reread the problem to understand the question.

The problem asks you to find the number of miles David rode his bicycle on Saturday and Sunday combined.

STEP 2   Decide what information is needed.

You need to find the total number of miles David biked that weekend.

STEP 3   Choose the most appropriate operation.

The key word *altogether* gives you the clue that you should probably add 17 and 25.

STEP 4   Solve the problem.

17 + 25 = 42

Answer: David rode a total of 42 miles this weekend.

STEP 5   Check your answer.

To check an addition problem, you could subtract one of the numbers in the problem from the answer. In this case, if you subtract 25 from 42, the answer is 17 (the other number in the problem). The answer checks out.

EXAMPLE 2   Lucinda ran 9 miles on Saturday. On Sunday she ran 26 more miles. How many more miles did Lucinda run on Sunday than on Saturday?

STEP 1   Reread the problem to understand the question.

The problem asks you to compare the number of miles Lucinda ran on Saturday and Sunday.

STEP 2   Decide what information is needed.

You need to find how many more miles Lucinda ran on Sunday than she ran on Saturday.

STEP 3   Choose the most appropriate operation.

The key phrase *more than* tells you that you should subtract.

STEP 4   Solve the problem.

26 − 9 = 17

Answer: Lucinda ran 17 more miles on Sunday than she ran on Saturday.

STEP 5   Check your answer.

To check a subtraction problem, you could add one of the numbers in the problem and the answer. In this case, if you add 9 and 17, the answer is 26 (the other number in the problem). The answer checks.

EXERCISE 7

Directions: Underline the key word, phrase, or idea in each problem. Then solve each problem. Show your work.

1. In May, Jackie's rent is increasing $30. If she pays $415 now, how much will her new rent cost a month?

2. Carmella's car weighs 2,975 pounds. When her trailer is empty, it weighs 475 pounds. What is the combined weight of the car and trailer?

3. Guillaume and three of his friends went out to eat. The check came to $26.56. If they split the check equally, how much does each person pay?

4. Abdul usually averages fifteen service calls a day. Marty can make twice as many. How many service calls does Marty average?

5. Garbage service in the town of Kankakee costs $156 a year. What is the monthly charge for garbage collection?

6. Hector borrowed $1,500 in student loans. He has managed to pay back $985. How much does he have left to pay?

7. If unleaded gasoline is advertised for $1.39 per gallon, how much would 12 gallons cost?

8. How many pieces 8 inches long can be cut from a 96-inch board?

9. In 1992, the Chicago O'Hare Airport, the world's busiest airport that year, flew 64,441,087 passengers. The Dallas/Ft. Worth Airport, ranking second that year, flew 51,943,567 passengers. How many more passengers flew out of Chicago O'Hare than Dallas/Ft. Worth?

10. As of 1993, the highest recorded temperature in June was 127° Fahrenheit (F) on June 15, 1896 at Fort Mojave, Arizona. The lowest recorded temperature in June was 2°F on June 13, 1907 in Tamarack, California. Find the difference between the highest and lowest June temperatures.

ANSWERS ARE ON PAGE 291.

EXERCISE 8

Directions: Write each of the following amounts using a dollar sign and decimal point. Then round each amount to the nearest dollar.

1. Nineteen dollars and seventy-eight cents _____

2. Thirty-one dollars and twenty-six cents _____

3. Fifty-three dollars and eighty-two cents _____

4. Forty dollars and twelve cents _____

5. Seventy-four dollars and three quarters _____

6. Thirteen dollars and sixty-one cents _____

7. Ninety-nine dollars and ninety-nine cents _____

8. Sixty-five cents _____

Directions: Fill in each blank with one of the choices within parentheses.

9. A liter holds _____ than a quart. (less, more)

10. A yard is _____ than a meter. (longer, shorter)

11. A pound is _____ than a kilogram. (heavier, lighter)

12. A speed of 50 miles per hour is _____ than a speed of 50 kilometers per hour. (slower, faster)

Directions: Fill in each blank below.

13. The shortest metric unit of length is the _____.

14. The smallest metric unit of weight is the _____ .

15. The smallest metric unit of liquid measure is the _____.

Directions: Circle the larger of each pair of measures.

16. 15 meters *or* 15 yards

17. 8 liters *or* 8 quarts

18. 22 kilograms *or* 22 pounds

19. one-half yard *or* one-half meter

20. 10 liters *or* 10 quarts

21. one-half kilogram *or* one-half pound

ANSWERS ARE ON PAGE 292.

MENTAL MATH STRATEGIES

Sometimes problems are so simple or easy to solve that a solution can be determined without using paper or pencil or other materials such as a calculator. When you find an answer without writing any numbers, you are applying certain *mental math strategies*. Knowing and practicing these strategies will save you time when you need it such as when taking a test having a time limit.

A strategy that you probably already know involves shortcuts for adding or multiplying when zeros are involved. For example, to multiply 48 and 100, first write 48. Since 100 *ends in two zeros*, insert two zeros after the 48.

Think: "48 × 1<u>00</u> = 4,8<u>00</u>."

Another example would be to add 5,000, 14,000, and 6,000 by thinking "5 + 14 + 6 = 25 and then insert three zeros."

EXAMPLE 1 Multiply 60 and 200.

You can do this mentally by multiplying 6 and 2 and then inserting **3 zeros** (**1** zero in 60 + **2** zeros in 200).

$$60 \times 200 = 12,000$$
$$6 \times 2 = 12$$

> **TIP:** Remember that when applying this mental math strategy, the zeros must be *ending* zeros. To add, the numbers must have the same number of ending zeros.

Another strategy is known as ***breaking apart numbers***. You apply this strategy when it is easier to think of a number as the sum of two numbers. For example, to add 73 + 25 mentally think of 73 as 70 + 3 and 25 as 20 + 5. Then you may be able to add 70 + 20 and 3 + 5 to get an answer of 98.

EXAMPLE 2   Jolene bought three cans of fruit juice. If each can cost 58 cents, how much did she spend?

STEP 1   Choose an appropriate operation.

Since you are finding the price of several items when one is given, you will multiply.

STEP 2   Apply the mental math strategy of breaking apart numbers.

Think: "$58 = 50 + 8$ so $50 \times 3 = 150$ and $8 \times 3 = 24$. $150 + 24 = 174$."

STEP 3   Write or state your answer to the problem.

174 cents is more commonly referred to as $1.74.
Jolene spent $1.74 for three cans of juice.

Another mental math strategy is called finding ***compatible numbers***. These numbers can be grouped together to form a number that may be easier to use such as 10, 30, 100, 400, and 1,000.

EXAMPLE 3   Jose has 59 baseball cards, Roseanne has 82 cards, and Aram has 41 cards. How many cards do the three friends have altogether?

STEP 1   Choose an operation.

You want to *add* 59, 82, and 41.

STEP 2   Apply a mental math strategy.

You notice that $59 + 41 = 100$ so think "$\mathbf{59} + 82 + \mathbf{41} = \mathbf{100} + 82 = 182$."

STEP 3   Write or state your answer to the problem.

The three friends have 182 baseball cards altogether.

The last most common strategy is referred to as ***substitution*** (or compensation). To apply this strategy, you change one number so it is easier to perform the necessary operation and then change the other number by its opposite. (The opposite of addition is subtraction and vice versa. The opposite of multiplication is division and vice versa.) For example,

$$57 + 34 = (57 + \mathbf{3}) + (34 - \mathbf{3}) = 60 + 31 = 91.$$

EXAMPLE 4   Miguel drove 101 miles to the airport. Connie only had to drive 28 miles. How much farther did Miguel drive than Connie?

STEP 1   Choose an appropriate operation.

The key words *farther than* indicate that you will subtract.

STEP 2   Apply the mental math strategy of compensation.

Think: "$101 - 28 = 101 - \mathbf{1} - 28 + \mathbf{1} = 100 - 28 + \mathbf{1} = 72 + 1 = 73$."

STEP 3   Write or state your answer to the problem.

Miguel drove 73 miles farther than Connie.

STEP 4   Check your answer. Since subtraction and addition are opposite, the answer + 28 should equal 101.

Add 28 + 73 mentally. Think: "20 + 8 + 70 + 3 = 90 + 11 = 101." The answer checks.

After you have practiced the different mental math strategies, they should help you save time by allowing you to take shortcuts whenever possible. But remember that you still must know your basic addition and multiplication facts to achieve the correct solution.

EXERCISE 9

Directions: Apply one of the mental math strategies and write the answer.

1. 27 + 52 _____

2. 19 × 10 _____

3. 60 × 90 _____

4. 7 + 36 + 3 _____

5. 7 × 5 × 20 _____

6. 99 + 53 _____

7. 102 + 14 _____

8. 43 + 28 _____

9. 99 − 37 _____

10. 1,000 × 32 _____

11. 16 + 42 + 34 _____

12. 500 × 8,000 _____

13. 800 × 300 _____

14. 13 + 5 + 15 + 7 _____

15. 399 − 12 _____

16. 37 + 99 _____

17. A carpet is 12 feet long and 10 feet wide. Find the area of the carpet. (Remember that area = length × width.) _____

18. Find the perimeter of the carpet in Question 17. (Remember that perimeter equals 2 (length + width).) _____

19. Mrs. O'Rourke is the guidance counselor for 28 adults, Mr. Martinez assists 32 adults, and Ms. Wolfe advises 41 adults. How many adults are being assisted by these guidance counselors? _____

20. Using the numbers in Question 19, how many more adults does Ms. Wolfe advise than Mr. Martinez? _____

ANSWERS ARE ON PAGE 292.

EXERCISE 10

Directions: Write the value of each digit for each number.

1. 97,104

2. 7,506,138

3. 890,468

4. 5,280

5. 13,090

6. 6,614,231

7. 158,620

ANSWERS ARE ON PAGE 292.

ESTIMATION

Estimation can often save you time when an exact answer is not needed or when you want to check whether an exact answer is reasonable.

We have already used the strategy of rounding. Another estimation strategy involves using the far left digits or **_front-end digits_**.

EXAMPLE 1 Estimate the sum of 259, 673, and 110.

STEP 1 Rewrite each number using its front-end digit followed by zeros to replace the other numbers.

$$259 \rightarrow 200 \quad 673 \rightarrow 600 \quad 110 \rightarrow 100$$

STEP 2 Perform the appropriate operation. (In this case, add.)

$$
\begin{array}{r}
259 \\
673 \\
+ 110 \\
\end{array}
\quad \text{becomes} \quad
\begin{array}{r}
200 \\
600 \\
+ 100 \\
\hline
900 \\
\end{array}
$$

Answer: The sum of 259, 673, and 110 is **about** 900.

TIP: When you add, make sure that you line up the numbers correctly.

Sometimes you will be able to apply a mental math strategy during your estimation process.

Sometimes numbers that are close to the original numbers are used instead of the numbers to make the solution easier or quicker to achieve. As with the mental math strategy, these numbers are called **_compatible numbers_**.

EXAMPLE 2 Estimate the quotient of 1,239 divided by 37.

STEP 1 Change 1,239 and 37 to numbers that are easier to divide.

$$1,239 \rightarrow 1,200 \quad 37 \rightarrow 40$$

STEP 2 Divide using the new numbers.

$$
\begin{array}{r}
30 \\
40\overline{)1,200} \\
\underline{120} \\
00 \\
\end{array}
$$

Answer: 1,239 divided by 37 is about 30.

STEP 3   Check the estimate.

Multiply 30 and 40 (mentally if possible). The product 1,200 is close to 1,239, so the estimate is reasonable.

TIP: Remember that estimates are only approximations. Often there are several different ways to estimate an answer, and these estimates may or may not be the same.

EXERCISE 11

Directions: Estimate each answer using one of the estimation strategies. Then list the strategy you used (rounding, front-end digits, or compatible numbers).

1. Round 68 to the nearest ten. _____
Strategy used:

_____

2. Round 352 to the nearest ten. _____
Strategy used:

_____

3. Round 416 to the nearest hundred. _____
Strategy used:

_____

4. Estimate the sum of 56 and 71. _____
Strategy used:

_____

5. Estimate the sum of 278, 318, and 594. _____
Strategy used:

_____

6. Estimate the quotient of 1,475 and 319. _____
Strategy used:

_____

Directions: Estimate each answer using each of the estimation strategies. Show your work.

7. 98 × 57

rounding: _____ front-end digits: _____ compatible numbers: _____

8. 2,783 + 907 + 1,346

rounding: _____ front-end digits: _____ compatible numbers: _____

9. 587 divided by 24

rounding: _____ front-end digits: _____ compatible numbers: _____

ANSWERS ARE ON PAGE 292.

EXERCISE 12

Directions: Estimate the answer for each problem below. Name the strategy you used and show your work.

1. During a drive to collect money for a charity, Juan turned in $695. He collected $315 by himself; the rest of this money he collected with Marsha. Marsha turned in $478 (the money she collected by herself). About how much did they collect together?

2. A pet store received a shipment of 105 cartons of dog food. Each carton contained 48 cans. About how many cans of dog food did the pet store receive?

3. The average cheetah can run 70 miles per hour. The average man can run about 28 miles per hour (for a short period of time). On the average, how much faster is the cheetah than man?

4. The Washington Monument is over 403 feet taller than the Statue of Liberty, which is 152 feet high. How tall is the Washington Monument?

ANSWERS ARE ON PAGE 292.

PROBLEM-SOLVING STRATEGIES

The mental math and estimation strategies you have learned are types of problem-solving strategies. These and others you will learn will help you become more successful when you solve problems (both when you are studying mathematics and in your everyday life).

Sometimes to solve a problem you may have drawn a sketch or diagram to help you understand what is being asked. When you do this, you are using the problem-solving strategy called ***drawing a picture***. Many people find this strategy the easiest to remember and use.

EXAMPLE 1   Matthew had driven 12 miles toward his girlfriend's house when he remembered that he had left his concert tickets at home. He went back home and, after a quick phone call to explain why he was late, drove the 25 miles back to her house. How many miles had he added to his odometer when he finally arrived at her house?

STEP 1   Understand the question.

You want to figure out how many miles Matthew drove to get to his girlfriend's house.

STEP 2   Find the necessary information.

If you just write the two numbers that are in the problem (12 and 25), you will probably get the wrong answer. If you draw a picture, you should be able to see that you really have three numbers involved: 12, 12, and 25.

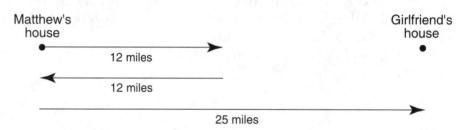

STEP 3   Choose an arithmetic operation.

By looking at the picture above plus noticing the key word *added*, you should see that you want to add 12, 12, and 25.

STEP 4   Solve the problem. (Make sure you answer the question asked.)

One way to add the numbers (but not the only way) is to think **12 + 12** + 25 = **24** + 25 = 49.

Answer: Matthew added 49 miles to the odometer driving to his girlfriend's house.

STEP 5   Check your answer.

Add the numbers again, or find an estimate and compare it to your answer. One possible estimate is to think that you were about half way to your girlfriend's house when you had to turn around. Traveling halfway to her house and then returning is about the same as traveling to her house (25 miles). Then you went straight to her house (another 25 miles), so 25 miles + 25 miles = 50 miles. Your answer, 49 miles, is close to your estimate, 50 miles. Your answer is reasonable.

> **TIP:** You do not have to be an artist to practice this strategy. If you know what you are drawing and why, this method can be very useful!

Another very popular problem-solving strategy is called ***guess and check***. You are probably using this method quite often but perhaps did not know that it was an acceptable way to solve problems!

EXAMPLE 2　Which two 2-digit numbers made from the digits 1, 2, 3, 4, and 5, give the largest sum when added together? No single digit may be used more than once.

STEP 1　Understand the question.

You want to find out which two 2-digit numbers give the largest sum when added together.

STEP 2　Find the necessary information.

You can only use the digits 1, 2, 3, 4, and 5. No digit may be used more than once.

STEP 3　Choose an arithmetic operation.

Since you are finding a sum, you should add the digits 1, 2, 3, 4, and 5.

STEP 4　Solve the problem.

First guess:　　　　　　　　　　Second guess:
54 + 32 = 86　　　　　　　　　　53 + 42 = 95

Answer: 53 + 42 = 95

STEP 5　Check your answer.

Test your first guess. Ask yourself: Is 86 a reasonable sum? No, adding 5 and 3 in the tens place gives 80. If you change 3 to 4 and then add 5 and 4 in the tens place, you get 90; 90 is greater than 80.

Test again. Ask yourself: Is 95 a reasonable sum? Yes, 5 and 4 are the largest digits that can appear in the tens column. The numbers 2 and 3 are the largest digits that can appear in the ones column. Therefore, choosing 53 and 42 or 52 and 43 is correct.

Using information from a table is the name of another valuable problem-solving strategy. When a chart, drawing, table, or map is part of a problem, it probably includes some information necessary to solve the problem. After reading the problem carefully, it usually pays to study the table and interpret or sort out what is useful information.

EXAMPLE 3   Kieron passed the sign shown to the right. He decided to change the oil in his car, rotate his tires, and have his car washed and waxed. How much did he spend on his car?

Special Weekend Rates	
Oil & Filter Change	$12.95
Rotation of Tires	$ 6.95
Car Lubricated	$ 8.75
Wash & Wax	$19.95

STEP 1   Understand the question.

You want to determine the total amount of money Kieron spent on his car.

STEP 2   Find the necessary information.

By looking at the chart, you know that it costs $12.95 for an oil and filter change, $6.95 to rotate tires, and $19.95 to wash and wax a car. (You also know that you do *not* need to use the $8.75 amount.)

STEP 3   Choose an arithmetic operation.

Since you are finding a total, you should add the three prices: $12.95, $6.95, and $19.95.

STEP 4   Solve the problem.
$$\begin{array}{r} \$12.95 \\ \$\ 6.95 \\ +\ \$19.95 \\ \hline \$39.85 \end{array}$$

Answer: Kieron spent $39.85 on his car.

STEP 5   Check your answer.

One way to check the answer is to round the prices to the nearest dollar and add. The estimate is $13 + $7 + $20, or $20 + $20 = $40. Since $40 is very close to the answer of $39.85, your answer is reasonable.

> **TIP:** It is wise to use estimation either before or after you have found an exact answer to determine if your answer is reasonable.

EXERCISE 13

Directions: Select a strategy to solve each problem. Show your work and state the strategy you used.

1. Five people are in a room. If everyone shakes hands with everyone else once, how many handshakes will there be in all?

2. Which two 3-digit numbers made from the digits 1, 2, 3, 4, 5, and 6 give the largest sum when added together? No single digit may be used more than once.

3. Nadia is driving from Pittsburgh to St. Louis. If she wants to save time, which route should she take?

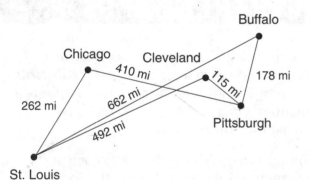

4. Three turtles are in a race. Turtle A was 2 feet behind Turtle B. Turtle C was 4 feet ahead of Turtle A. Turtle B was 6 feet from the starting line. Which turtle was ahead?

5. Which 3-digit and 1-digit number made with the digits 3, 4, 5, and 6 give the largest product when multiplied together? No single digit may be used more than once.

6. Honda was the biggest seller between 1989 and 1992. In what year were the largest number of cars of that make sold?

**TOP SELLING PASSENGER
CARS IN THE U.S.**

Year	Make	Number sold
1989	Honda Accord	362,707
1990	Honda Accord	417,179
1991	Honda Accord	399,297
1992	Ford Taurus	409,751

7. Which 3-digit and 2-digit numbers made with the digits 1, 2, 3, 4, and 5 give the largest product when multiplied together? No single digit may be used more than once.

8. Five basketball players are in a circle. Each player throws the basketball to every other player once. How many times is the ball thrown?

9. Which two 2-digit numbers made from the digits 5, 6, 7, and 8 give the largest sum when added together? No single digit may be used more than once.

10. Wanda had to hike 20 miles. She walked half the distance the first day. She walked half of the remaining distance the second day. How far did she have to walk the third day to finish the trip?

11. Give the windchill factor for the following.

WINDCHILL FACTOR

		Temperature in degrees Fahrenheit					
		15	10	5	0	−5	−10
wind speed (mph)	5	12	7	0	−5	−10	−15
	10	−3	−9	−15	−22	−27	−31
	15	−11	−18	−25	−31	−38	−45

a. Wind speed is 5 mph, temperature is 5 degrees. _____

b. Wind speed is 15 mph, temperature is 0 degrees. _____

c. Wind speed is 10 mph, temperature is −10 degrees. _____

d. Wind speed is 15 mph, temperature is 15 degrees. _____

ANSWERS ARE ON PAGES 292–293.

PROBLEMS HAVING MULTIPLE STEPS

At times you have to choose more than one operation to solve a problem. To simplify this type of problem, you can first write a **solution sentence**. This sentence is written by identifying phrases and numbers to state the solution in a simple manner. Once a solution sentence is identified, you can determine what information is missing.

EXAMPLE Last month Louise bought 5 compact discs (CDs) for $19.95 each and 3 cassettes for $9.99 each. How much did she spend altogether on music?

STEP 1 Write a solution sentence.

Summarize what you know into short phrases.
total cost of music = cost of CDs plus cost of cassettes

STEP 2 Substitute known values and symbols for the phrases.

Known values:
cost of CDs → 5 CDs for $19.95 → 5 × $19.95
cost of cassettes → 3 cassettes for $9.99 → 3 × $9.99

total cost of music = (**5** × **$19.95**) + (**3** × **$9.99**)

STEP 3   Complete the appropriate operations.

First operation: multiply to find the cost of each type of music.
total cost of music = (**$99.75**) + (**$29.97**)

Second operation: add the two costs.
total cost of music = (**$99.75**) + (**$29.97**) = $129.72

EXERCISE 14

Directions: Write a solution sentence for each problem. Then solve the problem.

1. Alfredo bought 5 pounds of potatoes at $0.75 per pound and 3 pounds of bananas at $0.45 per pound. How much did he spend altogether?   *5.10*

2. Maria purchased 3 cans of vegetables at $0.89 per can. How much change should she get from a $10 bill?   *7.33*

3. Wong bought 4 adult tickets to a pop concert at $25 per ticket and three children tickets at $10.50 per ticket. How much did he spend altogether for the tickets?   *131.50*

4. Barb spent $11.25 at one store, $15.50 at another store, and $10.75 at a third store. If she has $35 in her checking account, will she have enough money to cover her purchases?   *NO (37.50)*

5. Hal deposited $80 in his checking account. He then wrote checks for $5.35, $35.60, $20, $10, and $15. Did he deposit enough money to cover these five checks?   *NO (85.95)*

6. Shirley bought 2 tires for her car at $95 each and 6 spark plugs at $1.25 each. How much did she spend altogether?   *197.50*

7. Rosario is buying a 1996 Viper that costs $28,500. The auto dealer will give him $1,900 on a trade-in, and Rosario plans to put $1,200 in cash down. How much will he have to finance?   *25,400*

8. Magda plans to fly to Washington, D.C. Kiwi Airlines is offering fares at $89 one way, and Valujet $188 round trip. Which is the better buy?   *178*

9. Valencia rented three movies with a 3-for-$6.50 coupon. She rented a fourth one for two nights only at $3.25. How much should she get back if she pays with a $20-dollar bill?   *10.25*

10. Bobby Ray pumped nine gallons of gas at $1.27 per gallon. Will he have enough to pay for the gas if he has $12.00 in his wallet?   *YES (11.43)*

ANSWERS ARE ON PAGE 293.

EXERCISE 15

Directions: Add, subtract, multiply, or divide.

1. 16,394
+ 8,067

4. 803,497
− 197,868

7. 86,942
1,738
+ 54

10. 7)4,995

2. 803
× 95

5. 3,042
× 15

8. 69,304
− 17,290

11. 95,403
− 6,771

3. 6)1,926

6. 24)840

9. 346
× 13

12. 456,208
121,113
+ 55,158

Directions: Fill in the blanks with the correct digits.

13. 106 has _____ hundreds, _____ tens, and _____ ones.

14. 4,296 has _____ thousands, _____ hundreds, _____ tens, and _____ ones.

15. 27,865 has _____ ten thousands, _____ thousands, _____ hundreds, _____ tens, and _____ ones.

16. 406,918 has _____ hundred thousands, _____ ten thousands, _____ thousands, _____ hundreds, _____ tens, and _____ ones.

17. 97 has _____ hundreds, _____ tens, and _____ ones.

18. 16,875 has _____ ten thousands, _____ thousands, _____ hundreds, _____ tens, and _____ ones.

19. 8,656,422 has _____ millions, _____ hundred thousands, _____ ten thousands, _____ thousands, _____ hundreds, _____ tens, and _____ ones.

20. 55,800,250 has _____ ten millions, _____ millions, _____ hundred thousands, _____ ten thousands, _____ thousands, _____ hundreds, _____ tens, and _____ ones.

ANSWERS ARE ON PAGE 293.

WHOLE NUMBER AND PROBLEM SOLVING REVIEW

Directions: Write the value of each underlined digit.

1. <u>2</u>75 _____

2. 1,79<u>6</u> _____

3. 28,4<u>0</u>2 _____

4. 7<u>8</u>9,040 _____

5. <u>6</u>,748 _____

6. <u>4</u>,869,302 _____

Directions: Solve each problem by estimating. Show your work. Then solve the problems using the actual numbers. Compare your best estimate with the actual answer.

7.   297
     +112

8.   6,928
     − 3,014

9.   2,165
     × 498

10. 31)11,935

11. 318 + 21 + 594

12. 12,878 − 9,142

Directions: Write each of the following number phrases in symbols.

13. Nineteen hundred fifty-six _____

14. Eight hundred thousand, three hundred, forty-three _____

15. One million, four hundred three thousand, one _____

16. Twenty-three thousand, two hundred fifteen _____

Directions: Change each quantity to the unit indicated.

17. 60 in. = _____ ft

18. 4 qt = _____ pt

19. 128 oz = _____ lb

20. 56 hr = _____ d _____ hr

ANSWERS ARE ON PAGES 293–294.

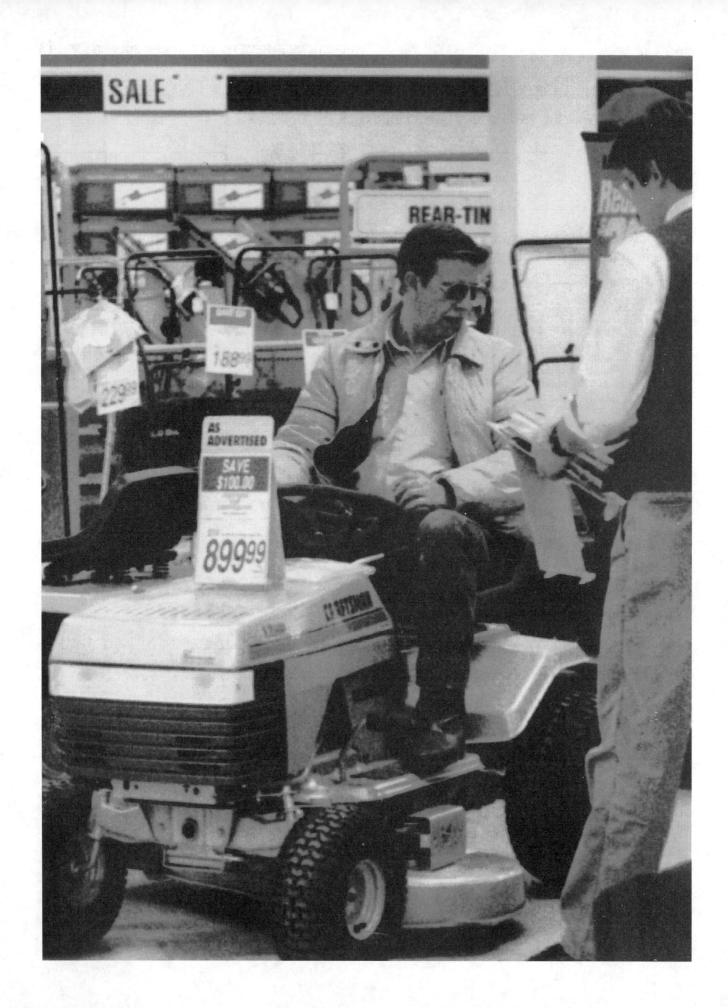

2 Decimals

DECIMALS

The U.S. monetary system is based on the ***decimal system***. Decimals are based on a whole being split into ten equal parts one or more times.

Let's start by thinking of dollars as whole numbers and cents as one type of decimal. When we think about values less than 1, think about money values less than a dollar.

1 dollar = 10 dimes = 100 pennies,
so
1 dime = 1 tenth of a dollar
and
1 penny = 1 hundredth of a dollar.

Since our money system is based on decimals, you should notice a similarity.

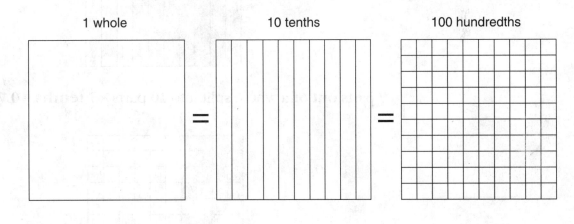

1 whole   10 tenths   100 hundredths

so

1 tenth = $\frac{1}{10}$ of a whole and 1 hundredth = $\frac{1}{100}$ of a whole.

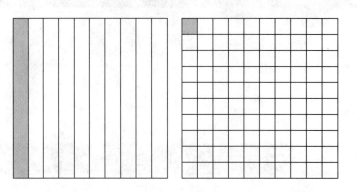

You can describe more precise values by splitting the whole into smaller and smaller parts. Decimals are wholes split into ten parts or multiples of ten parts (100, 1000, 10,000, and so on).

Using money as an example, a quarter is written as 25 cents or $0.25, so 25 **hundredths** written in the form of a decimal is 0.25.

EXAMPLE 1   Write the decimals shown.

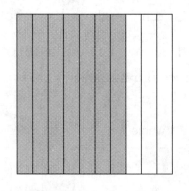

7 parts **out of** a whole split into **10** parts = 7 **tenths** = **0.7**

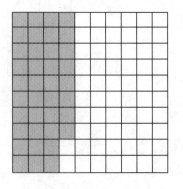

38 parts **out of** a whole split into **100** parts = 38 **hundredths** = **0.38**

We can extend the whole number place value chart to include decimal values. (The decimal point is read as *and*.)

| thousands (X 1,000 ones) | hundreds (X 100 ones) | tens (X 10 ones) | ones | ● | tenths (out of 10 parts) | hundredths (out of 100 parts) | thousandths (out of 1,000 parts) |

Remember that each decimal place stands for part of a whole.

Example	Value	Meaning
0.1	1 tenth	1 out of 10 parts
0.01	1 hundredth	1 out of 100 parts
0.001	1 thousandth	1 out of 1,000 parts
0.0001	1 ten-thousandth	1 out of 10,000 parts
0.00001	1 hundred-thousandth	1 out of 100,000 parts
0.000001	1 millionth	1 out of 1,000,000 parts

EXAMPLE 2   Use words to express the value of the decimal shown.

2.73 is read *two and seventy-three hundredths*.

To compare two or more values, first compare the whole number digits (the digits to the left of the decimal point) and ignore the decimal digits (to the right). Order the whole number digits. If two or more have the same whole number digits, compare the decimal digits.

EXAMPLE 3   Which has a greater value: 0.4 or 0.38?

STEP 1   Determine the more precise decimal place.

0.4 has a place value of tenths.
0.38 has a place value of hundredths.
Hundredths is more precise than tenths.

STEP 2 Insert zeros to the right of the decimals as needed so the decimals are written to the same place value.

$$0.4 \quad = \quad 0.40$$

4 tenths is the same as 40 hundredths.

STEP 3 Compare the decimals. Which is the larger of the two?

40 hundredths *is greater than* **38** hundredths.
Another way to express this is 0.40 > 0.38 or 0.4 > 0.38.

SUMMARY FOR COMPARING DECIMALS

To compare two or more decimals:

1) Determine the most precise decimal place.

2) Insert zeros to the right of the decimals as needed so the decimals are written to the same place value.

3) Rewrite the decimals using > or < (symbols for *greater than* or *less than*).

EXERCISE 1

Directions: In the space provided, write the decimals shown or described.

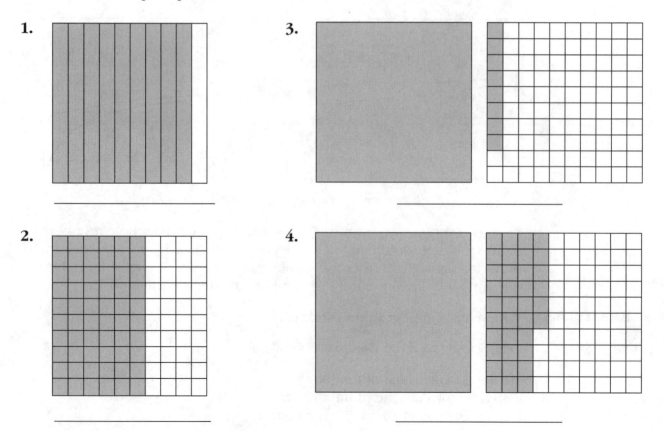

1.

2.

3.

4.

5. 4 out of 10 parts _____

6. 39 out of 100 parts _____

7. 82 out of 1,000 parts _____

8. 5 out of 100 parts _____

9. 7 out of 1,000 parts _____

10. 6 wholes and 48 out of 1,000 parts _____

11. 9 wholes and 81 out of 100 parts _____

12. 23 wholes and 105 out of 1,000 parts _____

Directions: Use words to express the value of each decimal.

13. 4.07 _____

14. 15.38 _____

15. 0.169 _____

16. 7.205 _____

17. 9.1 _____

18. 12.86 _____

Directions: Compare each pair of decimals. Write an expression using > or < when comparing.

19. 0.5, 0.8 _____   **28.** 3.2, 4 _____

20. 0.47, 0.39 _____   **29.** 0.99, 0.954 _____

21. 4.7, 4.82 _____   **30.** 8.09, 8.9 _____

22. 5.5, 5.05 _____   **31.** 6.50, 6.57 _____

23. .001, .010 _____   **32.** 1.33, 1.303 _____

24. 7.75, .075 _____   **33.** 9.08, 9.9 _____

25. 3.101, 3.1 _____   **34.** .03, .25 _____

26. 0.25, 0.257 _____   **35.** 99.9, 0.999 _____

27. 1.9, 1.999 _____   **36.** .503, 0.5 _____

ANSWERS ARE ON PAGE 294.

EXERCISE 2

Directions: Write each of the following amounts using a dollar sign and a decimal point. Then round each amount to the nearest dollar.

1. Nine dollars and forty-two cents

_____

2. Nineteen dollars and three quarters

_____

3. Forty-three dollars and five dimes

_____

4. Five quarters, a dime, and six pennies

_____

5. Two ten-dollar bills and eight dimes

_____

ANSWERS ARE ON PAGE 294.

ROUNDING DECIMALS

Decimals are rounded just as whole numbers are; however, when an amount of money is rounded, the value is usually rounded up to the next nearest cent.

EXAMPLE 1 Round 1.537 to the nearest whole number; round 1.537 to the nearest tenth; round 1.537 to the nearest hundredth.

STEP 1 Identify the place-value digit to be rounded.

Nearest one	Nearest tenth	Nearest hundredth
1.537	1.537	1.537
↑	↑	↑
Digit to be rounded	Digit to be rounded	Digit to be rounded

STEP 2 Look at the digit immediately to the right of the value to be rounded. If this digit is 5 or greater, round *up* to the next higher digit. If this digit is less than 5, round *down*. In other words, leave the digit to be rounded alone. In both cases, the digits to the right of the rounded digit become 0 (if they are part of the whole number) or are eliminated (if they are part of the decimal).

Nearest one	Nearest tenth	Nearest hundredth
1.537	1.537	1.537
↑	↑	↑
Round 1 up to 2.	The 5 stays as a 5.	Round 3 up to 4.
1.537 rounds up to 2.	1.537 rounds down to 1.5.	1.537 rounds up to 1.54.

EXAMPLE 2 While Eric was waiting in line at the store, he computed the sales tax on the items he bought. His calculator displayed the figure 2.0830. How much tax did he pay?

STEP 1 Look at the first digit to the right of the hundredths place. If it is greater than zero, round the decimal to the next higher hundredth (or cent).

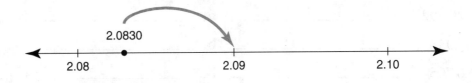

STEP 2 Write the calculator display as dollars and cents.

$$2.0830 \rightarrow \$2.09$$

SUMMARY FOR ROUNDING DECIMALS

To round decimal values:

1) For money, round up to the nearest cent.

2) Round as you would whole numbers.

EXAMPLE 3 The ad shown to the right appeared in a local newspaper. What is the unit price of the markers?

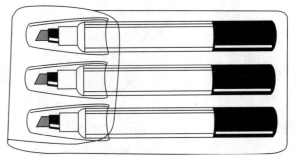

3 markers / $4

The price of one item is its *unit price*. To find the unit price of an item, divide the total price by the number of items. In this case, divide $4 by 3. Since $4 is the same as 400 cents, divide 400 by 3. 400 ÷ 3 = 133 R1. If the store sells one marker, the price is rounded up to 134 cents, or $1.34.

EXERCISE 3

Directions: Round each decimal.

	Nearest whole	**Nearest tenth**	**Nearest hundredth**
1. 5.892	a. _____	b. _____	c. _____
2. 20.492	a. _____	b. _____	c. _____
3. 1.038	a. _____	b. _____	c. _____
4. 6.705	a. _____	b. _____	c. _____

Directions: Round the following amounts to the nearest cent.

5. $1.333 _____

6. 28.7¢ _____

7. $68.5409 _____

8. $0.815 _____

9. $3.739 _____

10. 53.19¢ _____

Directions: Find the unit price for each situation. Show your work.

11. 5 notebook folders for $1

12. 6 pencils for 49 cents

13. 3 kiwis for $1

14. 3 packs of film for $9.49

15. 12-pack spring water for $8.99

16. a dozen doughnuts for $2.52

ANSWERS ARE ON PAGE 294.

EXERCISE 4

Directions: Solve each problem. Show any work you do.

1. One inch equals 2.54 centimeters. What is this length to the nearest tenth of a centimeter?

2. A $\frac{3}{8}$-inch drill bit has a diameter of 0.375 inch. What is the diameter to the nearest hundredth of an inch? What is its diameter to the nearest tenth of an inch?

3. A 12-can pack of soft drinks is on sale for $3.99. What is the price of each soft-drink can when you buy 12 of them?

4. Ten packs of gum usually cost $1.39 but are on sale for 99 cents. How much does a person save on each pack by buying the gum on sale? How much is saved altogether by buying ten packs of gum on sale?

ANSWERS ARE ON PAGE 294.

ADDING AND SUBTRACTING DECIMALS

Add or subtract decimals the same way you add or subtract whole numbers. Look at the following example.

EXAMPLE 1 Add three quarters and six dimes.

STEP 1 Change each amount of money to cents.

3 quarters → 3 × 25 cents → 75 cents or $0.75

6 dimes → 6 × 10 cents → 60 cents or $0.60

STEP 2 Add the cents.

75 cents		$0.75
+ 60 cents	or	+ $0.60
135 cents		$1.35

EXAMPLE 2 Add 3.4, 17.062, and 0.85.

STEP 1 Write the numbers vertically, aligning the decimal points and each place value.

tens	ones	tenths	hundredths	thousandths
	3 .	4		
1	7 .	0	6	2
	0 .	8	5	

STEP 2 Starting at the right, add as you do whole numbers. (Insert zeros to help you align places if necessary.)

$$\begin{array}{r} 3.400 \\ 17.062 \\ \underline{0.850} \\ 21.312 \end{array}$$ Move the decimal point straight down.

> **TIP:** When adding or subtracting decimals, write the numbers vertically, align the decimal points, and insert any necessary zeros.

EXAMPLE 3 Subtract 3.87 from 10.

STEP 1 Write the subtraction problem. $\begin{array}{r} 10 \\ \underline{-\ 3.87} \end{array}$ Remember to align digits.

STEP 2 Insert a decimal point and zeros if necessary after a whole number. Subtract.

$\begin{array}{r} 10.00 \\ \underline{-\ 3.87} \end{array}$ → $\begin{array}{r} \mathbf{9.90} \\ \underline{-\ 3.87} \\ 6.13 \end{array}$ Think of 10 ones as 9 ones, 9 tenths, and 10 hundredths.

SUMMARY FOR ADDING OR SUBTRACTING DECIMALS

To add or subtract decimals:

1) Line up the decimal points and all digits. If a number does not have a decimal point, add one at the far right. Add zeros to make subtraction (or addition) easier.

2) Add or subtract as with whole numbers.

3) Bring down the decimal point in the final answer.

EXERCISE 5

Directions: Add the following amounts of money. Show your work.

1. Three dimes and six nickels

3. Eight dimes and one quarter

_____

_____

2. Two quarters and nine nickels

4. Three quarters, two dimes, and seven nickels

_____

_____

Directions: Add the following decimals.

5.   0.3
    + 0.6

8.   17.35
    + 50.927

11.   6.8
    14.23
    + 20.079

14.   885.61
    37.0
    + 101.2

6. $0.23
    + $0.68

9.   0.18
    8.921
    + 0.58

12.   54.499
    8.67
    + 39.6

15.   5.8
    + 0.5

7.   1.09
    + 0.735

10.   15.7
    7.682
    + 3.09

13.   9.05
    .63
    + .01

16. $0.75
    $1.33
    +$ .06

Directions: Subtract the following decimals.

17.   9.7
        – 2.1

19.   3.985
         – 0.007

21.   42
        – 36.498

23. $27
        – $ 5.72

18.   42.16
         – 9.7

20. $8.10
        – $0.73

22.   9.8
         – 1.032

24.   500.7
        – 138.459

ANSWERS ARE ON PAGE 294.

EXERCISE 6

Directions: Add or subtract as necessary. Show your work.

1. 4.7 + 0.98 + 13.2

4. Subtract 1.967 from 4.83.

2. 100 – 98.7

5. Find the difference between $13 and $7.38.

3. Add $12, $7.57, and $5.25.

6. Find the sum of 98.175 and 7.08.

Directions: Solve each problem. Show your work.

7. In 1992, the unemployment rate for single men 16 years of age was 13.1 percent. If the unemployment rate for single women was 2.4 percent lower, what was that rate?

9. Regular unleaded gas is selling for $1.269 per gallon. What is the price to the nearest cent per gallon?

8. The number of motor vehicle registrations in Texas in 1992 was 8.655 million for automobiles, 4.057 million for trucks and buses, and 0.19 million for motorcycles. Find the total number of registrations.

10. Colleen's share of the bill for dinner was $12.93. She left a $2 tip. She spent $6.75 to watch a movie. How much did she spend that evening?

ANSWERS ARE ON PAGE 295.

MULTIPLYING DECIMALS

Multiply decimals the same way you multiply whole numbers. You must be careful to put the decimal point in the correct place in the product. To do this, add the number of decimal places in each number being multiplied. Starting at the far right of the product, count that number of decimal places to the left, and insert the decimal point. Look at the following examples.

EXAMPLE 1   Find the value of 15 quarters by multiplying.

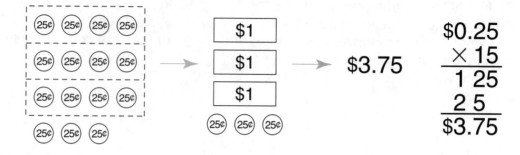

$$\begin{array}{r} \$0.25 \\ \times\ 15 \\ \hline 1\ 25 \\ 2\ 5 \\ \hline \$3.75 \end{array}$$

EXAMPLE 2   Multiply 2.3 and 1.2.

STEP 1   Count the number of decimal places in the original numbers.

2.3 has **1** number to the right of the decimal place.
1.2 has **1** number to the right of the decimal place.
The product should have **2** (1 + 1) decimal places.

STEP 2   Multiply as whole numbers.

STEP 3   Start at the far right of the product. Move 2 places to the left. Insert the decimal point between the 2 and the 7.

$$\begin{array}{r} 2.3 \\ \times\ 1.2 \\ \hline 46 \\ 2\ 3 \\ \hline 2.76 \end{array}$$

STEP 4   Check your answer by estimating the product.

2.3 is about 2. 1.2 is about 1. The product of 2.3 and 1.2 should be slightly greater than 2, so 2.76 seems reasonable. The answer checks.

EXAMPLE 3   Multiply 3.7 and 0.15. (0.15 can be written simply as .15.)

STEP 1   Count the number of decimal places in the original problem.

3.7 has **1** decimal place (1 number to the right of the decimal point). 0.15 has **2** decimal places (2 numbers to the right of the decimal point). The final product will have **3** (the sum of 1 and 2) decimal places.

STEP 2   Write the problem and multiply as with whole numbers.

STEP 3   Starting at the far right (since 555 could be written as 555.), move the point **3** places (from Step 1) to the left.

$$\begin{array}{r} 3.7 \\ \times\ .15 \\ \hline 185 \\ 37 \\ \hline 555 \end{array}$$

3.7 × .15 = .555 or 0.555

STEP 4   Check by estimating the product.

3.7 is about 4. Since multiplication is repeated addition, add .15 four times. Since .60 is close to .555 (the product), the answer checks out.

$$\begin{array}{r} .15 \\ .15 \\ .15 \\ + .15 \\ \hline .60 \end{array}$$

MULTIPLICATION OF DECIMALS SUMMARY

To multiply decimals:

1) Count the total number of decimal places in the original problem.

2) Multiply as with whole numbers.

3) Starting at the far right of the product, count required number of places to the left, and insert the decimal point.

EXERCISE 7

Directions: Find the value of the following amounts. Show your work.

1. 23 dimes

2. 40 quarters

3. 350 pennies

4. 75 nickels

5. 18 nickels

6. 11 half dollars

7. 11 dimes

8. 8 half dollars

Directions: Find each product. Show your work.

9. .5 × .3   **12.** 3 × 6.8   **15.** .25 × 1.3   **18.** 5.37 × .22

10. 1.4 × 1.2   **13.** .9 × 1.5   **16.** 6.9 × 1.05   **19.** $4.35 × 9

11. 1.5 × 2.1   **14.** 3 × 8.72   **17.** 4.7 × .31   **20.** .985 × 2.1

ANSWERS ARE ON PAGE 295.

EXERCISE 8

Directions: Add, subtract, multiply, or divide the following decimals and whole numbers.

1. 192 ÷ 8

2. 290.58
     + 843.9

3. $43.82
     + $59.68

4. 60.2
      × .6

5. $95.00
     − $ 8.57

Directions: Find the unit price for each situation. Show your work.

6. 8-pack AA batteries for $5.99   **7.** 3 packs of tissue for $2.69

Directions: Solve each problem. Show your work.

8. The average annual snowfall in Jackson, Mississippi is 1.2 inches. Madison, Wisconsin averages 34 times this amount. First estimate its average annual snowfall. Then find the exact average based on this information.

9. In 1973, leaded regular gasoline averaged 38.8 cents per gallon. In 1990, unleaded regular gasoline sold for 3 times this price. What was the 1990 average gasoline price?

ANSWERS ARE ON PAGE 295.

DIVIDING DECIMALS

Divide decimals the same way you divide whole numbers. When the divisor is a decimal, however, move the decimal point to the right, writing the divisor as a whole number. Next, move the decimal point in the dividend the same number of places as in the divisor. Put a decimal point in the quotient directly above the dividend's decimal point, and divide. Look at the following example.

EXAMPLE 1   Divide 17.5 by 1.25.

STEP 1   Move the decimal point in the divisor in order to make it a whole number. In this case, move the decimal point **2 places to the right**.

STEP 2   At the same time, move the decimal point in the dividend (remember, there is a decimal point at the end of a whole number) the same number of places as in Step 1. Insert zeros if necessary.

$$1.25{\overline{\smash{)}17.50.}}$$

STEP 3   Insert a decimal point in the quotient directly above the "final" decimal point position of the dividend.

STEP 4   Divide as with whole numbers.

$$
\begin{array}{r}
14. \\
125{\overline{\smash{)}1750.}} \\
\underline{125} \\
500 \\
\underline{500} \\
0
\end{array}
$$

STEP 5   Check your answer by multiplying the quotient (answer) by the original divisor. This product should be the original dividend.

$$
\begin{array}{r}
14 \leftarrow \text{quotient} \\
\times\ 1.25 \leftarrow \text{divisor} \\
\hline
17.50 \leftarrow \text{dividend.}
\end{array}
$$

EXAMPLE 2   Yumi and two of her friends earned $22.95 one Saturday washing cars. If they split the money equally, how much did each one receive?

STEP 1   Divide the dollars equally. Each friend receives $7 with $1 plus the original 95 cents left over.

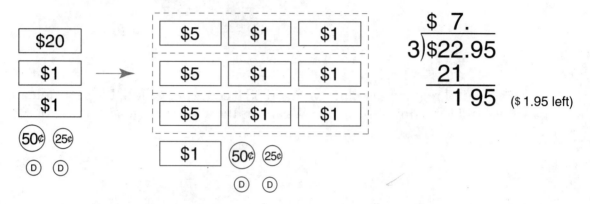

STEP 2   The $1.95 left over can be changed into 19 dimes and 1 nickel. Now divide 19 by 3. Each friend receives 6 dimes, or 60 cents with 1 dime and the nickel left over.

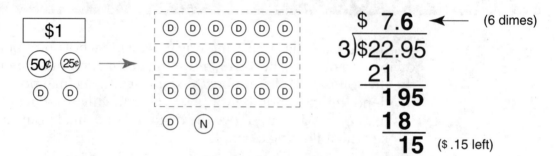

STEP 3   If we change the dime and nickel to 15 pennies, we can now divide by 3. Each friend receives 5 pennies (plus the 7 dollars and 6 dimes they received earlier). Each friend receives $7.65.

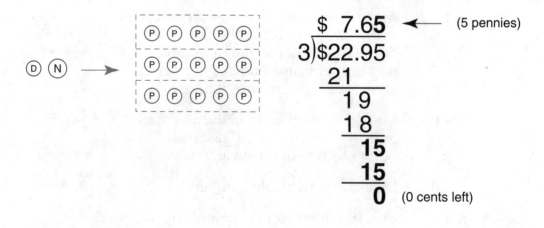

STEP 4   Check your answer by finding an estimate using compatible numbers.

Since $24 divided by 3 is $8, the three friends should each receive about $8. The quotient, $7.65, rounded to the nearest dollar is $8 (your estimate), so your answer is reasonable.

DIVISION OF DECIMALS SUMMARY

To divide decimals:

1) If the divisor is a decimal, move the decimal point to the right to rewrite the divisor as a whole number.

2) Move the decimal point in the dividend the same number of places as the divisor's decimal point was moved. Add zeros as needed.

3) Insert a decimal point in the quotient directly above the new decimal point in the dividend.

4) Divide as with whole numbers.

EXERCISE 9

Directions: Divide

1. Divide $28.35 by 5. Show your work.

Directions: Divide. Show your work.

2. $3\overline{)4.8}$

3. $.3\overline{)48}$

4. $.3\overline{).48}$

5. $.3\overline{)4.8}$

6. $1.6\overline{)4.8}$

7. $1.6\overline{)48}$

8. $.7\overline{)42}$

9. $.9\overline{)5.4}$

10. $8\overline{).72}$

11. $.07\overline{)49}$

12. $.3\overline{)1.47}$

13. $.3\overline{)1.44}$

14. 57.5 ÷ 2.5   **15.** 9.72 ÷ 1.2   **16.** 315 ÷ 4.5   **17.** 84.8 ÷ .53

18. The average annual precipitation in Fargo, North Dakota is 19.59 inches. However, there is only precipitation about 100 days out of the year. For these days of precipitation, find the average amount of precipitation.

19. In 1993, the third-class, single-piece cost to mail a 14-ounce letter or package was $1.67. About how much was this cost per ounce?

20. The machinist's blueprint showed that a key should be 2.136 inches long. What is this length to the nearest tenth of an inch? What is this length to the nearest hundredth of an inch?

21. Jennifer can either buy 3 audio tapes for $4.99 or 7 tapes for $5.99. Which is the better buy? Why?

22. According to the U.S. Bureau of the Census, Phoenix, Arizona had increased its 1980 population of 789,704 by 193,699 people by 1990. How many people lived in this city in 1990?

23. The Moffat Railroad in the Rocky Mountains of Colorado is 6.2 miles long. If the Seikan Railroad is 26.9 miles longer, how long is this Japanese railroad?

ANSWERS ARE ON PAGE 295.

DECIMALS REVIEW

Directions: For questions 1–10, answer each question. Show your work to the right.

1. What digit is in the ten-thousandths place in the number 45,832.09617?

2. Which has the greatest value: 0.9, 0.89, or 0.859?

3. What is the value of five ten-dollar bills, seven one-dollar bills, six quarters, and nine nickels?

4. Round 97.635 to
   a) the nearest one
   b) the nearest tenth
   c) the nearest hundredth

5. Determine the unit price of 10 items that are on sale for $38.92.

6. Find the sum of 53.9, 8.25, and .294.

7. Find the difference between 45 and 9.82.

8. What is the product of 3.45 and .9?

9. What is .75 divided by 1.5?

10. What is the quotient of 75 divided by .15?

Directions: Questions 11–16 include whole numbers as well as decimals. Choose the correct answer to each problem. Remember the problem-solving skills you have learned.

11. A baseball player had a .328 batting average at the end of the first month. At the end of the second month, the batting average was .382. The average

    (1) decreased by .54
    (2) decreased by .066
    (3) increased by .054
    (4) increased by .54
    (5) increased by .066

12. The rates for parking a car at the airport are given below. How much would it cost to park the car for six hours?

Airport Parking Rates	
Hourly rate:	$1.75
Daily rate:	$16
Weekly rate:	$100

    (1) $16
    (2) $96
    (3) $2.67
    (4) $16.67
    (5) $10.50

13. Enrique uses pieces of solid wire to make jewelry. He wants to cut a piece of wire 23.2 centimeters long into 8 equal parts. How long would each part be?

    (1) 31.2 cm
    (2) 2.9 cm
    (3) 15.2 cm
    (4) 3.9 cm
    (5) not enough information is given

14. Enrique has another piece of wire that is 127.4 centimeters long. If he cuts off a piece of wire that is 32.8 centimeters, how long is the piece that is left?

    (1) 105.4 cm
    (2) 160.21 cm
    (3) 9.46 cm
    (4) 95.4 cm
    (5) none of the above

15. You want to check your answer to Problem 13 by estimating. How could you find a reasonable estimate?

    (1) Multiply 3 cm by 8.
    (2) Divide 24 cm by 8.
    (3) Divide 23.2 cm by 10.
    (4) all of the above
    (5) none of the above

16. Karen drove 385 miles on 20 gallons of gas. How many miles per gallon did she average?

    (1) About 20 mi/gal
    (2) 19.25 mi/gal
    (3) 17.7 mi/gal
    (4) 1 and 2 are both acceptable answers.
    (5) 1 and 3 are both acceptable answers.

17. Karen's friend Richard averages 28.5 miles per gallon. How far can he drive using 17.4 gallons?

    (1) 11.1 mi
    (2) 45.9 mi
    (3) 285 mi
    (4) 495.9 mi
    (5) none of the above

18. Use the drawing to find the length of bolt C.

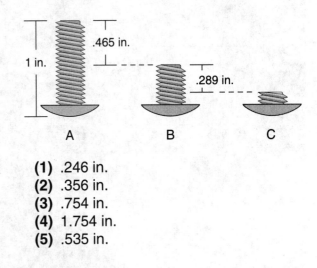

    (1) .246 in.
    (2) .356 in.
    (3) .754 in.
    (4) 1.754 in.
    (5) .535 in.

ANSWERS ARE ON PAGE 295.

3 Fractions and Mixed Numbers

FRACTIONS

Decimals involve any number of parts out of a whole made up of 10, 100, 1000, or so on parts. Fractions are another way of showing parts of a whole. A fraction is made up of two numbers. For example, the fraction $\frac{3}{4}$ has a **numerator** of 3 and a **denominator** of 4. The numerator indicates the number of parts. The denominator refers to the number of parts in the whole.

$$\frac{3}{4}$$

3 → number of parts shaded
→ out of
4 → number of parts in the whole

Decimals can be written as fractions. For example, 0.7 means 7 tenths or 7 parts out of 10 parts, so $0.7 = \frac{7}{10}$. This is expressed in the diagram at the right.

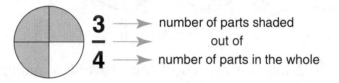

The whole number 1 can be expressed as any number divided by itself, such as $\frac{12}{12}$, $\frac{9}{9}$, $\frac{16}{16}$, or $\frac{100}{100}$.

Values between two whole numbers are **mixed numbers**, or the combination of a whole number and a fraction. For example, $2\frac{3}{5}$ is the same as $1 + 1 + \frac{3}{5}$ or $\frac{5}{5} + \frac{5}{5} + \frac{3}{5}$. From the diagram shown, we see that $2\frac{3}{5}$ is the same as $\frac{13}{5}$.

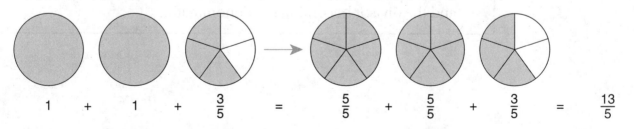

$$1 \quad + \quad 1 \quad + \quad \frac{3}{5} \quad = \quad \frac{5}{5} \quad + \quad \frac{5}{5} \quad + \quad \frac{3}{5} \quad = \quad \frac{13}{5}$$

A fraction with a numerator equal to or greater than its denominator is an **improper fraction**.

EXAMPLE 1   Rewrite $\frac{23}{6}$ as a whole or mixed number.

STEP 1   First divide the numerator by the denominator.

$$\text{denominator} \rightarrow 6\overline{)23} \leftarrow \text{numerator}$$
$$\begin{array}{r} 3 \text{ R}5 \\ 6\overline{)23} \\ \underline{18} \\ 5 \end{array}$$

STEP 2   Make the amount left over a fraction by writing the remainder as the numerator and the divisor as the denominator.

$$\frac{23}{6} \rightarrow 3 \text{ R}5 \rightarrow 3\frac{5}{6}$$

STEP 3   Check the answer. One way to check it is to draw a diagram of 3 wholes divided into sixths with an additional 5 sixths. Then add the total number of sixths.

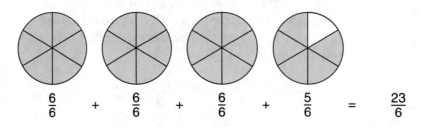

$$\frac{6}{6} \quad + \quad \frac{6}{6} \quad + \quad \frac{6}{6} \quad + \quad \frac{5}{6} \quad = \quad \frac{23}{6}$$

Another way to check the answer is to multiply the whole number by the denominator of the mixed number answer and then add the numerator. This number should be the same as the numerator of the original improper fraction.

$$3\frac{5}{6} \rightarrow \frac{3 \times 6 + 5}{6} \rightarrow \frac{23}{6}$$

SUMMARY OF CHANGING IMPROPER FRACTIONS TO WHOLE OR MIXED NUMBERS

To change an improper fraction to a whole or mixed number:

1) Divide the numerator of the improper fraction (the dividend) by its denominator (the divisor).

2) If the quotient has a remainder, the improper fraction is rewritten as a mixed number with the remainder becoming the numerator and the divisor becoming the denominator.

EXAMPLE 2   Rewrite $4\frac{1}{3}$ as an improper fraction.

STEP 1   Multiply the whole number by the denominator.

In this case we multiply 4 by 3 because 4 wholes (or ones) are split into thirds.

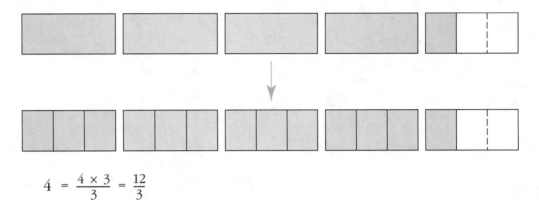

$$4 = \frac{4 \times 3}{3} = \frac{12}{3}$$

STEP 2   Now add the numerator of the original mixed number to the product from Step 1. The denominator stays the same.

In this example, we are simply adding 1 third to 12 thirds.

$$4\frac{1}{3} = \frac{12}{3} + \frac{1}{3} = \frac{13}{3}$$

SUMMARY OF CHANGING MIXED NUMBERS TO IMPROPER FRACTIONS

To change a mixed number to an improper fraction:

1) Multiply the whole number by the denominator.

2) Add the numerator. This result becomes the numerator of the improper fraction. The denominator is the same as that of the mixed number.

EXERCISE 1

Directions: Rewrite each improper fraction as a whole or mixed number. Show your work.

1. $\frac{15}{3}$

2. $\frac{21}{4}$

3. $\frac{17}{3}$

4. $\frac{33}{5}$

5. $\frac{41}{6}$

6. $\frac{38}{7}$

7. $\frac{85}{9}$

8. $\frac{99}{8}$

9. $\frac{56}{6}$

Directions: Rewrite each mixed or whole number as an improper fraction. Show your work.

10. $3\frac{5}{8}$

11. $6\frac{2}{3}$

12. $4\frac{1}{8}$

13. $4\frac{3}{4}$

14. $7\frac{5}{6}$

15. $9\frac{3}{5}$

16. $10\frac{11}{12}$

17. 9 (denominator of 10)

18. $12\frac{4}{7}$

Directions: Solve each problem. Show your work.

19. At Anthony's Pizza by the Slice, pizzas are cut into eight slices. If five pizzas are taken out of the oven and then sliced, how many slices are ready to be sold?

20. Sari has $\frac{17}{2}$ yards of material. Does she have more or less than 8 yards of cloth?

21. On July 1, 1981, approximately 15,560,000 Hispanics resided in the United States. By July 1, 1991, the number of Hispanic residents was estimated to be 23,350,000. What was the population change for Hispanics during this decade?

22. The restaurant bill totaled $37.84. Four friends decided to split the cost equally. How much was each person's share of the meal?

23. Jane wants to double a recipe that calls for $1\frac{1}{3}$ cups of flour. How much flour will she need?

24. Pi is the ratio of the circumference of a circle to the diameter. Pi is expressed as $\frac{22}{7}$. If expressed as a mixed number, what would Pi be?

ANSWERS ARE ON PAGE 295.

EQUIVALENT FRACTIONS

Equivalent fractions are fractions that have the same value. Any fraction multiplied by some form of 1 will yield an equivalent fraction. Look at the illustration below.

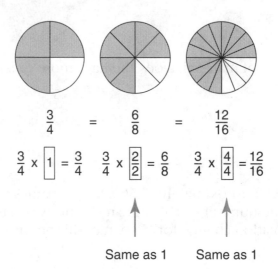

$$\frac{3}{4} = \frac{6}{8} = \frac{12}{16}$$

$$\frac{3}{4} \times \boxed{1} = \frac{3}{4} \qquad \frac{3}{4} \times \boxed{\frac{2}{2}} = \frac{6}{8} \qquad \frac{3}{4} \times \boxed{\frac{4}{4}} = \frac{12}{16}$$

Same as 1　　Same as 1

EXAMPLE 1　Name several fractions equivalent to $\frac{4}{5}$.

Multiply $\frac{4}{5}$ by different forms of 1.

$$\frac{4}{5} \times \frac{4}{4} = \frac{16}{20} \qquad \frac{4}{5} \times \frac{20}{20} = \frac{80}{100} \qquad \frac{4}{5} \times \frac{50}{50} = \frac{200}{250}$$

$$\frac{4}{5} = \frac{16}{20} = \frac{80}{100} = \frac{200}{250}$$

At times we want to identify a specific equivalent fraction.

EXAMPLE 2　What fraction having a denominator of 12 is equivalent to $\frac{21}{36}$?

Multiply or divide by a form of 1. Think: "36 divided by what number is 12?" Since $36 \div 3 = 12$, we can divide both the numerator and the denominator by 3 ($\frac{3}{3} = 1$).

$$\frac{21}{36} = \frac{?}{12}$$

$$\frac{21 \div 3}{36 \div 3} = \frac{7}{12}$$

A fraction is *in lowest terms* if the numerator and denominator cannot be divided evenly (remainder of zero) by any whole number other than 1. Since fractions can be written as many equivalent fractions, writing a fraction in lowest terms makes comparing answers easier.

EXAMPLE 3 Rewrite $\frac{20}{24}$ as a fraction in lowest terms.

Divide the numerator and denominator by a number or numbers until it can no longer be divided.

$$\frac{20}{24} = \frac{20 \div 2}{24 \div 2} = \frac{10 \div 2}{12 \div 2} = \frac{5}{6} \text{ or}$$

$$\frac{20}{24} = \frac{20 \div 4}{24 \div 4} = \frac{5}{6}$$

TIP: When rewriting a fraction in lowest terms, try to identify the greatest number by which both the numerator and denominator are evenly divisible.

EXERCISE 2

Directions: Write three equivalent fractions for each given fraction. Show your work.

1. $\frac{3}{8} =$ _____ = _____ = _____

2. $\frac{1}{6} =$ _____ = _____ = _____

3. $\frac{7}{10} =$ _____ = _____ = _____

4. $\frac{11}{12} =$ _____ = _____ = _____

Directions: Write the missing numerator for each equation.

5. $\frac{15}{25} = \frac{}{5}$

8. $\frac{23}{25} = \frac{}{100}$

11. $\frac{96}{100} = \frac{}{50}$

6. $\frac{20}{60} = \frac{}{3}$

9. $\frac{9}{10} = \frac{}{30}$

12. $\frac{88}{96} = \frac{}{24}$

7. $\frac{28}{32} = \frac{}{8}$

10. $\frac{16}{28} = \frac{}{7}$

13. $\frac{45}{80} = \frac{}{16}$

ANSWERS ARE ON PAGE 296.

CHANGING FRACTIONS TO DECIMALS AND DECIMALS TO FRACTIONS

Often a fraction has to be changed to a decimal or a decimal to a fraction.

EXAMPLE 1   Write $\frac{5}{8}$ as a decimal.

To change $\frac{5}{8}$ to a decimal, divide the numerator by the denominator. Add a decimal point and zeros as needed.

$\frac{5}{8} = 0.625$ or .625

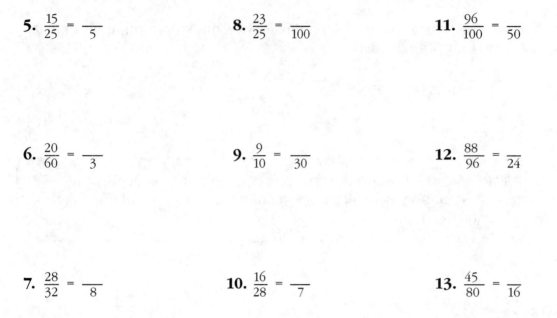

$$\begin{array}{r} 0.625 \\ 8\overline{)5.000} \\ \underline{4\,8} \\ 20 \\ \underline{16} \\ 40 \\ \underline{40} \\ 0 \end{array}$$

SUMMARY FOR CHANGING FRACTIONS TO DECIMALS

To change a fraction to a decimal:

1) Divide the numerator of the fraction by its denominator.

2) Insert a decimal point after the numerator, and add additional zeros if necessary. If the fraction is improper, the decimal will be 1 (when the numerator is equal to the denominator) or greater than 1 (when the numerator is greater than the denominator).

Sometimes no matter how many zeros you add in the dividend, the answer either does not end or repeats one or more digits (called a ***repeating decimal***).

EXAMPLE 2   Rewrite $\frac{7}{9}$ as a decimal.

Divide the numerator by the denominator. Since the numbers keep repeating, round the answer to a certain place (usually rounding to the nearest hundredth is adequate). Remember that this means you must divide to the thousandths place.

$$\begin{array}{r} 0.777 \\ 9\overline{)7.000} \\ \underline{6\,3} \\ 70 \\ \underline{63} \\ 70 \\ \underline{63} \\ 7 \end{array}$$

$\frac{7}{9}$ = 0.777 . . . (symbol for continues in this pattern) → 0.78

EXAMPLE 3   Write 1.76 as a mixed number in lowest terms.

$$1.76 = 1\frac{76}{100} = 1\frac{76 \div 4}{100 \div 4} = 1\frac{19}{25}$$

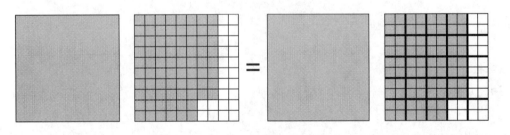

SUMMARY FOR CHANGING DECIMALS TO FRACTIONS

To change a decimal to a fraction or mixed number:

1) Write the decimal as a fraction (or mixed number) with a denominator having a multiple of 10.

2) Write the fraction in lowest terms.

EXERCISE 3

Directions: Rewrite each fraction as a decimal. Show your work.

1. $\frac{3}{12}$

4. $\frac{12}{16}$

7. $\frac{4}{32}$

10. $\frac{8}{11}$

2. $\frac{7}{8}$

5. $\frac{33}{50}$

8. $\frac{17}{40}$

11. $\frac{7}{15}$

3. $\frac{22}{8}$

6. $\frac{1}{8}$

9. $\frac{3}{8}$

12. $\frac{4}{5}$

Directions: Rewrite each decimal as a fraction or mixed number. Show your work.

13. .35

16. 2.4

19. 1.78

22. 7.0125

14. .068

17. 6.52

20. 9.045

23. 4.920

15. 0.75

18. 5.47

21. 1.925

24. 8.5

ANSWERS ARE ON PAGE 296.

CHOOSING A COMMON DENOMINATOR

Before adding or subtracting fractions or mixed numbers, first find a common denominator. Usually the least or lowest common denominator is used.

EXAMPLE Find equivalent fractions for $\frac{2}{3}$ and $\frac{3}{4}$ using a common denominator.

STEP 1 Identify the given denominators.

The denominators for $\frac{2}{3}$ and $\frac{3}{4}$ are 3 (or thirds) and 4 (or fourths).

STEP 2 Determine a common denominator by listing some multiples of each denominator.

Multiples of 3: **3** (3×1), **6** (3×2), **9** (3×3), **<u>12</u>** (3×4)
15 (3×5), **18** (3×6), **21** (3×7), **<u>24</u>** (3×8)

Multiples of 4: **4** (4×1), **8** (4×2), **<u>12</u>** (4×3) **16** (4×4)
20 (4×5), **<u>24</u>** (4×6), **28** (4×7), **32** (4×8)

STEP 3 Write equivalent fractions using any of the common denominators (12, 24, 36, and so on).

$$\frac{2}{3} = \frac{?}{12} \rightarrow \frac{2 \times 4}{3 \times 4} = \frac{8}{12}$$

$$\frac{3}{4} = \frac{?}{12} \rightarrow \frac{3 \times 3}{4 \times 3} = \frac{9}{12}$$

SUMMARY FOR CHOOSING A COMMON DENOMINATOR

To determine a common denominator of two or more fractions:

1) Write multiples of each denominator, and identify one or more common multiples.

2) Write equivalent fractions using one of the common multiples.

EXERCISE 4

Directions: List multiples for each set of numbers. Then identify two common multiples.

1. Multiples of 6: _____

　　Multiples of 5: _____

　　Common multiples: _____

2. Multiples of 8: _____

　　Multiples of 12: _____

　　Common multiples: _____

3. Multiples of 9: _____

　　Multiples of 36: _____

　　Common multiples: _____

4. Multiples of 7: _____

　　Multiples of 21: _____

　　Common multiples: _____

Directions: Write equivalent fractions using a common denominator of each set of fractions.

5. $\dfrac{1}{2} = \dfrac{}{8}$

　　$\dfrac{3}{8} = \dfrac{}{8}$

6. $\dfrac{4}{5} = \dfrac{}{15}$

　　$\dfrac{1}{3} = \dfrac{}{15}$

7. $\dfrac{7}{9} = \dfrac{}{36}$

　　$\dfrac{3}{12} = \dfrac{}{36}$

8. $\dfrac{1}{2} = \dfrac{}{6}$

　　$\dfrac{2}{3} = \dfrac{}{6}$

9. $\dfrac{5}{6} = —$

　　$\dfrac{11}{30} = —$

10. $\dfrac{7}{10} = —$

　　$\dfrac{19}{45} = —$

11. $\dfrac{8}{15} = —$

　　$\dfrac{13}{18} = —$

12. $\dfrac{5}{9} = —$

　　$\dfrac{3}{10} = —$

13. $\dfrac{15}{16} = —$

　　$\dfrac{21}{40} = —$

14. $\dfrac{13}{20} = —$

　　$\dfrac{19}{45} = —$

15. $\dfrac{17}{25} = —$

　　$\dfrac{5}{8} = —$

16. $\dfrac{1}{15} = —$

　　$\dfrac{1}{20} = —$

ANSWERS ARE ON PAGE 296.

COMPARING AND ORDERING FRACTIONS

We often want or need to compare fractions. When we have more than two fractions involved, we usually list the fractions in order from least to greatest or greatest to least.

The marks of a ruler or yardstick indicate fractions ordered from left (least) to right (greatest) as shown below.

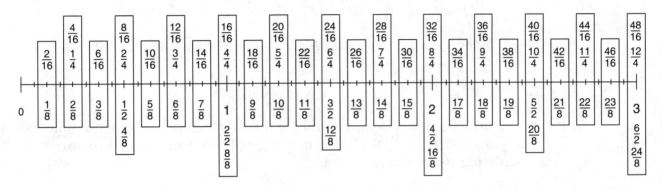

A number line can be used to help compare or order fractions.

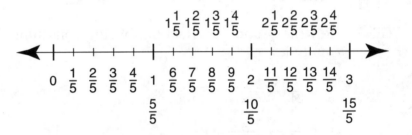

The fractions $1\frac{2}{5}$ and $\frac{9}{5}$ can be compared easily. Since $1\frac{2}{5}$ (or $\frac{7}{5}$) is to the left of $\frac{9}{5}$, $1\frac{2}{5}$ is *less than* $\frac{9}{5}$. This can be written as $1\frac{2}{5} < \frac{9}{5}$.

To compare $\frac{7}{10}$ and $\frac{3}{5}$, a number line showing fifths and tenths must be drawn.

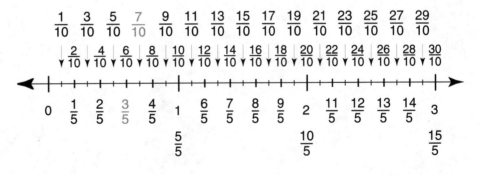

Since $\frac{7}{10}$ is to the right of $\frac{3}{5}$, $\frac{7}{10}$ is greater than $\frac{3}{5}$. Write $\frac{7}{10} > \frac{3}{5}$.

EXAMPLE 1   Compare $1\frac{6}{10}$ and $1\frac{4}{5}$.

Draw a number line with both fifths and tenths or draw two diagrams.

$$1\frac{6}{10}$$

Since $1\frac{4}{5}$ is greater than $1\frac{6}{10}$, or $1\frac{4}{5}$ is to the right of $1\frac{6}{10}$, write $1\frac{4}{5} > 1\frac{6}{10}$.

EXAMPLE 2   Compare $\frac{5}{6}$ and $\frac{7}{8}$.

STEP 1   Identify a common denominator for the two fractions. The denominators of $\frac{5}{6}$ and $\frac{7}{8}$ are 6 and 8. List the multiples of 6 and 8 until a **common multiple** is identified.

Multiples of 6: **6** (6 × 1), **12** (6 × 2), **18** (6 × 3), **24** (6 × 4)

Multiples of 8: **8** (8 × 1), **16** (8 × 2), **24** (8 × 3)

STEP 2   Rewrite $\frac{5}{6}$ and $\frac{7}{8}$ as fractions having denominators of 24 (the common multiple).

$$\frac{5}{6} = \frac{?}{24} \rightarrow \frac{5 \times 4}{6 \times 4} = \frac{20}{24}$$

$$\frac{7}{8} = \frac{?}{24} \rightarrow \frac{7 \times 3}{8 \times 3} = \frac{21}{24}$$

STEP 3   Compare the numerators.

Since $20 < 21$, $\frac{20}{24} < \frac{21}{24}$ and $\frac{5}{6} < \frac{7}{8}$.

EXERCISE 5

Directions: Compare each pair of mixed numbers or fractions using a ruler or a number line. Write a statement using > or <.

1. $\frac{1}{4}, \frac{3}{16}$ _____

2. $\frac{5}{8}, \frac{11}{16}$ _____

3. $\frac{3}{4}, \frac{13}{16}$ _____

4. $1\frac{1}{4}, 1\frac{1}{8}$ _____

5. $1\frac{4}{5}, \frac{8}{5}$ _____

6. $\frac{16}{10}, \frac{6}{5}$ _____

Directions: Compare each pair of fractions using common denominators. Then write a statement using > or <. Show your work.

7. $\frac{3}{8}, \frac{3}{5}$

_____

8. $\frac{1}{4}, \frac{1}{6}$

_____

9. $\frac{5}{12}, \frac{1}{3}$

_____

10. $\frac{13}{16}, \frac{7}{8}$

_____

11. $\frac{7}{10}, \frac{7}{9}$

_____

12. $\frac{9}{10}, \frac{11}{12}$

_____

ANSWERS ARE ON PAGE 297.

ADDING AND SUBTRACTING FRACTIONS THAT HAVE LIKE DENOMINATORS

When adding or subtracting fractions, look to see if the denominators are the same (***like denominators***) or different (***unlike denominators***).

EXAMPLE 1   Add $\frac{5}{12}$ and $\frac{7}{12}$.

STEP 1   Look at the denominators. If they are the same (12), the sum will have this denominator (12).

$$\frac{5}{12} + \frac{7}{12} = \frac{\square}{12}$$

STEP 2   Think: "How many twelfths result from combining the parts?" 12 *twelfths*

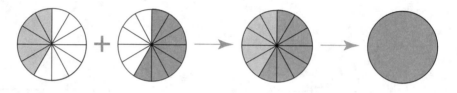

STEP 3   Write the sum as a fraction.

$$\frac{5}{12} + \frac{7}{12} = \frac{12}{12}$$

STEP 4   Simplify the answer. (Reduce to lowest terms or change to a whole or mixed number.)

$$\frac{12}{12} = \mathbf{1}, \text{ so } \frac{5}{12} + \frac{7}{12} = \frac{12}{12} = 1$$

> **TIP:** When adding or subtracting fractions that have like denominators, the denominators remain the same. However, if the answer can be simplified (reduced to lowest terms), the final denominator will change.

EXAMPLE 2   Subtract $\frac{1}{10}$ from $\frac{7}{10}$.

STEP 1   Look at the denominators. The denominators are the same (10), so the difference will have the same denominator (10).

$$\frac{7}{10} - \frac{1}{10} = \frac{\square}{10}$$

STEP 2   Think: "How many tenths result from removing 1 tenth from 7 tenths?" 6 *tenths*

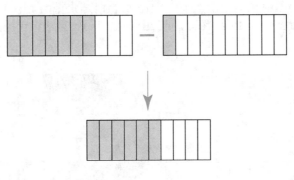

STEP 3   Write the difference as a fraction.

$$\frac{7}{10} - \frac{1}{10} = \frac{6}{10}$$

STEP 4   Simplify the answer ($\frac{6}{10}$).

$$\frac{6 \div 2}{10 \div 2} = \frac{3}{5}, \text{ so } \frac{7}{10} - \frac{1}{10} = \frac{6}{10} = \frac{3}{5}$$

Now review Examples 1 and 2 looking for a general method to add or subtract fractions with like denominators.

SUMMARY OF ADDING OR SUBTRACTING FRACTIONS THAT HAVE LIKE DENOMINATORS

To add or subtract fractions with like denominators:

1) Add or subtract the numerators. (The denominators will be the same as the original ones.)

2) If necessary, write the answer in lowest terms.

3) Change any improper fractions to whole or mixed numbers.

EXERCISE 6

Directions: Write the addition or subtraction problem illustrated by each diagram. Then find the sum or difference. Be sure every answer is written in lowest terms.

1.

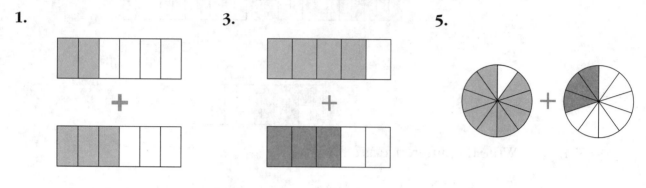

3.

5.

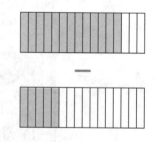

2.

4.

6.

Directions: Find the sum or difference. Reduce every answer to lowest terms. Show your work.

7. $\frac{5}{12} + \frac{3}{12}$

8. $\begin{array}{r} \frac{7}{8} \\ -\frac{1}{8} \end{array}$

9. $\begin{array}{r} \frac{9}{16} \\ -\frac{3}{16} \end{array}$

10. $\frac{9}{10} - \frac{3}{10}$

11. $\frac{7}{16} + \frac{3}{16}$

12. $\begin{array}{r} \frac{7}{18} \\ -\frac{1}{18} \end{array}$

13. $\frac{5}{8} + \frac{7}{8}$

14. $\begin{array}{r} \frac{11}{20} \\ +\frac{9}{20} \end{array}$

15. $\frac{14}{15} - \frac{11}{15}$

16. $\frac{11}{12} + \frac{5}{12}$

17. $\frac{23}{25} - \frac{18}{25}$

18. $\begin{array}{r} \frac{33}{50} \\ -\frac{18}{50} \end{array}$

19. $\begin{array}{r} \frac{8}{9} \\ +\frac{7}{9} \end{array}$

20. $\frac{31}{36} - \frac{5}{36}$

21. $\begin{array}{r} \frac{43}{100} \\ +\frac{87}{100} \end{array}$

ANSWERS ARE ON PAGES 297–298.

ADDING AND SUBTRACTING FRACTIONS THAT HAVE UNLIKE DENOMINATORS

When adding or subtracting fractions with denominators that are not the same, first find equivalent fractions with common denominators. Then add or subtract the fractions.

EXAMPLE 1   Add $\frac{7}{12}$ and $\frac{2}{3}$.

STEP 1   Look at the denominators. They are different (12 and 3). Find a common denominator of these two numbers. *12*

$$\frac{7}{12} = \frac{\square}{12}$$
$$+ \frac{2}{3} = \frac{\square}{12}$$

STEP 2   Find an equivalent fraction for $\frac{2}{3}$ using a denominator of 12.

$\frac{2}{3} = \frac{\square}{12}$ Think: $3 \times ? = 12$

$\frac{2}{3} \times \frac{4}{4} = \frac{8}{12}$ Multiply by $\frac{4}{4}$ or 1.

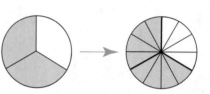

STEP 3   Add using twelfths.

$\frac{7}{12} = \frac{7}{12}$ Add the new numerators.

$+ \frac{2}{3} = \frac{8}{12}$

$\frac{15}{12}$ The new denominator is 12.

STEP 4   Reduce the answer to lowest terms.

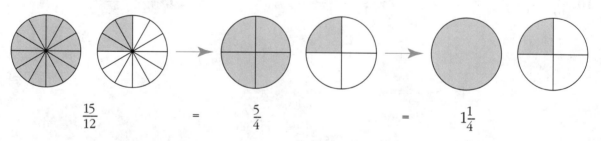

$$\frac{15}{12} \qquad = \qquad \frac{5}{4} \qquad = \qquad 1\frac{1}{4}$$

EXAMPLE 2 Subtract $\frac{1}{5}$ from $\frac{3}{4}$.

STEP 1 Look at the denominators. They are different (5 and 4). One common denominator is 20, since $5 \times 4 = 20$ and $4 \times 5 = 20$.

$$\frac{3}{4} = \frac{\square}{20}$$
$$-\frac{1}{5} = \frac{\square}{20}$$

STEP 2 Find equivalent fractions for $\frac{1}{5}$ and $\frac{3}{4}$ with 20 as the denominators.

$\frac{3}{4} = \frac{\square}{20}$ Think: $4 \times ? = 20$ $\frac{1}{5} = \frac{\square}{20}$ Think: $5 \times ? = 20$

$\frac{3}{4} \times \frac{5}{5} = \frac{15}{20}$ Multiply by $\frac{5}{5}$ or 1. $\frac{1}{5} \times \frac{4}{4} = \frac{4}{20}$ Multiply by $\frac{4}{4}$ or 1.

$\frac{3}{4} = \frac{15}{20}$ $\frac{1}{5} = \frac{4}{20}$

STEP 3 Subtract using twentieths.

$$\frac{3}{4} = \frac{15}{20}$$ Subtract the new numerators.
$$-\frac{1}{5} = \frac{4}{20}$$
$$\frac{11}{20}$$ The new denominator is 20.

STEP 4 The answer is already in lowest terms.

TIP: To find a common denominator when adding or subtracting fractions with unlike denominators, multiply the original denominators by each other. Remember to simplify or reduce the answer to lowest terms.

ADDING OR SUBTRACTING FRACTIONS THAT HAVE UNLIKE DENOMINATORS

To add or subtract fractions with unlike denominators:

1) Find a common denominator.

2) Add or subtract the new numerators. The common denominator will be the denominator.

3) If necessary, write the answer in lowest terms.

4) Change any improper fractions to whole or mixed numbers.

EXERCISE 7

Directions: Write the addition or subtraction problem illustrated by each diagram. Then find the sum or difference. Reduce every answer to lowest terms.

1.

3.

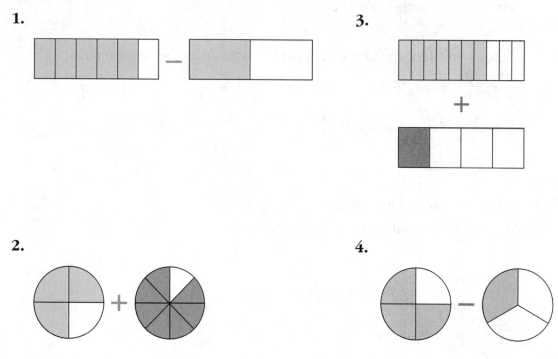

2.

4.

Directions: Write the missing numerators. Then find the sum or difference. Reduce every answer to lowest terms.

5. $\dfrac{2}{3} = \dfrac{10}{15}$

$-\dfrac{1}{5} = \dfrac{}{15}$

7. $\dfrac{1}{8} = \dfrac{}{24}$

$+\dfrac{2}{3} = \dfrac{}{24}$

9. $\dfrac{3}{10} = \dfrac{}{30}$

$-\dfrac{1}{6} = \dfrac{}{30}$

11. $\dfrac{3}{16} = \dfrac{3}{16}$

$\dfrac{1}{2} = \dfrac{}{16}$

$+\dfrac{1}{4} = \dfrac{}{16}$

6. $\dfrac{1}{6} = \dfrac{2}{12}$

$+\dfrac{1}{2} = \dfrac{}{12}$

8. $\dfrac{3}{4} = \dfrac{}{28}$

$-\dfrac{3}{7} = \dfrac{}{28}$

10. $\dfrac{11}{12} = \dfrac{}{60}$

$-\dfrac{4}{15} = \dfrac{}{60}$

12. $\dfrac{4}{15} = \dfrac{4}{15}$

$\dfrac{1}{3} = \dfrac{}{15}$

$+\dfrac{1}{5} = \dfrac{}{15}$

Directions: Find the sum or difference. Reduce every answer to lowest terms.

13. $\dfrac{3}{8}$

$+\dfrac{1}{2}$

17. $\dfrac{3}{4}$

$+\dfrac{2}{5}$

21. $\dfrac{3}{5}$

$+\dfrac{5}{6}$

14. $\dfrac{13}{16}$

$-\dfrac{5}{32}$

18. $\dfrac{5}{8}$

$-\dfrac{1}{6}$

22. $\dfrac{8}{9}$

$-\dfrac{3}{4}$

15. $\dfrac{4}{5}$

$+\dfrac{3}{10}$

19. $\dfrac{11}{12}$

$-\dfrac{3}{4}$

23. $\dfrac{1}{12}$

$\dfrac{1}{3}$

$+\dfrac{1}{4}$

16. $\dfrac{2}{3}$

$+\dfrac{5}{6}$

20. $\dfrac{3}{8}$

$+\dfrac{2}{3}$

24. $\dfrac{13}{16}$

$-\dfrac{2}{3}$

ANSWERS ARE ON PAGE 298.

EXERCISE 8

1. Rewrite $5\frac{7}{8}$ as an improper fraction. _____

2. Change $\frac{54}{10}$ to a mixed number in lowest terms. _____

3. Write three equivalent fractions for $\frac{5}{6}$. _____

4. Rewrite $\frac{5}{12}$ as a decimal. _____

5. Change 0.072 to a fraction in lowest terms. _____

6. Write equivalent fractions for $\frac{7}{10}$ and $\frac{5}{8}$ using a common denominator. _____

7. Write a statement comparing $\frac{4}{5}$ and $\frac{3}{4}$ using < or >. _____

Directions: Solve each addition or subtraction problem below using any method. Reduce every answer to lowest terms.

8. Nelida ordered carpet that was $\frac{11}{16}$-inch thick. The pad underneath it was $\frac{5}{8}$-inch thick. How much thicker is the carpet than the pad?

9. It rained $\frac{5}{8}$ of an inch last Saturday. The next day it rained another $\frac{7}{8}$ inch. How much rain fell during those two days?

10. According to the blueprint, a spring should be $\frac{9}{32}$-inch long. When Lars measured it, the spring was $\frac{5}{16}$-inch long. Is the actual spring longer or shorter than the blueprint measure and by how much?

ANSWERS ARE ON PAGE 299.

ADDING MIXED NUMBERS

To add mixed numbers, look at the denominators. If they are different, rename them using a common denominator. Next, add the whole number parts first; then add all the fractional parts of each mixed number. If the sum of the fractions results in an improper fraction, change it to a mixed number. Add the whole number part of the mixed number to the whole number part of the original sum.

EXAMPLE   Add $2\frac{4}{5}$ and $1\frac{1}{3}$.

STEP 1   Look at the denominators. They are different (5 and 3).

STEP 2   Find equivalent fractions for $\frac{4}{5}$ and $\frac{1}{3}$ with 15 as the denominator.

$$2\frac{4}{5} = 2\frac{12}{15}$$

STEP 3   Add the renamed fractions.

$$+1\frac{1}{3} = 1\frac{5}{15}$$
$$\overline{\phantom{+1\frac{1}{3} = }\ 3\frac{17}{15}}$$

STEP 4   Add the whole numbers.

STEP 5   Reduce the answer to lowest terms.

Since $\frac{17}{15}$ is an improper fraction, think:

$$3\frac{17}{15} = 3 + 1 + \frac{2}{15} = 4\frac{2}{15}.$$

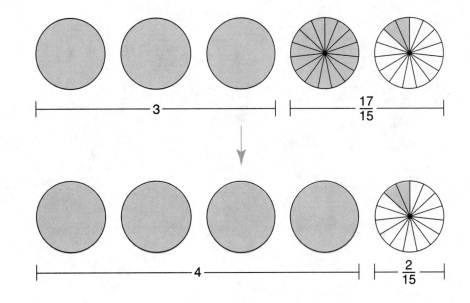

> ## SUMMARY FOR ADDING MIXED NUMBERS
>
> To add mixed numbers:
>
> **1)** Rename the fractions using a common denominator.
>
> **2)** Add the whole numbers, and add the new fractions.
>
> **3)** Simplify the fraction, changing any improper fraction to a mixed number.
>
> **4)** Add the whole number part of the mixed number to the whole number part of the original sum.

EXERCISE 9

Directions: Fill in any missing blanks and add.

1. $5\frac{7}{10}$

$+\ 3\frac{1}{10}$

$\overline{}\frac{}{10} = \underline{}\frac{}{}$

2. $1\frac{1}{4} = \underline{}\frac{}{4}$

$+\ 2\frac{1}{2} = \underline{}\frac{}{4}$

$\underline{}\frac{}{4}$

3. $3\frac{7}{8} = \underline{}\frac{}{16}$

$+\ 4\frac{5}{16} = \underline{}\frac{}{16}$

$\underline{}\frac{}{16} = \underline{}\frac{}{16}$

4. $6\frac{5}{9} = \underline{}\frac{}{18}$

$+\ 8\frac{5}{6} = \underline{}\frac{}{18}$

$\underline{}\frac{}{18} = \underline{}\frac{}{18}$

5. $7\frac{2}{3} = \underline{}\frac{}{9}$

$+\ 5\frac{4}{9} = \underline{}\frac{}{9} =$

$\underline{}\frac{}{9} = \underline{}\frac{}{9}$

6. $11\frac{2}{3} = \underline{}\frac{}{15}$

$+\ 2\frac{4}{5} = \underline{}\frac{}{15}$

$\underline{}\frac{}{15} = \underline{}\frac{}{15}$

Directions: Add each set of mixed numbers. Show your work.

7. $8\frac{2}{3}$

    $+ \ 4\frac{3}{8}$

10. $12\frac{9}{10}$

    $+ \ 8\frac{2}{3}$

8. $7\frac{4}{5}$

    $+ \ 9\frac{3}{4}$

11. $9\frac{7}{12}$

    $+10\frac{4}{5}$

9. $5\frac{5}{6}$

    $+ \ 4\frac{7}{8}$

12. $20\frac{3}{4}$

    $+16\frac{19}{25}$

ANSWERS ARE ON PAGE 300.

SUBTRACTING MIXED NUMBERS

To subtract mixed numbers, we sometimes have to rename mixed numbers.

EXAMPLE Subtract $1\frac{3}{4}$ from $3\frac{1}{6}$.

STEP 1 Look at the denominators. They are different (4 and 6).

STEP 2 Find equivalent fractions for $\frac{3}{4}$ and $\frac{1}{6}$ with 12 as the denominator.

$$3\frac{1}{6} = 3\frac{2}{12}$$
$$-1\frac{3}{4} = 1\frac{9}{12}$$

STEP 3   Subtract the fractional parts and whole numbers. If this is not possible, rename the first mixed number.

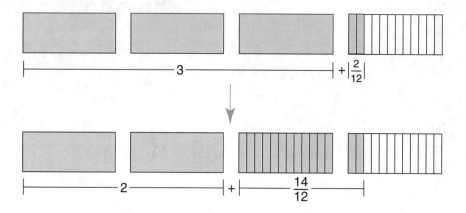

STEP 4   Subtract renamed fractions and the new whole numbers.

STEP 5   Simplify the answer if necessary.

$$3\frac{1}{6} = 3\frac{2}{12} = 2\frac{14}{12}$$
$$-1\frac{3}{4} = 1\frac{9}{12} = 1\frac{9}{12}$$
$$1\frac{5}{12}$$

SUMMARY FOR SUBTRACTING MIXED NUMBERS

To subtract mixed numbers:

1) Rename the fractions using a common denominator.

2) Rename the first mixed number if the first numerator is less than the second numerator.

3) Subtract the new fractions and the whole numbers. Simplify the fractional part of the difference, if necessary.

TIP: To rename the first (or top) mixed number, decrease the whole number by 1, and add the numerator and denominator to get the new numerator of the improper fraction. The denominator stays the same.

EXERCISE 10

Directions: Fill in the missing blanks and subtract.

1. $5\dfrac{9}{10} = \dfrac{\quad 9}{\quad 10}$

   $- \ 3\dfrac{1}{2} = \dfrac{\quad}{\quad 10}$

   $\dfrac{\quad}{\quad 10} = \dfrac{\quad}{\quad}$

2. $3\dfrac{1}{6} = \dfrac{\quad}{\quad 12} = \dfrac{\quad}{\quad 12}$

   $- \ 1\dfrac{3}{4} = \dfrac{\quad}{\quad 12} = \dfrac{\quad}{\quad 12}$

   $\dfrac{\quad}{\quad 12}$

3. $9\dfrac{1}{3} = \dfrac{\quad}{\quad 12} = \dfrac{\quad}{\quad 12}$

   $- \ 6\dfrac{5}{12} = \dfrac{\quad}{\quad 12} = \dfrac{\quad}{\quad 12}$

   $\dfrac{\quad}{\quad 12}$

4. $8\dfrac{3}{8} = \dfrac{\quad}{\quad 24} = \dfrac{\quad}{\quad 24}$

   $- \ 4\dfrac{5}{6} = \dfrac{\quad}{\quad 24} = \dfrac{\quad}{\quad 24}$

   $\dfrac{\quad}{\quad 24}$

Directions: Subtract each set of mixed numbers. Show your work.

5. $10\dfrac{4}{5}$

   $- \ 6\dfrac{3}{4}$

6. $15\dfrac{3}{10}$

   $- \ 9\dfrac{7}{12}$

7. $5\dfrac{1}{6}$

   $- \ 4\dfrac{7}{9}$

8. 14

   $- \ 8\dfrac{18}{25}$

9. $39\dfrac{7}{20}$

   $-10\dfrac{4}{5}$

10. $20\dfrac{4}{35}$

   $-16\dfrac{2}{3}$

Directions: Solve each problem below. Show your work.

11. Janelle made a fruit salad with $1\frac{1}{4}$ pounds of grapes, $2\frac{3}{8}$ pounds of apples, and $1\frac{2}{3}$ pounds of strawberries. How much fruit did she use?

12. Ravi bought two rolls of 100 stamps. If stamps cost 32 cents each, estimate the cost of the stamps. Exactly how much did he spend on stamps?

13. In the 1992 Summer Olympic Games, Michael Stulze from the United States won the shot put event with a throw of 71 feet $2\frac{1}{2}$ inches. Sixty years earlier, the event was won by American John Kuck with a throw of 52 feet $11\frac{11}{16}$ inches. Who threw the shot put farther and by how much?

ANSWERS ARE ON PAGE 300.

MULTIPLYING FRACTIONS AND MIXED NUMBERS

Two fractions can be multiplied by simply multiplying the numerators and denominators and simplifying the answer. Look at the following example.

EXAMPLE 1   Multiply $\frac{5}{8}$ and $\frac{3}{4}$.

STEP 1   Multiply the numerators. $\frac{5}{8} \times \frac{3}{4} = \frac{5 \times 3}{8 \times 4} = \frac{15}{32}$

Multiply the denominators.

STEP 2   Rewrite the answer in lowest terms if necessary. In this case, the answer is already in lowest terms.

SUMMARY OF MULTIPLYING FRACTIONS

To multiply fractions:

1) Multiply the numerators and multiply the denominators.

2) Simplify the result, if necessary.

When multiplying mixed numbers, change the mixed numbers to improper fractions. Then follow the steps for multiplying fractions.

EXAMPLE 2   Multiply $1\frac{2}{3}$ and $2\frac{1}{5}$.

STEP 1   Change the mixed numbers to improper fractions.

$$1\frac{2}{3} = \frac{(1 \times 3) + 2}{3} = \frac{5}{3}; \, 2\frac{1}{5} = \frac{(2 \times 5) + 1}{5} = \frac{11}{5}$$

STEP 2   Multiply the improper fractions by multiplying the numerators and the denominators.

$$1\frac{2}{3} \times 2\frac{1}{5} = \frac{5}{3} \times \frac{11}{5} = \frac{55}{15}$$

STEP 3   Change the improper fraction to a mixed number, and simplify the fraction.

$$\frac{55}{15} = 3\frac{10}{15} = 3\frac{2}{3}$$

SUMMARY OF MULTIPLYING MIXED NUMBERS

To find a product involving mixed numbers:

1) Change all mixed numbers to improper fractions.

2) Multiply the numerators and multiply the denominators.

3) Simplify the result, if necessary.

EXERCISE 11

Directions: Find each product. Reduce all mixed numbers or fractions to lowest terms.

1. $\frac{1}{5} \times \frac{3}{8}$

2. $\frac{7}{12} \times \frac{2}{3}$

3. $\frac{9}{10} \times \frac{5}{6} = \frac{3}{4}$

4. $\frac{3}{4} \times \frac{7}{8}$

5. $\frac{8}{15} \times \frac{3}{10}$

6. $\frac{4}{5} \times \frac{11}{20}$

7. $\frac{3}{8} \times \frac{12}{50}$

8. $1\frac{2}{5} \times \frac{3}{8}$

9. $2\frac{3}{4} \times 4\frac{1}{3}$

10. $2\frac{5}{8} \times 1\frac{1}{2}$

11. $5\frac{9}{10} \times 4$

12. $4\frac{4}{15} \times 6\frac{5}{9}$

13. $9\frac{11}{18} \times 3\frac{2}{3}$

14. $19 \times 7\frac{5}{36}$

15. $15\frac{8}{25} \times 10\frac{7}{8}$

Directions: Solve each problem. Show your work.

16. To convert temperature measured as Fahrenheit to Celsius, subtract 32 and then multiply by $\frac{5}{9}$. What is the Celsius temperature if the Fahrenheit temperature is 104 degrees?

17. Kieron's exercise workout takes him $1\frac{1}{2}$ hours to complete. If he exercises three days a week, how much time does he spend exercising in a week?

ANSWERS ARE ON PAGE 300.

DIVIDING FRACTIONS AND MIXED NUMBERS

To divide fractions or mixed numbers, you must invert the divisor and multiply. The divisor is the number that goes into the other number.

EXAMPLE 1   Find $3 \div \frac{1}{16}$.

Divide 3 into sixteenths. Think "How many sixteenths are in 3 wholes (or 3 inches)?"

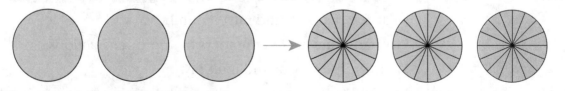

1 whole is the same as 16 (1 × 16) sixteenths.
2 wholes is the same as 32 (2 × 16) sixteenths.
3 wholes is the same as 48 (3 × 16) sixteenths.
Therefore, $3 \div \frac{1}{16}$ is the same as 3×16.

$$3 \div \frac{1}{16} = 3 \times \frac{16}{1} = 48$$

By studying this example, we notice that *dividing by* $\frac{1}{16}$ became *multiplying by 16 or* $\frac{16}{1}$. The divisor, $\frac{1}{16}$, was inverted to become $\frac{16}{1}$.

EXAMPLE 2   Find $1\frac{3}{8} \div \frac{1}{2}$.

STEP 1   Change any mixed numbers to improper fractions.

$$1\frac{3}{8} \div \frac{1}{2} = \frac{11}{8} \div \frac{1}{2}$$

STEP 2   Change the division symbol to multiplication and invert the second fraction (the divisor).

$$1\frac{3}{8} \div \frac{1}{2} = \frac{11}{8} \div \frac{1}{2} = \frac{11}{8} \times \frac{2}{1}$$

STEP 3   The problem is now a multiplication problem. Complete the problem.

$$1\frac{3}{8} \div \frac{1}{2} = \frac{11}{8} \div \frac{1}{2} = \frac{11}{8} \times \frac{2}{1} = \frac{22}{8} = \frac{11}{4} = 2\frac{3}{4}$$

STEP 4   Check by estimating. Think: "How many $\frac{1}{2}$s are in $1\frac{3}{8}$?"

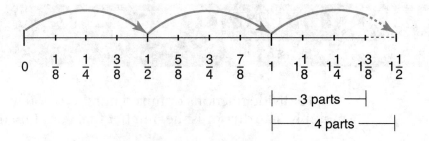

By drawing a number line, we can determine that the answer is about 3. Since $2\frac{3}{4}$ is about 3, the answer is reasonable.

SUMMARY OF DIVIDING FRACTIONS AND MIXED NUMBERS

To divide fractions and mixed numbers:

1) Change any mixed numbers to improper fractions.

2) Invert the divisor and multiply.

3) Simplify the result, if necessary, by writing the answer in lowest terms.

4) Change any improper fraction to a mixed or whole number.

EXERCISE 12

Directions: Write the inverse of each fraction, mixed number, or whole number.

1. $\frac{5}{12}$ **2.** 3   **3.** $6\frac{9}{10}$ **4.** 27

Directions: Use the number line below to find the following.

5. How many fourths are in 3? _____

6. How many eighths are in $2\frac{1}{2}$? _____

7. How many sixteenths are in $1\frac{3}{4}$? _____

8. How many $\frac{3}{4}$-inch pieces are in $2\frac{1}{4}$ inches? _____

9. How many $\frac{1}{8}$-inch pieces are in $1\frac{5}{16}$ inches? _____

Directions: Find each quotient. Show your work.

10. $\frac{3}{8} \div \frac{2}{3} = \frac{3}{8} \times$ ____ = ____

11. $\frac{5}{6} \div \frac{10}{17} =$ ____ $\times$ ____ = ____ = ____ = ____

12. $2\frac{1}{3} \div \frac{4}{9} = \frac{}{3} \div \frac{4}{9} = \frac{}{3} \times$ ___ = ____ = ____ = ____

13. $1\frac{3}{4} \div 2\frac{7}{18} = \frac{}{4} \div \frac{}{18} = \frac{}{} \times \frac{}{} = \underline{\qquad} = \underline{\qquad}$

14. $4\frac{7}{12} \div 3\frac{1}{10}$

15. $6 \div 2\frac{9}{25}$

16. $10\frac{23}{40} \div 5$

Directions: Solve each problem. Show your work.

17. A pica is a measure of $\frac{1}{6}$ inch. If a length is measured as 21 picas, how many inches is this length?

18. Horsepower is defined to be the power needed to lift 33,000 pounds a distance of one foot in one minute. If this is about $1\frac{1}{2}$ times the power an average horse can exert, how much would a horse be expected to lift one foot in one minute?

ANSWERS ARE ON PAGE 301.

FRACTIONS AND MIXED NUMBERS REVIEW

Directions: In questions 1–15, solve each problem. Show your work to the right.

1. What fraction is represented by the decimal .81?

2. What improper fraction is the equivalent of $5\frac{9}{10}$?

3. What mixed number is the equivalent of $\frac{49}{12}$?

4. Name three fractions equal to $\frac{6}{23}$.

5. What fraction with a denominator of 90 is the equivalent of $\frac{11}{18}$?

6. Rewrite the fraction $\frac{63}{72}$ in lowest terms.

7. Change the fraction $\frac{17}{25}$ to a decimal.

8. Change 4.96 to a mixed number in lowest terms.

9. Name a common denominator of $\frac{3}{10}$ and $\frac{11}{15}$.

10. Write a statement using < or > comparing $1\frac{7}{12}$ to $1\frac{9}{16}$.

11. Joyce studied for two and a half hours. Jose made the claim that he studied three times as long. For how long would Jose have studied?

12. Martin lives $\frac{7}{8}$ of a mile from school. If Christy rides the bus for another $1\frac{3}{4}$ miles after Martin gets off, how far away from school does Christy live?

13. How many thirds are in 4?

14. Subtract $\frac{7}{16}$ from $1\frac{3}{8}$.

15. Find $\frac{9}{10} \div 1\frac{7}{8}$.

Directions: Questions 16–25 include whole numbers, decimals, and fractions. Choose the correct answer to each problem. Remember the problem-solving skills you have learned.

16. Last week Kevin worked 40 hours for his usual pay rate of $8 an hour. For the next 6 hours of work, he was paid one and a half times his usual rate. You are to find his total pay for the week. Which is the correct expression for solving this problem?

(1) (40 × $8) + (6 × 1.5)
(2) (40 × $8) + ($8 × 1.5)
(3) (40 × $8) + (6 × $8 × 1.5)
(4) (46 × $8) + (6 × 1.5)
(5) (46 × $8) + (8 × 1.5)

17. Which of the following is in order from least to greatest?

(1) .87, 8.7, 8.07, 8.77
(2) $\frac{3}{10}, \frac{3}{8}, \frac{3}{4}, \frac{3}{2}$
(3) .1, .01, .001, .0001
(4) $8\frac{1}{7}, 8\frac{1}{8}, 8\frac{1}{9}, 8\frac{1}{10}$
(5) $\frac{10}{3}, \frac{8}{3}, \frac{4}{3}, \frac{2}{3}$

18. Which of the following represents the largest amount?

(1) $3.52
(2) three and a half dollars
(3) three dollars and two quarters
(4) two dollars and three quarters
(5) $3.50

19. A recipe calls for 1 cup shortening, $1\frac{1}{2}$ cups sugar, $1\frac{3}{4}$ cups flour, and 1 cup of raisins. If Bryan doubles the recipe, how much flour should he use?

(1) $2\frac{1}{2}$ cups
(2) $5\frac{1}{4}$ cups
(3) $1\frac{3}{4}$ cups
(4) $3\frac{1}{2}$ cups
(5) $\frac{7}{8}$ cup

20. How many pieces $\frac{3}{4}$ inch long can be cut from a foot-long cord?

(1) 9 pieces
(2) 36 pieces
(3) 16 pieces
(4) 20 pieces
(5) 12 pieces

21. If "lean hamburger" is $\frac{1}{5}$ fat, how many ounces of fat are in a 12-ounce hamburger steak?

(1) $\frac{5}{12}$ oz
(2) $\frac{12}{5}$ oz
(3) 60 oz
(4) 5 oz
(5) 12 oz

22. To add $\frac{2}{5}$ and $\frac{5}{12}$, you would

   (1) multiply both $\frac{2}{5}$ and $\frac{5}{12}$ by some form of 1

   (2) find equivalent fractions for $\frac{2}{5}$ and $\frac{5}{12}$

   (3) determine a common denominator and add renamed numerators

   (4) all of the above

   (5) none of the above

23. Which expression represents the correct comparison of $\frac{30}{5}$, 6.00, and 4.2 divided by .7?

   (1) $\frac{30}{5} < 6.00 < 4.2$ divided by .7

   (2) $\frac{30}{5} > 6.00 > 4.2$ divided by .7

   (3) $\frac{30}{5} = 6.00$ and both are less than 4.2 divided by .7

   (4) $\frac{30}{5} = 6.00$ and both are greater than 4.2 divided by .7

   (5) They all are equal.

24. Which is cheaper: 4 items for $1.60 or $5 for 12 items?

   (1) Four items for $1.60 is slightly cheaper

   (2) Five dollars for 12 items is considerably cheaper

   (3) They are the same.

   (4) Four items for $1.60 is considerably cheaper

   (5) Five dollars for 12 items is slightly cheaper

25. One rod is $8\frac{15}{16}$ inches long. Another rod is $7\frac{5}{8}$ inches long. If the two rods are placed end to end, what is their total length?

   (1) $15\frac{20}{24}$ in.

   (2) $1\frac{5}{16}$ in.

   (3) $16\frac{20}{24}$ in.

   (4) $16\frac{9}{16}$ in.

   (5) $16\frac{9}{24}$ in.

ANSWERS ARE ON PAGE 301.

GARAGE
22'7 x 27'5

FAMILY
13'1 x 19'1

CLOSET
2'2 x 7'5

BATH
8'6 x 5'6

PORCH
15'7 x 5'6

4 Measurement and Geometry

STANDARD MEASUREMENT

We use different *units* to measure length, capacity, weight, and time. Standard units of measure and their relationships are given in the chart below. Use this information to change from one unit to another.

STANDARD UNITS OF MEASURE

Length
1 foot (ft) = 12 inches (in.)
1 yard (yd) = 3 feet = 36 inches
1 mile (mi) = 1,760 yards = 5,280 feet

Capacity
1 cup (c) = 8 fluid ounces (fl oz)
1 pint (pt) = 2 cups
1 quart (qt) = 2 pints
1 gallon (gal) = 4 quarts

Weight
1 pound (lb) = 16 ounces (oz)
1 ton (T) = 2,000 pounds

Time
1 minute (min) = 60 seconds (sec)
1 hour (hr) = 60 minutes
1 day = 24 hours
1 week (wk) = 7 days
1 year (yr) = 365 days

EXAMPLE 1   Change 105 days to weeks.

STEP 1   Find the relationship between the two units.

There are 7 days in 1 week.

STEP 2   To change from a smaller unit (days) to a larger unit (weeks), divide.

105 days ÷ 7 = 15 weeks

EXAMPLE 2   Change 3 gallons to cups.

STEP 1   Find the relationship between the two units.

There are 4 quarts in 1 gallon, 2 pints in 1 quart, and 2 cups in 1 pint. Use these relationships.

STEP 2   To change from a larger unit to a smaller unit, multiply.

3 gallons × 4 = 12 quarts   12 quarts × 2 = 24 pints

24 pints × 2 = 48 cups

SUMMARY FOR CHANGING UNITS OF MEASURE

To change units of measure:

1) Find the relationship between the two units.

2) To change from a smaller unit to a larger unit, divide.

3) To change from a larger unit to a smaller unit, multiply.

EXERCISE 1

Directions: Circle the larger unit.

1. cups or pints

2. pounds or ounces

3. inches or feet

4. gallons or quarts

5. minutes or seconds

6. yards or miles

7. days or hours

8. quarts or pints

9. days or weeks

10. yards or feet

Directions: Change each measurement to the unit indicated. Refer to the chart on page 109, if necessary.

11. 12 gallons = _____ quarts

12. 84 days = _____ weeks

13. 30 feet = _____ yards

14. 5 tons = _____ pounds

15. 3 pounds = _____ ounces

16. 60 inches = _____ feet

17. 240 seconds = _____ minutes

18. 6 cups = _____ pints

19. 12 miles = _____ feet

20. 300 minutes = _____ hours

Directions: Answer each question below. Show your work.

21. How many inches are in 3 yards?

22. How many hours are in 1 week?

23. How many cups are in 6 quarts?

24. How many tons are in 8,000 pounds?

25. How many ounces are in 5 pounds?

26. How many seconds are in 1 day?

27. How many miles are in 15,840 feet?

28. How many gallons are in 32 cups?

29. Which unit is not smaller than a quart?

    (1) pint
    (2) cup
    (3) gallon
    (4) fluid ounce

30. Which unit is not larger than a minute?

    (1) hour
    (2) second
    (3) day
    (4) week

ANSWERS ARE ON PAGE 301.

MIXED UNITS

Some measurements are given in mixed units. For example, a person's height is given as 5 feet 4 inches. Changing from mixed units or to mixed units is an important skill.

EXAMPLE 1   Change 5 feet 4 inches to inches.

Use the relationship: 12 inches = 1 foot.

$$5 \text{ feet 4 inches} = (5 \text{ feet}) + (4 \text{ inches})$$
$$= (5 \text{ feet} \times 12) + (4 \text{ inches})$$
$$= 60 \text{ inches} + 4 \text{ inches}$$
$$= 64 \text{ inches}$$

EXAMPLE 2   Change 200 minutes to hours and minutes.

Use the relationship: 60 minutes = 1 hour.
200 minutes = 200 ÷ 60 = 3 R20 or 3 hours and 20 minutes

EXERCISE 2

Directions: Change each measurement to the unit(s) indicated.

1. 6 feet 2 inches = _____ inches

2. 54 inches = _____ feet _____ inches

3. 2 hours 15 minutes = _____ minutes

4. 300 minutes = _____ hours _____ minutes

5. 11 cups = _____ quarts _____ cups

6. 10,000 feet = _____ miles _____ feet

7. $3\frac{1}{3}$ minutes = _____ minutes _____ seconds

8. 1 year = _____ weeks _____ days

9. 50 ounces = _____ pounds _____ ounces

10. 7 minutes 35 seconds = _____ seconds

Directions: Solve each problem below. Show your work.

11. Enrique is 6 feet 1 inch tall. Simon is 70 inches tall. Who is taller?

12. Ria worked 8 hours 45 minutes. Sue worked 600 minutes. Who worked longer?

13. Can A contains 10 fluid ounces of sauce. Can B contains 1 cup of sauce. Which can contains more sauce?

14. Nadia made 20 cups of punch and filled a 1-gallon container. How many cups of punch are left?

ANSWERS ARE ON PAGE 301.

THE METRIC SYSTEM

The **metric system** of measurement is used widely throughout the world. It is based on the decimal system of numbers. The basic units of metric measure are **meter** for length, **liter** for liquid capacity, and **gram** for mass. Prefixes used with these units form other units. The common prefixes are **milli-** for $\frac{1}{1000}$ or 0.001, **centi-** for $\frac{1}{100}$ or 0.01, and **kilo-** for 1,000 times the basic unit.

EXAMPLE 1   Use the prefixes to find the number of millimeters in 1 meter.

Millimeter is the smaller unit, and 1 millimeter is $\frac{1}{1000}$ or 0.001 of a meter. So, there are 1,000 millimeters in 1 meter.

The diagram below can help you change from one metric unit to another.

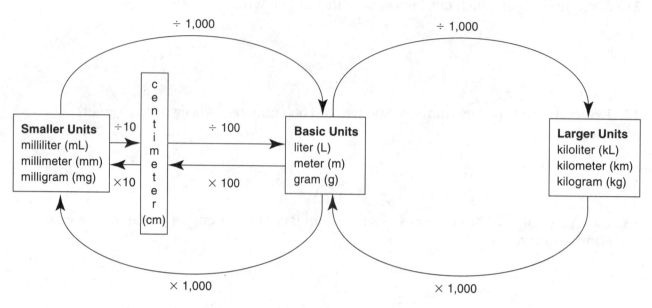

EXAMPLE 2 Change 70 centimeters to meters.

As with standard units of measure, divide to change from a smaller unit to a larger unit.

There are 100 centimeters in 1 meter, so divide by 100.

70 cm ÷ 100 = 0.70 m = 0.7 m

EXAMPLE 3 Change 5.2 liters to milliliters.

Multiply to change from a larger unit to a smaller unit. Since 1,000 milliliters are in 1 liter, multiply by 1,000.

5.2 L × 1,000 = 5,200 mL

TIP: When multiplying or dividing by a multiple of 10, just move the decimal point the same number of places as the number of zeros in the multiple of 10.

EXERCISE 3

Directions: Complete the chart below.

Metric Units of Measure

Length

1. 1 meter (m) = _____ centimeters (cm)

2. 1 meter = _____ millimeters (mm)

3. 1 centimeter = _____ millimeters

4. 1 kilometer (km) = _____ meters

Liquid Capacity

5. 1 liter (L) = _____ milliliters (mL)

6. 1 kiloliter (kL) = _____ liters

Mass

7. 1 gram (g) = _____ milligrams (mg)

8. 1 kilogram (kg) = _____ grams

Directions: Change each measurement to the unit indicated.

9. 320 cm = _____ m

10. 40 cm = _____ mm

11. 0.4 kL = _____ L

12. 5,500 g = _____ kg

13. 6 m = _____ cm

14. 89 mm = _____ cm

15. 6.5 L = _____ mL

16. 2 km = _____ m

17. 342,000 mg = _____ g

18. 1.4 kL = _____ L

19. 10 kg = _____ g

20. 750 mL = _____ L

21. 5kg = _____ g

22. 600 cm = _____ m

23. 7.2g = _____ mg

24. 240m = _____ km

25. 2,000 L = _____ kL

26. 512 mL = _____ L

Directions: Solve each problem below. Show your work.

27. Write four metric units for length in order from smallest to largest.

28. Write three metric units for mass in order from largest to smallest.

29. How many milliliters of liquid are in a half-liter bottle?

30. A glass holds 250 milliliters of water. How many liters of water are needed to fill 10 glasses?

31. The mass of a person is about 70 kilograms. How many grams is this?

32. An orange contains about 60 milligrams of protein. How many grams is this?

ANSWERS ARE ON PAGE 302.

GEOMETRIC DEFINITIONS

In the study of geometry there are many definitions to learn. Skills of geometry include drawing shapes, identifying shapes, and understanding relationships among shapes. You will learn some basic definitions and practice these skills in this section. First, carefully study the definitions and figures below.

Line: a set of points continuing in opposite directions

Segment: a set of points forming the shortest path between two points

Ray: a set of points continuing in one direction only

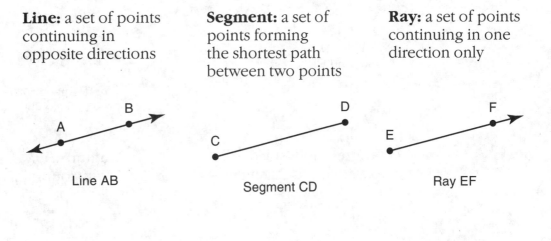

Line AB

Segment CD

Ray EF

Angle: a figure made of two rays extending from the same point

Right angle: an angle that measures 90°

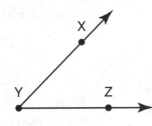

Angle XYZ

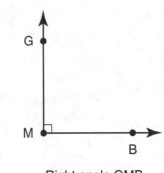

Right angle GMB

Parallel lines: lines that run in the same direction and that do not cross or intersect

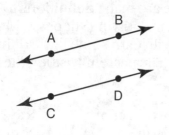

Parallel lines
AB and CD

Perpendicular lines: lines that intersect to form right angles

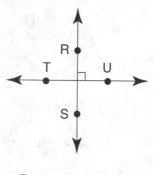

Perpendicular Lines
RS and TU

Rectangle: a four-sided figure with four right angles

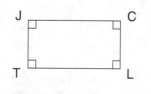

Rectangle JTLC

Square: a four-sided figure with four right angles and four equal sides

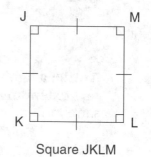

Square JKLM

Triangle: a three-sided figure

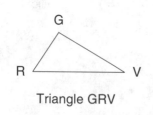

Triangle GRV

Circle: a curved flat figure every point of which is the same distance from the center

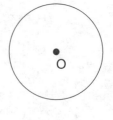

Circle O

EXERCISE 4

Directions: Draw and label each figure described.

1. Segment MN

2. Circle C

3. Right angle RST

4. Ray PQ

5. Parallel lines

6. Line ST

7. An angle formed by rays FG and FK

8. Perpendicular lines intersecting at point B

9. A triangle no two sides of which have the same length

10. A triangle that has a right angle

11. Square WXYZ

12. Rectangle ABCD with parallel sides AB and DC

Directions: Fill in each blank with the appropriate word.

13. A right angle is an angle that measures _____.

14. A _____ is a curved flat figure every point of which is the same distance from the center.

15. A _____ is a set of points continuing in opposite directions.

16. A rectangle is a four-sided figure with four _____ angles.

17. A _____ is a set of points forming the shortest path between two points.

18. Lines that run in the same direction and that do not cross or intersect are _____.

19. An _____ is a figure made of two rays extending from the same point.

20. A _____ is a three-sided figure.

21. A square is a four-sided figure with four right angles and four _____ sides.

22. _____ lines intersect to form right angles.

23. A _____ is a set of points continuing in one direction only.

ANSWERS ARE ON PAGE 302.

MEASURING LINE SEGMENTS

To measure a given distance or length, you can use a meter stick or a centimeter ruler. A centimeter ruler is shown below. Centimeters are labeled 1, 2, 3, . . . , 15. The shorter lines are millimeters.

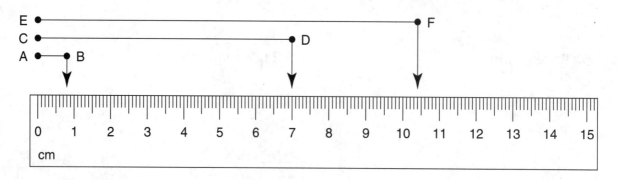

EXAMPLE   Write the length of segments AB, CD, and EF shown above.

STEP 1   Count millimeters from 0 to the end of segment AB: 8 mm, or 0.8 cm.

STEP 2   Read centimeters from 0 to the end of segment CD: 7 cm.

STEP 3   Read centimeters, then count millimeters, from 0 to the end of segment EF:
10 cm + 4 mm, or 10.4 cm.

> **TIP:** Remember that the metric system is based on decimals. Use decimal numbers to write metric measurements.

EXERCISE 5

Directions: Write the length of each segment shown below.

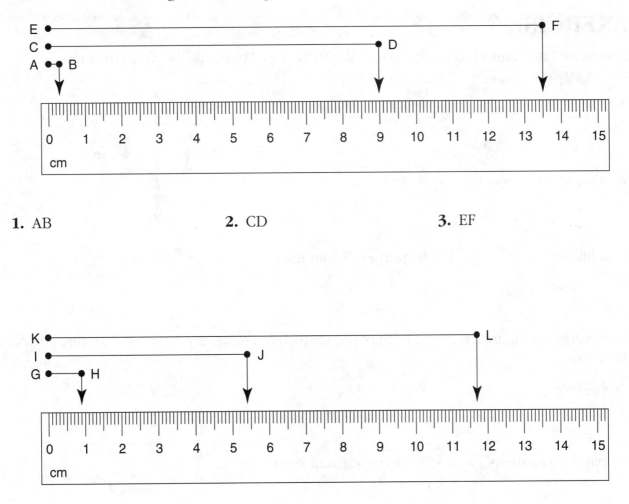

1. AB   **2.** CD   **3.** EF

4. GH   **5.** IJ   **6.** KL

Directions: Write the appropriate metric unit: m, cm, mm, or km.

7. Ashur is an avid runner. Today he ran 12 ____ in about an hour.

8. Kerstin's mother's height is about 1.6 ____.

9. A sheet of notebook paper measures about 22 ____ wide.

10. A dime is about 2 ____ wide and 1 ____ thick.

11. The distance from Miami to Chicago is about 2,000 ____.

12. The length of a queen-size bed is about 200 ____, or 2 ____.

ANSWERS ARE ON PAGE 303.

EXERCISE 6

Directions: Use Figure 1 to name each of the following. There may be more than one correct answer.

1. a ray

2. a segment

3. a line

4. a right angle

5. a circle

6. perpendicular lines

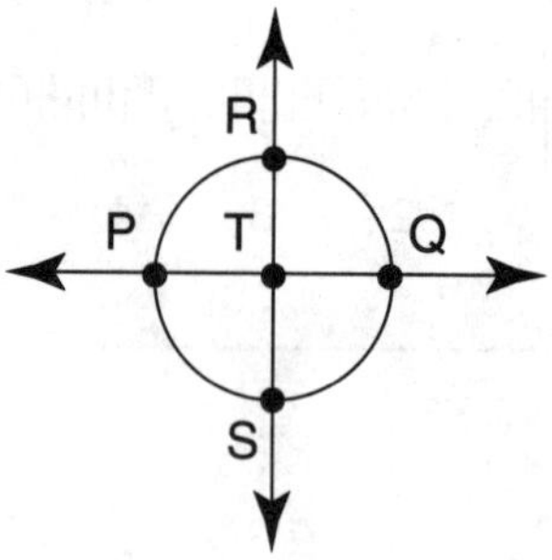

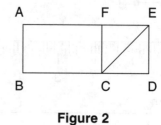

Figure 1

Directions: Use Figure 2 to name each of the following. There may be more than one correct answer.

7. a square

8. parallel segments

9. a triangle

10. perpendicular segments

Figure 2

11. an angle that is not a right angle

12. a rectangle that is not a square

13. three segments having the same length

14. three angles having the same measure

Directions: Circle *T* if the statement is true, or *F* if it is false.

15. **T** **F** A square has perpendicular sides.

16. **T** **F** A 30° angle is larger than a right angle.

17. **T** **F** Parallel lines are always the same distance from each other.

18. **T** **F** A rectangle is a square.

19. **T** **F** A rectangle has parallel sides.

20. **T** **F** A triangle can have parallel sides.

21. **T** **F** A triangle can have more than one right angle.

22. **T** **F** Perpendicular lines do not intersect.

23. **T** **F** Lines in the same plane either intersect or are parallel.

24. **T** **F** Two perpendicular lines form four 90° angles.

ANSWERS ARE ON PAGE 303.

PERIMETER AND CIRCUMFERENCE

The distance around a figure such as a triangle, rectangle, or square is its ***perimeter***. To find the perimeter of a figure, simply add the lengths of all the sides.

EXAMPLE 1 Find the perimeter of the rectangle shown.

28 cm

10 cm ☐ 10 cm

28 cm

Perimeter = 28 + 10 + 28 + 10 = 76 cm

EXAMPLE 2 Find the perimeter of a square with sides 5 ft long.

STEP 1 Draw a diagram.

5 ft

STEP 2   A square has four equal sides, so each side is 5 ft long.

Perimeter = 5 + 5 + 5 + 5 = 20 ft

The distance around a circle is its **circumference**. This measure depends on the radius or diameter of the circle. The **radius** of a circle is the distance from the center to any point on the curve of the circle. The **diameter** is a line segment that crosses the circle through its center from one side to the other.

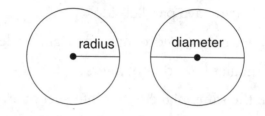

If you know the radius of a circle, multiply by 2 to find its diameter. If you know the diameter of a circle, divide by 2 to find its radius.

EXAMPLE 3   Find the radius and diameter of the circle shown.

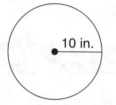

The radius is labeled: 10 in.
The diameter is twice the radius: 10 in. × 2 = 20 in.

To find the circumference of a circle, multiply its diameter by π (pi), which is about 3.14 or $\frac{22}{7}$.

TIP: Use $\pi \approx \frac{22}{7}$ when the diameter or radius is a multiple of 7. Otherwise, use $\pi \approx 3.14$.

EXAMPLE 4   Find the circumference of a circle with a diameter of 21 ft.
Since the diameter is a multiple of 7, use $\pi \approx \frac{22}{7}$.

Circumference = $\pi \times d \approx \frac{22}{7} \times 21 = 66$ ft

EXAMPLE 5   Find the circumference of a circle with a radius of 12 cm.

STEP 1   Find the diameter.

d = 12 cm × 2 = 24 cm

STEP 2   Since the diameter is not a multiple of 7, use $\pi \approx 3.14$.

Circumference = $\pi \times d \approx 3.14 \times 24 = 75.36$ cm

SUMMARY FOR FINDING PERIMETER AND CIRCUMFERENCE
To find the perimeter of a triangle, square, or rectangle: Add the lengths of its sides. To find the circumference of a circle: Multiply its diameter by π (pi).

EXERCISE 7

Directions: Find the perimeter or circumference of each figure shown. Show your work.

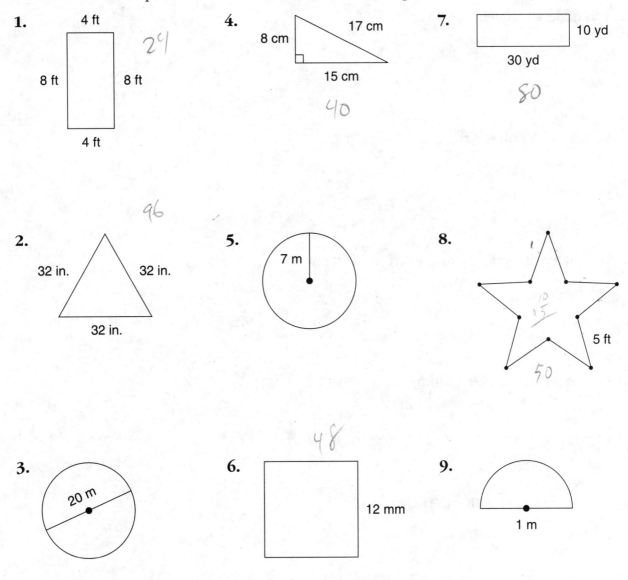

1.   4 ft

24

8 ft   8 ft

4 ft

4.   17 cm

8 cm

15 cm

40

7.   10 yd

30 yd

80

2.   96

32 in.   32 in.

32 in.

5.   7 m

8.   10 ×5

5 ft

50

3.   20 m

6.   48

12 mm

9.   1 m

Directions: Find the perimeter or circumference of each figure described.

10. A square with sides 9 in.

36

11. A rectangle with length 8 mm and width 11 mm

38

12. A triangle with each side 15 cm

45

13. A circle with radius 3 ft

14. A triangle with sides 30 cm, 40 cm, and 50 cm

120

15. A circle with diameter 42 mm

16. A six-sided figure with each side 12 m

72

ANSWERS ARE ON PAGE 303.

EXERCISE 8

Directions: Solve each problem below.

1. The perimeter of a square is 16 meters. What is the length of each side?

2. The perimeter of a rectangle is 24 feet. If the width is 7 feet, what is the length?

3. The perimeter of a triangle is 29 centimeters. Two of the sides are 10 centimeters long. What is the length of the third side?

4. A circle has a circumference of 22 inches. What is the radius of the circle? (HINT: Use $\pi \approx \frac{22}{7}$.)

3.5

$$C = \pi d$$

$$\frac{22}{7} = \frac{3.14 d}{1}$$

$$\frac{22}{1} = \frac{22}{7} d$$

$$\frac{22}{7} \qquad \frac{22}{7}$$

5. A rectangle has a perimeter of 50 feet. Which dimensions are not possible?

    (1) sides: 11 feet, 12 feet, 13 feet, 14 feet
    (2) sides: 5 feet, 20 feet, 5 feet, 20 feet
    (3) length 8 feet, width 17 feet
    (4) length 1 feet, width 24 feet

$$\frac{22 \div 22}{1 \qquad 7}$$

$$\frac{22}{1} \times \frac{7}{22} = 7$$

6. A circle has a circumference of 44 centimeters. Which dimension is possible?

    (1) radius 7.1 centimeters   14.2   44.588
    (2) radius 7 centimeters   14   43.96
    (3) diameter 15 centimeters   47.1
    (4) diameter 12 centimeters   37.68

ANSWERS ARE ON PAGE 303.

AREA

The **_area_** of a figure is the amount of surface covered by the figure. The shaded region of each shape below shows its area. Area is measured in square units.

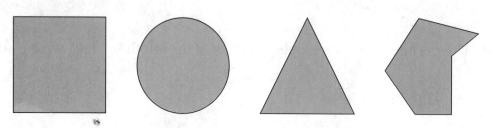

To find the area of a rectangle, multiply its length and width.

EXAMPLE 1   Find the area of the rectangle shown.

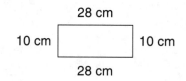

Area = length × width = 28 cm × 10 cm = 280 sq cm (or cm²)

To find the area of a square, multiply its length and width.

EXAMPLE 2   Find the area of a square with sides 5 feet long.

STEP 1   Draw a diagram.

5 ft

STEP 2   A square has four equal sides, so its length is 5 feet and its width is 5 feet.

Area = 5 ft × 5 ft = 25 ft²

To find the area of a triangle, first identify the base and height of the triangle. The base is always the side that the triangle rests on. The height is the length of the segment perpendicular to the base and extending to the "top" of the triangle. In each triangle shown below, the base is labeled b and the height is labeled h.

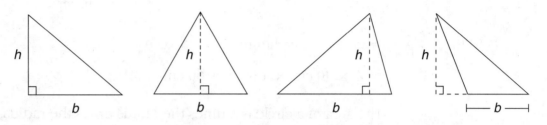

EXAMPLE 3   Find the base and height of a triangle with right angle ABC and sides AB = 3 meters, BC = 4 meters, and AC = 5 meters.

STEP 1   Draw a diagram.

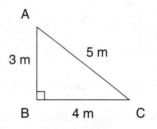

STEP 2   Since AB and BC are perpendicular, the height of the triangle is AB and has a measure of 3 meters. The base of the triangle is BC and has a measure of 4 meters.

TIP: Be careful to identify the base and height of a triangle before finding its area.

The area of a triangle is half its base times its height.

EXAMPLE 4   Find the area of the triangle shown.

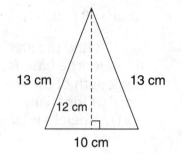

STEP 1   Identify the base and height.
base = 10 cm; height = 12 cm

STEP 2   Area = $\frac{1}{2}$ × base × height

   = $\frac{1}{2}$ × 10 cm × 12 cm = 60 cm²

The area of a circle is π times the radius times the radius again. Use π ≈ $\frac{22}{7}$ or π ≈ 3.14.

EXAMPLE 5   Find the area of the circle shown.

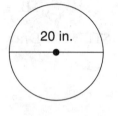

STEP 1   Find the radius.

Diameter ÷ 2 = 20 in. ÷ 2 = 10 in.

STEP 2   Since the radius is not a multiple of 7, use π ≈ 3.14.

Area = π × radius × radius
   ≈ 3.14 × 10 in. × 10 in. ≈ 314 in.²

SUMMARY FOR FINDING AREA

Rectangle: Area = length × width

Triangle: Area = $\frac{1}{2}$ × base × height

Circle: Area = π × radius × radius

EXERCISE 9

Directions: Find the area of each figure shown. Show your work.

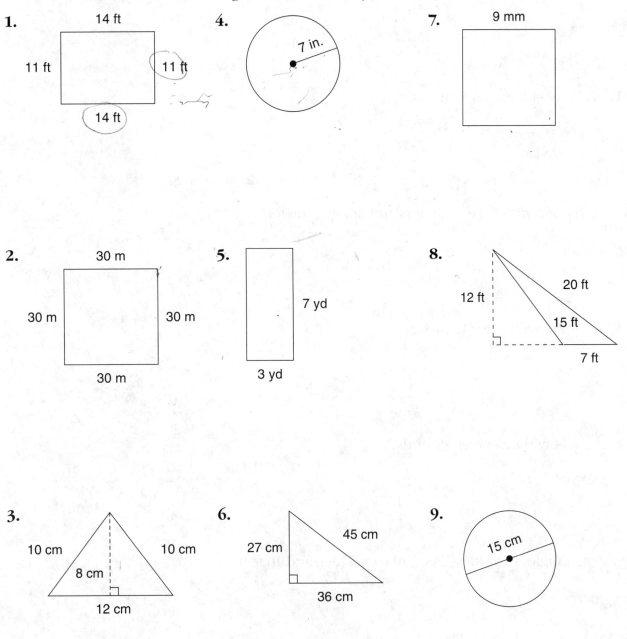

1.
14 ft
11 ft   11 ft
14 ft

4.
7 in.

7.
9 mm

2.
30 m
30 m   30 m
30 m

5.
7 yd
3 yd

8.
12 ft   20 ft
15 ft
7 ft

3.
10 cm   10 cm
8 cm
12 cm

6.
27 cm   45 cm
36 cm

9.
15 cm

Directions: Find the area of each figure described. Show your work.

10. A rectangle with length 9 millimeters and width 6 millimeters

11. A circle with radius 3 meters

12. A triangle with base 10 meters and height 3 meters

13. A square with sides 12 inches

14. A circle with diameter 28 yards

15. A rectangle with sides 3 feet, 10 feet, 3 feet, and 10 feet

16. A triangle with right angle ABC and sides AB = 8 centimeters, BC = 15 centimeters, and AC = 17 centimeters

ANSWERS ARE ON PAGE 303.

EXERCISE 10

Directions: Solve each problem below.

1. The area of a square is 16 square meters. What is the length of each side?

2. The area of a rectangle is 36 square feet. If the width is 4 feet, what is the length?

3. The area of a triangle is 30 square centimeters. Its base is 6 centimeters. What is its height?

4. A circle has an area of 120 square inches. Is its radius closer to 6 inches or 7 inches?

5. A rectangle has an area of 48 square feet. Which dimensions are not possible?

    (1) sides: 6 feet, 8 feet, 6 feet, 8 feet
    (2) sides: 2 feet, 24 feet, 2 feet, 24 feet.
    (3) length 3 feet, width 16 feet
    (4) length 4 feet, width 13 feet

6. A triangle has an area of 12 square centimeters. Which dimensions are possible?

    (1) base 12 centimeters, height 1 centimeter
    (2) base 12 centimeters, height 2 centimeters
    (3) base 3 centimeters, height 4 centimeters
    (4) base 6 centimeters, height 2 centimeters

ANSWERS ARE ON PAGE 304.

VOLUME

Volume is a measure of the space inside a three-dimensional figure. It is like capacity, the amount a container can hold. Volume is measured in cubic units.

The figure below is called a **rectangular solid** because it is made up of rectangles. We commonly call it a box.

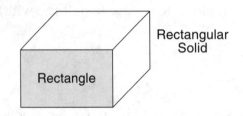

To find the volume of a rectangular solid, multiply its length, width, and height.

EXAMPLE 1   Find the volume of the rectangular solid shown.

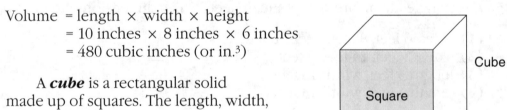

Volume = length × width × height
        = 10 inches × 8 inches × 6 inches
        = 480 cubic inches (or in.³)

A **cube** is a rectangular solid made up of squares. The length, width, and height of a cube are equal.

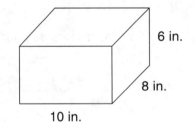

EXAMPLE 2   Find the volume of a cube with side 10 centimeters.

Volume = length × width × height

= 10 centimeters × 10 centimeters × 10 centimeters

= 1,000 cubic centimeters (or cm³)

SUMMARY FOR FINDING VOLUME

To find the volume of a rectangular solid:

1) Multiply its length, width, and height.

EXERCISE 11

Directions: Find the volume of each figure shown. Show your work.

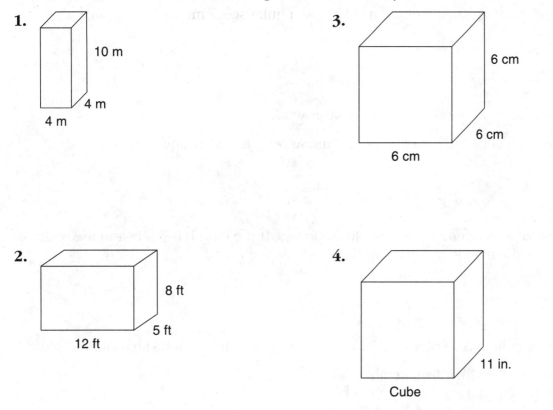

1.   10 m   4 m   4 m

2.   8 ft   5 ft   12 ft

3.   6 cm   6 cm   6 cm

4.   11 in.   Cube

Directions: Find the volume of each figure described. Show your work.

  5. A rectangular solid with length 4 feet, width 2 feet, and height 7 feet

  6. A rectangular solid with length 20 meters, width 5 meters, and height 1 meter

  7. A cube with side 2 centimeters

  8. A cube with side 14 inches

Directions: Solve each problem below. Show your work.

  9. The volume of a cube is 27 cubic meters. Find its length, width, and height.

  10. The volume of a rectangular solid is 126 cubic feet. If the length is 3 feet and the width is 7 feet, what is the height?

  11. A rectangular solid has a volume of 72 cubic feet. Which dimensions are not possible?

  (1) length 2 feet, width 4 feet, height 9 feet
  (2) length 6 feet, width 6 feet, height 2 feet
  (3) length 9 feet, width 8 feet, height 0 feet
  (4) length 3 feet, width 6 feet, height 4 feet

  12. A cube has a volume of 64 cubic centimeters. Which dimension is possible?

  (1) side 4 centimeters
  (2) side 16 centimeters
  (3) side 8 centimeters
  (4) side $21\frac{1}{3}$ centimeters

ANSWERS ARE ON PAGE 304.

MEASUREMENT AND GEOMETRY PROBLEMS

In this section you will combine your skills of measurement, geometry, and problem solving. Remember to use the five-step approach to solve each problem. With measurement and geometry problems, you need to pay attention to units. Also, if a diagram is not given, it may be helpful to draw your own.

EXAMPLE 1   A bowling lane, from the foul line to the first pin, is 60 feet long. A bowling ball measures 27 inches around. If a bowling ball is rolled straight down a bowling lane and hits the first pin, how many revolutions will the ball make?

STEP 1   Understand the question.

You must figure out how many times the ball will "rotate" while rolling from the foul line to the first pin.

STEP 2   Decide what information is needed.

The distance the ball will roll is 60 feet. The distance around the ball is 27 inches. Draw a diagram showing this information.

STEP 3   Choose the most appropriate operation.

Change 60 feet to inches so that both measurements are inches. Divide by 27 inches for the number of revolutions.

STEP 4   Solve the problem.

60 feet × 12 = 720 inches; 720 inches ÷ 27 inches = $26\frac{2}{3}$ revolutions

STEP 5   Check your answer.

Use feet, rather than inches, to check your answer.

27 inches ÷ 12 = $2\frac{1}{4}$ feet;

$2\frac{1}{4}$ feet × $26\frac{2}{3}$ revolutions = 60 feet

EXERCISE 12

Directions: Solve each problem below. Show your work.

1. The Russian space shuttle Buran has a wing-span of 79.2 feet. NASA's space shuttle wing-span is 78.6 feet. Which wing-span is greater? How much greater?

2. A pyramid near Cairo, Egypt is approximately 450 feet high. Its square base has sides 755 feet long. What is the area of the base of the pyramid?

3. The Sears Tower in Chicago is 443 meters high. The Empire State Building in New York City is 381 meters high. How much higher is the Sears Tower than the Empire State Building?

4. A "board foot" is a unit used for lumber. It measures 12 inches by 12 inches by 1 inch. What is the volume (cubic inches) of one board foot?

5. A football field is $53\frac{1}{3}$ yards wide. Express the width of a football field in feet.

6. Which figure has the greater area, a circle with a diameter of 2 inches or a square with a side of 2 inches? Draw a diagram to show your result.

7. In 4 weeks, a baby gained 3 pounds. On average, how many ounces did the baby gain each day?

8. At birth, Abby weighed 6 pounds 9 ounces. At her 1-month doctor checkup, she weighed 8 pounds 13 ounces. Gaining at this rate, how much will she weigh at her 2-month checkup?

9. A brownie recipe suggests the use of two 8-inch square pans or one rectangular pan that measures 13 inches by 9 inches. Which will result in thicker brownies?

10. This sentence is printed on a 5-pound sack of flour: "There are about four cups of flour in one pound." A recipe for a loaf of bread requires $1\frac{3}{4}$ cups of flour. How many loaves of bread can you make with this sack of flour?

ANSWERS ARE ON PAGE 304.

PERIMETER, CIRCUMFERENCE, AREA, AND VOLUME PROBLEMS

Many problems involve finding perimeter, circumference, area, or volume. Sometimes you need to decide which of these measures to calculate in order to solve a problem. Here are some useful hints.

- Perimeter and circumference are both distances around a figure. They are one-dimensional measures of length.

- Area is the amount of surface. Area is a two-dimensional measure, so use square units.

- Volume is the amount of space. Volume is a three-dimensional measure, so use cubic units.

Here's a problem that involves the three different types of measures. Suppose you buy a tiny present for someone and decide to wrap it in the box shown below. Refer to this box for the examples.

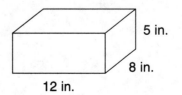

EXAMPLE 1   How much styrofoam filling will the box hold?

STEP 1   Decide which measure to calculate and which units to use.

The problem asks for the amount of space in the box, a three-dimensional measure. Find the volume (cubic inches, or in.^{3}).

STEP 2   Volume = length × width × height
= 12 inches × 8 inches × 5 inches
= 480 cubic inches
The box will hold 480 cubic inches (in.^{3}) of styrofoam filling.

EXAMPLE 2   How much wrapping paper will cover the box?

STEP 1   Decide which measure to calculate and which units to use.

The problem asks for the amount of surface on each rectangle of the box. Find its area (square inches).

STEP 2   Draw a diagram and calculate the area for each rectangle.

Top: Area = 12 × 8 = 96 in.^{2}
Bottom: Area = 12 × 8 = 96 in.^{2}

Front: Area = 12 × 5 = 60 in.^{2}
Back: Area = 12 × 5 = 60 in.^{2}

Left side: Area = 8 × 5 = 40 in.^{2}
Right side: Area = 8 × 5 = 40 in.^{2}

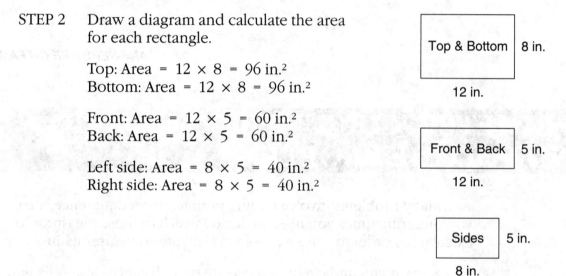

STEP 3   Add the areas: 96 + 96 + 60 + 60 + 40 + 40 = 392 in.^{2}
Therefore, 392 square inches of wrapping paper will cover the box.

EXAMPLE 3   How much ribbon will go around the box in two directions?

STEP 1   Decide which measure to calculate and which units to use.

The problem asks for the distance around the box, a measure of length. Find its perimeter (inches).

STEP 2   Draw a diagram and calculate the length of the ribbon going around the box.

Vertical direction:
5 + 8 + 5 + 8 = 26 in.

Horizontal direction:
5 + 12 + 5 + 12 = 34 in.

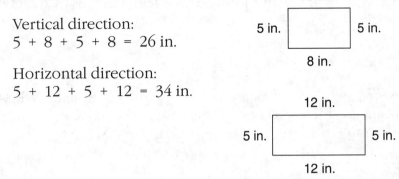

STEP 3   Add the lengths: 26 in. + 34 in. = 60 in. or 5 ft
Therefore, 60 inches (or 5 feet) of ribbon will go around the box.

EXERCISE 13

Directions: Solve each problem below. Show your work.

1. The Eichenbergers live on a corner lot that measures 120 feet by 80 feet. They must add sidewalks along the edge of their lot next to the street. New sidewalks cost $12 per foot. How much will their new sidewalks cost?

2. Sidewalks are 5 feet wide. They are divided into sections that are 5 feet long. How many sections will a sidewalk that is 120 feet long have?

3. The Eichenbergers' new sidewalk will be 200 feet long and 5 feet wide. How much area will the new sidewalk cover?

4. Sidewalks are 4 inches deep. One section of sidewalk is 5 feet long and 5 feet wide. How much concrete (ft³) will be used for one section?

5. Beth is decorating her bedroom. The floor measures 12 feet by 15 feet. How much carpet (yd²) does she need to cover the floor of her bedroom?

6. Beth will add trim along the edge of her room and around the door frame. The room measures 12 feet by 15 feet. The door measures 2 feet 6 inches by 6 feet 8 inches. How much trim does she need?

7. An ice cube tray makes 12 ice cubes. Each ice cube is 3 centimeters wide, 4 centimeters long, and 3 centimeters high. Will one liter of water fill two ice cube trays? (HINT: 1 cm^3 = 1 mL)

8. A college basketball court is 94 feet long and 50 feet wide. A high school basketball court is 84 feet long and 50 feet wide. How much more floor space does the college court have?

9. A 10-inch pizza costs $8, while a 12-inch pizza costs $10.50. Which size pizza is the better buy?

10. Annika's favorite part of a pizza is its crust around the edge. How much more crust does a 12-inch pizza have than a 10-inch pizza?

11. Which unit is appropriate for a perimeter measurement?

    (1) square yards
    (2) in.^{3}
    (3) cm
    (4) liter

12. Which unit is not appropriate for a volume measurement?

    (1) cubic centimeter
    (2) in.^{2}
    (3) m^3
    (4) cup

ANSWERS ARE ON PAGE 304.

MEASUREMENT AND GEOMETRY REVIEW

Directions: In questions 1–18, solve each problem. Show your work to the right.

1. Write the length of segment AB.

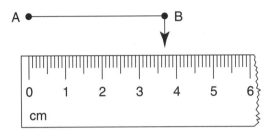

2. How many cups are in one gallon?

3. Find the perimeter of a rectangle with length 15 meters and width 10 meters.

4. What type of lines never intersect?

5. Change 2.5 kilograms to grams.

6. Find the diameter of a circle with radius 8 feet.

7. Find the area of the rectangle shown.

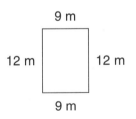

8. What figure is made up of the set of points all the same distance from a center point?

9. Change 80 ounces to pounds.

10. Find the volume of a cube whose side measures 7 meters.

11. Find the circumference of a circle with a diameter of 6 inches.

12. Change 300 centimeters to meters.

13. The perimeter of a square is 20 inches. Find the length of each side.

14. Find the area of triangle ABC.

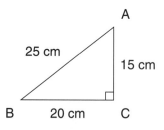

15. Draw and label a right angle formed by rays PT and PR.

16. Find the area of a circle that has a radius of 4 centimeters.

17. Find the volume of the rectangular solid shown.

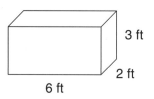

18. Change 64 inches to feet and inches.

Directions: Questions 19–30 include whole numbers, decimals, fractions, measurement, and geometry. Choose the correct answer to each problem. Remember the problem-solving skills you have learned.

19. Mia's quiz scores are 90, 82, 88, 89, and 74. Find the average, using the following grading scale.

A   90–100
B   80–89
C   70–79
D   60–69
F   0–59

(1) A
(2) B
(3) C
(4) D
(5) F

20. Which of the following is a set of equivalent numbers?

(1) $140\frac{1}{3}$, 47, $\frac{141}{3}$
(2) 0.04, $\frac{4}{10}$, $\frac{2}{5}$
(3) $\frac{1}{8}$, 1.25, $\frac{3}{16}$
(4) 12.5, $12\frac{1}{2}$, $\frac{24}{2}$
(5) 6.2, $6\frac{1}{5}$, $6\frac{2}{10}$

21. In her purse, Susan has two five dollar bills, five quarters, two dimes, and four pennies. In her purse, Patty has eight dollar bills, two quarters, eight dimes, and ten nickels. Which of the following statements is true?

(1) Susan and Patty have the same number of coins.
(2) Susan has more money in her purse than Patty.
(3) Patty and Susan each have under $10 in her purse.
(4) Patty has more money in her purse than Susan.
(5) The difference in the amount of money in their purses is less than a dollar.

22. The regulation home plate for a baseball field has dimensions shown. How much tape would you need to go around the home plate?

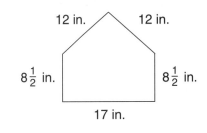

(1) 58 in.
(2) 144.5 in.
(3) 4 ft 10 in.
(4) 75 in.
(5) both (1) and (3) are correct

23. A cake mix suggests the use of two 9-inch circular pans for a layer cake, or one 13-inch by 9-inch rectangular pan for a sheet cake. If the sheet cake is about 2 inches high, how high would you expect each circular cake to be?

(1) slightly less than 2 in.
(2) slightly more than 2 in.
(3) 4 in.
(4) 1 in.
(5) none of the above

24. A weekday long-distance telephone call from Bozeman to Billings costs $0.41 for the first minute and $0.29 for each additional minute. At this rate, how much will a 15-minute phone call cost?

(1) $4.76
(2) $5.25
(3) $6.03
(4) $4.47
(5) not enough information is given

25. The area of a square is 81 in.^{2} Find the perimeter of the square.

(1) 18 in.
(2) 9 in.
(3) 36 in.
(4) 324 in.
(5) not enough information is given

26. Aram earns $5.50 per hour at a movie theater. One week he worked $2\frac{1}{2}$ hours on Friday, 6 hours on Saturday, and 8 hours on Sunday. How much money did he earn that week?

(1) $88.00
(2) $16.50
(3) $90.75
(4) $82.50
(5) none of the above

27. Which decimal number is rounded to the nearest thousandth?

(1) 6.8945 rounded to 6.895
(2) 3.61249 rounded to 3.6125
(3) 19.1406 rounded to 19.14
(4) 2,100 rounded to 2,000
(5) 48,000 rounded to 50,000

28. Tsung-Chi and Juanita are going on a 1,200-mile trip. If Juanita drives about $\frac{1}{4}$ of the distance, how many miles will Tsung-Chi drive?

(1) 300 miles
(2) 900 miles
(3) 240 miles
(4) 960 miles
(5) 4,800 miles

29. The diagram below shows a bowling lane. How wide is the lane, including the two gutters?

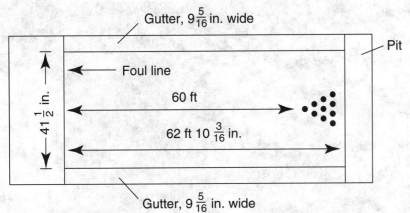

Note: measurements not to scale

(1) $41\frac{1}{2}$ in.

(2) $50\frac{13}{16}$ in.

(3) $18\frac{5}{8}$ in.

(4) $59\frac{11}{16}$ in.

(5) $60\frac{1}{8}$ in.

30. Use the diagram of the bowling lane in Problem 29. What is the distance from the first pin to the pit?

(1) 60 ft

(2) $10\frac{3}{16}$ in.

(3) 2 ft $10\frac{13}{16}$ in.

(4) 2 ft $10\frac{3}{16}$ in.

(5) not enough information is given

ANSWERS ARE ON PAGE 305.

5 Ratios, Proportions, and Percents

RATIOS

A ***ratio*** is a comparison of two numbers. For example, you can use a ratio to compare the numbers 2 and 7. There are three different ways to write the ratio:

by using the word *to*	by using a colon	by writing a fraction
2 to 7	2 : 7	$\frac{2}{7}$

Think of a ratio as a fraction. Just as the fractions $\frac{2}{7}$ and $\frac{7}{2}$ are not the same, the ratios "2 to 7" and "7 to 2" are not the same. So the *order* of the two numbers in a ratio is important. A ratio must be reduced to lowest terms.

EXAMPLE 1 In Bob's family, there are 2 boys and 4 girls. What is the ratio of boys to girls in Bob's family?

STEP 1 Write the ratio in one of these three ways.

Use the word *to*.	Use a colon.	Write a fraction.
2 boys to 4 girls	2 boys : 4 girls	$\frac{2 \text{ boys}}{4 \text{ girls}}$
2 to 4	2 : 4	$\frac{2}{4}$

STEP 2 Reduce to lowest terms.

Use the word *to*.	Use a colon.	Write a fraction.
1 boy to 2 girls	1 boy : 2 girls	$\frac{1 \text{ boy}}{2 \text{ girls}}$
1 to 2	1 : 2	$\frac{1}{2}$

STEP 3   Make a statement about the ratio.

The following statements are all appropriate.
The ratio of boys to girls in Bob's family is 1 to 2.
The ratio of boys to girls in Bob's family is 1 : 2.
The ratio of boys to girls in Bob's family is $\frac{1}{2}$.

SUMMARY FOR WRITING RATIOS

To write a ratio comparing two numbers:

1) Use the word to, use a colon, or write a fraction.

2) The order of the numbers is important.

3) Reduce the ratio to lowest terms.

Some ratio problems require calculation before you write the ratio.
See the example below.

EXAMPLE 2   In a class of 30 students, there are 14 boys. What is the ratio of boys to girls in the class?

STEP 1   Calculate the number of girls in the class since this number is not given.

30 students − 14 boys = 16 girls

STEP 2   Write the ratio of boys to girls.

$\frac{14}{16}$

STEP 3   Reduce the ratio to lowest terms.

$\frac{14}{16} = \frac{7}{8}$

STEP 4   Make a statement about the ratio.

The ratio of boys to girls in the class is 7 to 8.

EXERCISE 1

Directions: Write each ratio in two other ways.

1. 6 to 7

2. 1 : 50

3. $\frac{7}{3}$

4. $\frac{10}{19}$

5. 13 : 1

6. 2 to 5

Directions: Write a ratio for each situation described.

7. To make orange juice, combine 1 can of concentrate with 3 cans of water. Write the ratio of concentrate to water.

8. Drew takes home $2,000 a month. He saves $200 and spends the rest. Write a ratio of the amount Drew spends to the amount Drew saves each month.

9. The Bobcats lost 9 games and won 2 games this season. Write the ratio of wins to losses.

10. Pam sleeps 8 hours every night. Write a ratio of Pam's time spent sleeping to Pam's time spent not sleeping.

11. To make lemonade, add 4 cans of water to every can of concentrate. Write the ratio of water to concentrate.

12. A ski resort advertised that it had 23 snow days during January. Write a ratio of snow days to no-snow days.

13. In a local election, Marshall received 582 votes while Hawks received 366 votes. Write a ratio of the number of votes for Hawks to the number of votes for Marshall.

14. Write the ratio of vowels to consonants in the word *extravagant.*

Directions: Results from three survey questions are given in the table below. Use these results to write the ratios indicated in Problems 15 – 20.

	"Yes"	**"No"**
Question 1	76	32
Question 2	100	8
Question 3	25	83

15. "Yes" : "No" for Question 1

16. "No" : "Yes" for Question 2

17. "Yes" for Question 3 : "Yes" for Question 2

18. "No" for Question 1 : "No" for Question 2

19. Total "Yes" : Total "No" for Questions 1–3

20. "Yes" for Question 2 : "Yes" for Questions 1 and 3 combined

Directions: Choose the best answer.

21. Which statement does not have the same meaning as "the ratio of males to females is 1 to 2"?

    (1) Half are male, and half are female.
    (2) There are twice as many females as males.
    (3) For each male, there are two females.
    (4) Two out of three are female.
    (5) One out of three is male.

22. Three of Hannah's answers on a test of 30 problems were wrong. Which of the following is a ratio of right answers to wrong answers?

    (1) 30 to 3
    (2) 3 to 27
    (3) 27 to 30
    (4) 10 to 1
    (5) 9 to 1

ANSWERS ARE ON PAGE 305.

RATES

A **rate** shows a relationship between two quantities measured in different units. Rates are a commonly used type of ratio. A **unit rate** is the rate for one unit of a given quantity. To find a unit rate, you divide the two numbers in the ratio.

EXAMPLE 1   Ken and Barbara used 16 gallons of gasoline to drive 500 miles. Find the unit rate of gas mileage (miles per gallon).

STEP 1   Write the ratio of miles to gallons: $\frac{500 \text{ miles}}{16 \text{ gallons}}$.

Note that this is a rate, but not a unit rate.

STEP 2   Divide so that you have a unit rate.

500 miles ÷ 16 gallons = 31.25 miles per gallon

A **unit price** is the price per unit of an item. Divide to find a unit price.

EXAMPLE 2   Soap is priced at $1.19 for 4 bars. Find the unit price.

STEP 1   Write the ratio of price to number of bars: $\frac{\$1.19}{4 \text{ bars}}$.

STEP 2   Divide so that you have a unit price.

$1.19 ÷ 4 bars = $0.2975 per bar

STEP 3   Round to the nearest cent.

$0.2975 rounds up to $0.30.
The unit price is about $.30 per bar.

SUMMARY FOR FINDING RATES AND UNIT PRICES

To find a unit rate:

1) Write a ratio of the two quantities.

2) Divide to find the unit rate.

3) To find a unit price, divide price by the number of units.

EXERCISE 2

Directions: Write the unit rate for each situation described.

1. On a 15-minute typing test, Neysa typed 825 words. What was Neysa's typing rate (words per minute)?

2. This week, Ravi worked 20 hours and earned $130. What is his earning rate (dollars per hour)?

3. Louisa and Won drove 135 miles and used 6 gallons of gasoline. Find the gas mileage rate of their car (miles per gallon).

4. Les and Erna drove 210 miles in $3\frac{1}{2}$ hours. Find their rate of travel (miles per hour).

Directions: Write each unit price.

5. 5 pounds of potatoes for $1.49

6. 10 pencils for $.99

7. 3 rolls of film for $8

8. A dozen eggs for $1.09

Directions: Solve each problem.

9. Consuela's car used 12 gallons of gasoline for 330 miles of highway driving. Bill's car used 10 gallons for 300 miles of highway driving. Which car has better gas mileage?

10. Robin ran a 10-kilometer race in 42 minutes 30 seconds. What was her average rate (kilometers per minute)?

11. Brian ran 6 miles in 50 minutes. On average, did he run *faster* or *slower* than 8 minutes per mile?

12. Lorenzo normally types 80 words per minute. On his last test, he typed 416 words in 5 minutes. Is this *faster* or *slower* than his normal typing rate?

13. Suppose your favorite shampoo is sold in two sizes. The 15-oz bottle costs $2.79, and the 12-oz bottle costs $1.99. Is the bigger bottle the better buy?

14. You have three choices for buying soda: a 6-pack for $2.19, a 12-pack for $3.99, or a 24-pack for $8.49. Which is the best buy? Which is the worst buy?

ANSWERS ARE ON PAGE 306.

PROPORTIONS

A ***proportion*** is made up of two equal ratios. If you think of ratios as fractions, then the two ratios in a proportion are equivalent fractions.

EXAMPLE 1   Write a proportion, using "3 to 4" as one of the ratios.

STEP 1   Write the given ratio as a fraction: $\frac{3}{4}$

STEP 2   Write an equivalent fraction.

$$\frac{3}{4} = \frac{3 \times 2}{4 \times 2} = \frac{6}{8}$$

STEP 3   Write the proportion.

$$\frac{3}{4} = \frac{6}{8}$$

Sometimes you can use the idea of equivalent fractions to decide if two ratios form a proportion or not. "Do the two ratios form a proportion?" is the same as asking, "Are the two fractions equivalent?"

EXAMPLE 2   Do the two ratios $\frac{4}{10}$ and $\frac{5}{12}$ form a proportion?

STEP 1   Find a common denominator: 60.

STEP 2   Write each as a fraction with denominator 60.

$$\frac{4}{10} = \frac{4 \times 6}{10 \times 6} = \frac{24}{60}$$

$$\frac{5}{12} = \frac{5 \times 5}{12 \times 5} = \frac{25}{60}$$

STEP 3   Are the two fractions equivalent? No, since $\frac{24}{60} \neq \frac{25}{60}$.

Do the two ratios form a proportion? No.

A quick way to see if two ratios form a proportion or not is to check their two cross products. A **_cross product_** is the numerator of one ratio multiplied by the denominator of the other ratio. If the cross products are equal, the ratios form a proportion. If the cross products are not equal, the ratios do not form a proportion.

EXAMPLE 3   Do the two ratios $\frac{2}{15}$ and $\frac{3}{16}$ form a proportion?

STEP 1   Find cross products: $2 \times 16 = 32$, and $15 \times 3 = 45$

STEP 2   Are the cross products equal? No, since $32 \neq 45$.

Do the two ratios form a proportion? No.

You can use proportions to solve some rate problems.

EXAMPLE 4   On Monday, Sam drove 100 miles in 2 hours. On Tuesday, he drove 125 miles in $2\frac{1}{2}$ hours. Did he drive the same rate on Tuesday as on Monday? If so, write a proportion showing that the two ratios (rates) are equal.

STEP 1   Divide to find each rate.

100 miles ÷ 2 hours = 50 miles per hour

125 miles ÷ $2\frac{1}{2}$ hours = 50 miles per hour

STEP 2   Answer the question.

Yes, Sam drove the same rate on Tuesday as on Monday (50 miles per hour).

STEP 3   Write a proportion showing that the rates are equal.

$$\frac{100}{2} = \frac{125}{2.5}$$

STEP 4   Use cross products to check your answer.

$100 \times 2.5 = 250; 2 \times 125 = 250$

The cross products are equal, so the rates are equal.

> **TIP:** The two ratios that form a proportion must be equal. So, the two ratios must be equivalent fractions or equivalent rates. Also, their cross products must be equal.

EXERCISE 3

Directions: Do the two ratios form a proportion? If so, write the proportion.

1. $\frac{2}{3}, \frac{10}{15}$

5. 3 to 4, 5 to 8

2. $\frac{1}{4}, \frac{2}{9}$

6. 50 to 20, 10 to 4

3. $\frac{16}{3}, \frac{8}{1}$

7. 1 : 2, 6 : 9

4. $\frac{5}{5}, \frac{3}{3}$

8. 8 : 3, 24 : 9

Directions: Form a proportion, using the ratio given. There is more than one correct answer.

9. $\frac{1}{9}$

13. 13 to 1

10. $\frac{25}{20}$

14. $\frac{17}{3}$

11. 12 to 13

15. 5 : 11

12. 6 : 3

16. 10 : 3

Directions: Solve each problem.

17. Photographs measure either 3 inches by 5 inches, or 4 inches by 6 inches. Do the ratios of $\frac{width}{length}$ form a proportion? Show your work.

18. Barb mixed three parts of blue paint with one part of yellow paint to make green paint. Bonnie mixed five parts of blue paint with two parts of yellow paint to make green paint. Will the two shades of green paint be the same? Why or why not?

19. Tessa typed 650 words in 10 minutes. Suzie typed 780 words in 12 minutes. Do the two rates form a proportion? Is their typing speed the same?

20. A dozen large eggs cost $1.09. At the same rate, how much should two dozen large eggs cost? Express this as a proportion.

Directions: Choose the best answer.

21. Which of the following is the correct pair of cross products for the proportion $\frac{5}{6} = \frac{20}{24}$?

    (1) $5 \times 20, 6 \times 24$
    (2) $5 \times 24, 6 \times 20$
    (3) $5 \times 6, 20 \times 24$
    (4) $5 \times 4 = 20, 6 \times 4 = 24$
    (5) none of the above

22. Which ratio will not form a proportion with the ratio "1 to 5"?

    (1) 5 to 25
    (2) 2 to 10
    (3) 5 to 1
    (4) 1.5 to 7.5
    (5) 24 to 120

23. Which statement is true of the proportion $\frac{3}{4} = \frac{9}{12}$?

    (1) 3 : 4 and 9 : 12 are equal ratios.

    (2) $\frac{9}{12}$ and $\frac{3}{4}$ are equivalent fractions.

    (3) Cross products 3 × 12 and 4 × 9 are equal.

    (4) The ratios $\frac{3}{4}$ and $\frac{9}{12}$ form a proportion.

    (5) All the statements above are true.

24. The unit price of toothpaste is $.16 per ounce. Which of the following is a proportion that shows this?

    (1) $\frac{\$1.60}{10 \text{ oz}}$

    (2) $\frac{\$1.00}{16 \text{ oz}}$

    (3) $\frac{\$1.20}{10 \text{ oz}} = \frac{\$1.68}{14 \text{ oz}}$

    (4) $\frac{\$1.28}{8 \text{ oz}} = \frac{\$1.92}{12 \text{ oz}}$

    (5) all of the above

ANSWERS ARE ON PAGE 306.

SOLVING PROPORTIONS

To solve a proportion, you find the missing value in the proportion. You can use what you have already learned about proportions to solve them.

EXAMPLE 1   Solve the proportion $\frac{5}{8} = \frac{\square}{10}$.

    STEP 1   Find whichever cross product you can.

                5 × 10 = 50

    STEP 2   Divide by the number not yet used.

                50 ÷ 8 = 6.25

    STEP 3   Write the value into the proportion, and check cross products.

                $\frac{5}{8} = \frac{6.25}{10}$; 5 × 10 = 50; 8 × 6.25 = 50; cross products are equal.

    STEP 4   Write the missing value: 6.25

For many problems, you can write and solve a proportion.

EXAMPLE 2   A college advertises a 4 : 5 ratio of male students to female students. If there are about 1,200 male students, how many female students are there?

STEP 1   Write a proportion. Make sure the order of the numbers is the same for each of the two ratios. Leave a blank for the missing value (in this case, the number of female students).

$$\frac{\text{male}}{\text{female}} \quad \frac{4}{5} = \frac{1,200}{\square}$$

STEP 2   Solve the proportion.

$5 \times 1,200 \div 4 = 1,500$ female students

STEP 3   Check cross products in the proportion $\frac{4}{5} = \frac{1,200}{1,500}$.

$4 \times 1,500 = 6,000; 5 \times 1,200 = 6,000$

STEP 4   State your answer.

There are about 1,500 female students.

EXERCISE 4

Directions: Solve the proportion (find the missing value).

1. $\frac{1}{13} = \frac{10}{\square}$

2. $\frac{10}{3} = \frac{\square}{150}$

3. $\frac{\square}{42} = \frac{6}{7}$

4. $\frac{7}{\square} = \frac{5}{12}$

5. $\frac{4}{1} = \frac{16}{\square}$

6. $\frac{9}{2} = \frac{\square}{12}$

7. $\frac{\square}{5} = \frac{5}{25}$

8. $\frac{30}{\square} = \frac{4}{15}$

9. $\frac{9}{10} = \frac{\square}{36}$

10. $\frac{5}{7} = \frac{1}{\square}$

Directions: Solve each problem.

11. Etu earned $100 mowing 8 lawns. At this rate, how much will he earn mowing 10 lawns?

12. To make punch, combine 5 parts juice with 2 parts ginger ale. How much ginger ale should you add to 8 liters of juice?

13. The scale on a highway map is 1 in. : 50 miles. What is the distance between two cities that are $2\frac{1}{2}$ inches apart on the map?

14. Brendan's car gets 32 miles to the gallon. How many miles can Brendan drive on a full tank, which is about 12 gallons?

15. Gauri read on a cereal box that one serving, or $\frac{3}{4}$ cup of cereal, has 230 calories. But Gauri eats 1 cup as a serving. How many calories does 1 cup of the cereal have? Round to the nearest calorie.

16. Pat wants to use a copy machine to enlarge a small rectangular picture that measures $1\frac{1}{4}$ in. by 2 in. What is the largest Pat can make the picture and still have it fit on a piece of $8\frac{1}{2}$ in. by 11 in. paper?

ANSWERS ARE ON PAGE 306.

PERCENTS

A ***percent*** is another means of expressing a number as part of a whole. The word ***percent*** means "of 100." For example, you can write the ratio "3 to 100" as "3%" and read it as "3 percent."

Because a percent is a form of a ratio, and you can write any ratio as a fraction, then you can write a percent as a fraction. You can also write fractions and percents as decimals. It is very useful to be able to change among these three forms of a number: percents, fractions, and decimals.

EXAMPLE 1   The 10-by-10 grid below has 100 squares. What portion of the grid is shaded? Write a percent, a fraction, and a decimal.

STEP 1   Write a percent.

40 of the 100 squares are shaded: 40%

STEP 2   Write a fraction in lowest terms.

$$\frac{40}{100} = \frac{40 \div 20}{100 \div 20} = \frac{2}{5}$$

STEP 3   Write a decimal.

"forty hundredths" = 0.40 = 0.4

STEP 4   Summarize.

So 40%, or $\frac{2}{5}$, or 0.4, of the grid is shaded.

To calculate with a percent, you first need to change the percent to a fraction or a decimal. The next two examples show you how to do this.

EXAMPLE 2   Change 14% to a fraction.

STEP 1   Write the percent as a ratio that compares a number to 100 (a fraction with denominator 100).

$$14\% = \frac{14}{100}$$

STEP 2   Write the fraction in lowest terms.

$$\frac{14}{100} = \frac{14 \div 2}{100 \div 2} = \frac{7}{50}$$

STEP 3   Summarize.

$$14\% = \frac{7}{50}$$

EXAMPLE 3   Change 14% to a decimal.

STEP 1   Write the percent as a ratio that compares a number to 100 (a fraction with denominator 100). Do not write the fraction in lowest terms.

$$14\% = \frac{14}{100}$$

STEP 2   Write the fraction as a decimal.

$$\frac{14}{100} = \text{"fourteen hundredths"} = 0.14$$

STEP 3   Summarize.

$$14\% = 0.14$$

Here's a shortcut. To change a percent to a decimal, move the decimal point two places to the *left* and drop the percent symbol. To change a decimal to a percent, move the decimal point two places to the *right* and write the percent symbol.

EXAMPLE 4   Change 78% to a decimal.

STEP 1   Remember that the "decimal point" for a whole number is to the right of the ones digit.

78.

STEP 2   Move the decimal point two places to the left.

0.78

STEP 3   Summarize.

$$78\% = 0.78$$

EXAMPLE 5   Change 0.06 to a percent.

STEP 1   Move the decimal point two places to the right.

006.

STEP 2   Write the percent symbol (and remove unnecessary zeros).

6%

STEP 3   Summarize.

0.06 = 6%

To change a fraction to a percent, first divide to write the fraction as a decimal. Then write the decimal as a percent.

EXAMPLE 6   Change $\frac{2}{5}$ to a percent.

STEP 1   Divide to write the fraction as a decimal.

$2 \div 5 = 0.4$

STEP 2   Write the decimal as a percent.

0.4 = 40%

STEP 3   Summarize.

$\frac{2}{5} = 40\%$

SUMMARY FOR CHANGING PERCENTS, FRACTIONS, AND DECIMALS

To change a percent to a fraction: Write the percent as a ratio (a fraction with denominator 100), then reduce to lowest terms.

To change a percent to a decimal: Write the percent as a fraction, then as a decimal. Or, move the decimal point two places to the left and drop the percent symbol.

To change a decimal to a percent: Move the decimal point two places to the right, and write the percent symbol.

To change a fraction to a percent: Divide the fraction to express as a decimal, then write as a percent.

EXERCISE 5

Directions: Change each percent to a fraction and a decimal.

1. 25%

2. 8%

3. 10%

4. 66%

5. 1%

6. 90%

7. 37%

8. 3%

Directions: Change each fraction or decimal to a percent.

9. $\frac{1}{2}$

10. $\frac{3}{5}$

11. 0.09

12. 0.74

13. $\frac{1}{10}$

14. $\frac{3}{4}$

15. 0.7

16. 0.16

17. $\frac{7}{20}$

18. $\frac{1}{25}$

19. 0.02

20. 0.99

21. $\frac{3}{8}$

22. $\frac{15}{16}$

Directions: Which is greater?

23. $\frac{1}{4}$ or 20%

28. 100% or 0.01

24. 85% or $\frac{4}{5}$

29. $\frac{2}{10}$ or 22%

25. $\frac{1}{2}$ or 48%

30. 0.35 or 39%

26. 10% or 0.11

31. 42% or 0.7

27. 0.6 or 55%

32. 58% or $\frac{3}{5}$

Directions: Choose the best answer.

33. Which of the following is not equivalent to 65%?

(1) $\frac{65}{100}$

(2) $\frac{13}{20}$

(3) 6.50

(4) 0.65

34. Which of the following is the smallest?

(1) 1%
(2) 1
(3) 0.1
(4) 10%

ANSWERS ARE ON PAGES 306–307.

COMMON PERCENTS, FRACTIONS, AND DECIMALS

Some percents, fractions, and decimals are so commonly used that it's best to memorize them. Two of these fractions have decimals that repeat.

EXAMPLE 1 Change $\frac{1}{3}$ to a percent.

STEP 1 Divide to write the fraction as a decimal.

$1 \div 3 = 0.33333\ldots$

Note that the 3 continues to repeat, indicated by the dots . . .

STEP 2 Write the decimal as a percent (move the decimal point).

$0.33333\ldots = 33.333\ldots\%$

STEP 3 Write 33.333 . . . as a mixed number. To the left of the decimal point is the whole number 33. To the right is 0.333 . . . , or $\frac{1}{3}$.

$33.333\ldots\% = 33\frac{1}{3}\%$

STEP 4 Summarize.

$\frac{1}{3} = 33\frac{1}{3}\%$

EXAMPLE 2 Change $\frac{2}{3}$ to a percent.

STEP 1 Divide to write the fraction as a decimal.

$2 \div 3 = 0.66666\ldots$

STEP 2 Write the decimal as a percent.

$0.66666\ldots = 66.666\ldots\%$

STEP 3 Write 66.666 . . . as a mixed number.

$66.666\ldots\% = 66\frac{2}{3}\%$

STEP 4 Summarize.

$\frac{2}{3} = 66\frac{2}{3}\%$

EXERCISE 6

Directions: The table below includes commonly used percents, fractions, and decimals. Complete the table.

	Fraction	Percent	Decimal
1.	$\frac{1}{4}$		
2.	$\frac{1}{3}$		
3.	$\frac{1}{2}$		
4.	$\frac{2}{3}$		
5.	$\frac{3}{4}$		
6.		50%	
7.		$33\frac{1}{3}\%$	
8.		75%	
9.		25%	
10.		$66\frac{2}{3}\%$	
11.			0.75
12.			0.666…
13.			0.25
14.			0.333…
15.			0.5

ANSWERS ARE ON PAGE 307.

PERCENT OF A NUMBER

A percent is a portion of some number. Often you want to figure out what that portion *is*. For example, if you decide to leave a 15% tip at a restaurant, you need to calculate the *amount of money* that is 15% of the bill.

EXAMPLE 1   What is 15% of $25?

STEP 1   Write the percent as a decimal.

15% = 0.15

STEP 2   Multiply.

0.15 × $25 = $3.75

STEP 3   Summarize.

15% of $25 is $3.75.

To calculate with percents, you first need to change the percent to either a decimal or a fraction. The example above uses a decimal, and the example below uses a fraction. You may use whichever form of the number is easier for you to work with, since they will both give you the same answer.

EXAMPLE 2   What is 25% of $400?

STEP 1   Write the percent as a fraction.

$25\% = \frac{1}{4}$

STEP 2   Multiply.

$\frac{1}{4} \times \$400 = \$100$

STEP 3   Summarize.

25% of $400 is $100.

SUMMARY FOR FINDING THE PERCENT OF A NUMBER

To find the percent of a number:
1) Change the percent to a decimal or a fraction.
2) Multiply.

Some problems require you to find the percent of a number. Before you do any calculations, remember to read the problem carefully. With percent problems, look for the word *of* since most percent problems ask you to find the percent of a number. When the answer you need is the percent *of* a number, multiply to find the answer.

EXAMPLE 3   A state official predicts that 70% of the registered voters in Montana will vote on election day. If there are 514,000 registered voters in Montana, how many are predicted to vote?

STEP 1   Understand the question.

You must figure out how many of the 514,000 registered voters are predicted to vote on election day.

STEP 2   Decide what information is needed.

Use the percent of voters predicted to vote: 70%.
Also, use the number of registered voters: 514,000.

STEP 3   Choose the most appropriate operation.

This problem asks, "What is 70% of 514,000?"
The operation to use is multiplication.

STEP 4   Solve the problem.

70% of 514,000 = 0.70 × 514,000 = 359,800 voters

STEP 5   Check your answer.

To check, see if the ratio $\frac{359,800}{514,000}$ equals 70%.

359,800 ÷ 514,000 = 0.7 = 70%

So 359,800 voters are predicted to vote.

EXERCISE 7

Directions: Calculate each of the following.

1. 10% of 870

2. 75% of 16

3. 12% of $100

4. $33\frac{1}{3}$% of 99

5. 80% of 1,064

6. 5% of $60,000

7. 100% of 23

8. 2% of 8,750

9. 47% of 100

10. 50% of $50

11. 65% of 44,500

12. 1% of $800

13. 25% of 48

14. 30% of $68

15. $66\frac{2}{3}$% of 180

16. 98% of $1

Directions: Solve each problem.

17. The sales tax rate is 6%. Calculate the sales tax on an automobile purchase of $12,500.

18. Gerry wants to leave a 15% tip at a restaurant. His bill is $13.00. How much money should Gerry leave for a tip?

19. A store advertises "40% off" all shoes. How much money will you save on a pair of shoes priced at $45?

20. Christa is buying an $80 dress for "25% off." How much will the dress cost?

21. To pass an exam, you must get at least 70% of the 30 problems correct. How many problems must you get correct to pass?

22. A Realtor earns 5% commission on the sale of a home sold for $108,000. How much commission does the Realtor earn on this sale?

23. A women's basketball coach reported that 80% of the team's 20 games were wins. How many games were wins? How many were losses?

24. Heather puts 10% of her gross earnings into a savings account. Each month she earns $2,500. How much will she put into savings in one year?

25. A manufacturer claims that only 2% of its products are defective. If 1,000 of its products are sold to a store in a month, how many of these are defective? How many are not?

26. Of 600 voters surveyed, 42% favored Brown, 51% favored Sanchez, and the rest were undecided. What percent of the voters surveyed were undecided? How many were undecided?

ANSWERS ARE ON PAGE 307.

INTEREST PROBLEMS

When you put money into a savings account, the bank pays you *interest*. When you borrow money from a bank, you pay interest. The amount of the interest depends upon three things: principal, rate, and time. You can use the formula below to calculate interest.

$$\text{interest} = \text{principal} \times \text{rate} \times \text{time}$$

The *principal* is the amount of money invested or borrowed. The *rate* is the annual interest rate, usually given as a percent. The *time* is the length of time (years) the money is invested or borrowed.

EXAMPLE   Laurel put $1,000 into a savings account. The bank pays 3% interest annually on this account. How much interest will Laurel earn if she leaves the money in the account for 2 years?

STEP 1   Identify the principal, the rate, and the time.

Principal: $1,000
Rate: 3% = 0.03
Time: 2

STEP 2   Multiply.

Interest = principal × rate × time
= $1,000 × 0.03 × 2
= $60

STEP 3   Summarize.

Laurel will earn $60 in interest.

Make sure that time is expressed in terms of years.

EXAMPLES   Write the following times in terms of years.

4 months = $\frac{4}{12}$ years   9 months = $\frac{9}{12}$ years

200 days = $\frac{200}{365}$ years   31 days = $\frac{31}{365}$ years

EXERCISE 8

Directions: Calculate interest.

1. principal = $10,000
   rate = 8%
   time = 5 years

2. principal = $2,000
   rate = 10%
   time = 1 year

3. principal = $2,500
   rate = 4%
   time = 6 months

4. principal = $120,000
   rate = 9%
   time = 30 years

5. principal = $5,000
   rate = 11%
   time = 100 days

6. principal = $600
   rate = 5.5%
   time = 12 months

Directions: Solve each problem.

7. Kachina put $4,000 into a savings account that pays 4% annual interest. How much interest will she earn in 3 years?

8. Lila put $10,000 into a savings account that pays 3.5% annual interest. How much money will she have in the account after one year?

9. Jamil borrowed $75,000 from a mortgage company to buy a house. He will repay the loan at 8% annual interest in 30 years. How much will he pay the mortgage company in interest?

10. On her eighteenth birthday, Veda put $1,500 into a savings account. The annual interest rate on the account is 6%. How much money will she have in the account on her twenty-first birthday?

11. A credit card company charges 12% annual interest on any balance due. If the balance due on Mimi's credit card is $150 and she waits 30 days to pay the bill, how much interest will she owe the credit card company?

12. Zahur bought a car priced at $18,500. He made a 10% down payment and borrowed the rest of the money at a 9% annual interest rate. He will pay the balance due in five years. How much interest will he pay?

ANSWERS ARE ON PAGE 308.

PERCENT PROBLEMS AND PROPORTIONS

One way to solve percent problems is to use proportions. You write and solve a proportion that has the percent written as a ratio comparing a number to 100.

$$\frac{\text{part}}{\text{whole}} = \frac{\%}{100}$$

The next three examples show how to use this type of proportion to solve percent problems. By solving the proportion you find the missing value—the part, the whole, or the percent. The 100 is always in the proportion. Be careful to write the proportion correctly before you solve it. After solving the proportion, multiply to check your result.

EXAMPLE 1   What is 30% of 90?

STEP 1   Identify the part, the whole, and the percent.

Part: (this is the missing value)
Whole: 90
Percent: 30

STEP 2   Write the proportion $\frac{\text{part}}{\text{whole}} = \frac{\%}{100}$

$$\frac{\square}{90} = \frac{30}{100}$$

STEP 3   Solve the proportion.

$90 \times 30 \div 100 = 27$

STEP 4   Summarize.

30% of 90 is 27.

STEP 5   Use multiplication to check your answer.

$30\% \text{ of } 90 = 0.3 \times 90 = 27$

EXAMPLE 2   What percent of 90 is 18?

STEP 1   Identify the part, the whole, and the percent.

Part: 18
Whole: 90
Percent: (this is the missing value)

STEP 2   Write the proportion $\frac{part}{whole} = \frac{\%}{100}$.

$$\frac{18}{90} = \frac{\square}{100}$$

STEP 3   Solve the proportion.

$18 \times 100 \div 90 = 20$

STEP 4   Summarize.

20% of 90 is 18.

STEP 5   Use multiplication to check your answer.

20% of 90 $= 0.2 \times 90 = 18$

EXAMPLE 3   80% of what number is 20?

STEP 1   Identify the part, the whole, and the percent.

Part: 20
Whole: (this is the missing value)
Percent: 80

STEP 2   Write the proportion $\frac{part}{whole} = \frac{\%}{100}$.

$$\frac{20}{\square} = \frac{80}{100}$$

STEP 3   Solve the proportion.

$20 \times 100 \div 80 = 25$

STEP 4   Summarize.

80% of 25 is 20.

STEP 5   Use multiplication to check your answer.

80% of 25 $= 0.8 \times 25 = 20$

You can also use this method when solving word problems that involve percents. Carefully decide what is missing—the part, the whole, or the percent. Then write the proportion with the numbers given, and solve for the missing value.

EXAMPLE 4   In an election, 49% of the votes cast were against a constitutional amendment. This was 158,071 votes. How many votes were cast?

STEP 1   Understand the question.

You must figure out the total number of votes cast, for and against the amendment.

STEP 2   Decide what information is needed.

The percent of votes cast against the amendment: 49%.
The number of votes cast against the amendment: 158,071.

STEP 3   Write the proportion $\frac{\text{part}}{\text{whole}} = \frac{\%}{100}$.

Part: 158,071
Whole: (this is the missing value)
Percent: 49

$$\frac{158,071}{\square} = \frac{49}{100}$$

STEP 4   Solve the proportion.

$158,071 \times 100 \div 49 \approx 322,594$ votes

STEP 5   Summarize.

49% of 322,594 is about 158,071.

STEP 6   Use multiplication to check your answer.

$49\% \times 322,594 = 0.49 \times 322,594 \approx 158,071$

So, 322,594 votes were cast.

EXERCISE 9

Directions: Answer each question.

1. What number is 25% of 80?

2. 3 is 75% of what number?

3. What percent of 44 is 11?

4. 16% of what number is 200?

5. 3% of 500 is what number?

6. 12 is what percent of 24?

7. What percent of 16 is 12?

8. What number is 90% of 1,000?

9. 10% of what number is 8?

10. 6 is 25% of what number?

11. 9 is what percent of 100?

12. 50% of 62 is what number?

13. 7 is 1% of what number?

14. 17 is what percent of 51?

15. What is 100% of 49?

16. 15% of what number is 6?

ANSWERS ARE ON PAGE 308.

EXERCISE 10

Directions: Solve each problem. If necessary, round to the nearest percent or whole number.

1. Americans consume 340 million pounds of cranberries a year. They consume about 73 million pounds during Thanksgiving week alone. What percent of American cranberry consumption is attributed to Thanksgiving?

2. There are about 93 million households in America. Living in about 8% of the households are single parents with children. Find the number of households in America in which single parents with children live.

3. Adams received 52% of the votes to win an election. There were 215,405 voters. How many people voted for Adams?

4. Rivera got 13,407 votes, while the opponent got 6,309 votes. What percent of the votes did Rivera get?

5. One serving of wheat cereal provides 5 grams of dietary fiber. This is 21% of the Daily Value recommended for a 2,000-calorie diet. How many grams of dietary fiber are recommended daily for a person on a 2,000-calorie diet?

6. Barbara bought some mittens on sale for $12.00. She paid only 80% of the original price. What was the original price of the mittens? How much money did she save by buying the mittens on sale?

7. A baby's head is about 25% the length of its body, while an adult's head is about 17% the length of its body. Abigail is 4 months old and measures 24 inches long. About how long is her head?

8. A child's height at age 2 is usually about 50% of its full adult height. Eric is 2 years old and 32 inches tall. About how tall will Eric be as an adult?

9. A newborn baby sleeps an average of 16 hours in a 24-hour period. What percent of its time does a newborn baby spend sleeping?

10. Diana says that she spends about 30% of her time sleeping. How many hours does she sleep in a 24-hour period?

Directions: Choose the best answer.

11. Which of the following proportions could you use to find what percent 5 is of 8?

   (1) $\dfrac{5}{\square} = \dfrac{8}{100}$

   (2) $\dfrac{5}{8} = \dfrac{\square}{100}$

   (3) $\dfrac{\square}{8} = \dfrac{5}{100}$

   (4) none of the above

12. Which of the following proportions could you use to find what percent of 25 is 10?

   (1) $\dfrac{10}{25} = \dfrac{\square}{100}$

   (2) $\dfrac{10}{100} = \dfrac{25}{\square}$

   (3) $\dfrac{10}{\square} = \dfrac{25}{100}$

   (4) none of the above

13. Which calculation will NOT give 25% of 80?

   (1) 0.25×80
   (2) $\dfrac{1}{4} \times 80$
   (3) $80 \times 25 \div 100$
   (4) $80 \times 100 \div 25$

ANSWERS ARE ON PAGE 308.

RATIOS, PROPORTIONS, AND PERCENTS REVIEW

Directions: In questions 1–22, solve each problem. Show your work to the right.

1. Solve the proportion $\frac{3}{7} = \frac{\square}{63}$.

2. Change 0.23 to a percent.

3. Change 70% to a decimal.

4. Form a proportion using the ratio "1 to 3".

5. What is the unit price of 12 bagels for $5?

6. A football team won 8 games and lost 2 games. Write the ratio of wins to losses.

7. Write the ratio $\frac{6}{7}$ in two other ways.

8. Calculate 85% of 120.

9. Change $\frac{2}{3}$ to a percent.

10. Write the fraction and decimal that equals 25%.

11. What percent of 60 is 6?

12. The scale on a map is 1 cm : 100 km. What is the distance between 2 cities located 5 cm apart on the map?

13. Mina drove 130 miles in two hours. What was her average rate (miles per hour)?

14. Change 2% to a fraction.

15. How much is a 15% tip on a restaurant bill of $7?

16. 90% of what number is 18?

17. Do the two ratios $\frac{2}{5}$ and $\frac{3}{10}$ form a proportion? If so, write the proportion.

18. Change $\frac{1}{5}$ to a percent.

19. Calculate the interest earned on $2,000 invested for 2 years at an annual rate of 6%.

20. What number is 30% of 40?

21. The ratio of men to women at a company is 2 : 3. If there are 60 men, how many women are there?

22. 35 is what percent of 70?

Directions: Questions 23–38 include whole numbers, decimals, fractions, measurement, geometry, ratios, proportions, and percents. Choose the correct answer to each problem. Remember the problem-solving skills you have learned.

23. Each day Trinh buys a can of soda at a machine in her apartment building for 75¢. Instead, she could buy a 12-pack at the grocery store for $4.99. If she did this, how much money would she save in a month?

    (1) about $10
    (2) about $12
    (3) about $22
    (4) about $4
    (5) about $18

24. Daniel's bill at a restaurant was $19. He wants to leave a 15% tip. He will write a check for the total. For what amount should he write the check?

    (1) $2.85
    (2) $21.85
    (3) $28.50
    (4) $16.15
    (5) not enough information is given

25. How many seconds are there in one week?

    (1) 86,400
    (2) 10,080
    (3) 20,160
    (4) 604,800
    (5) none of the above

26. A meteorologist reported that 17 days in Boston during June were rainy. What percent of days in Boston during June were rainy?

    (1) 17%
    (2) about 17%
    (3) about 55%
    (4) about 57%
    (5) not enough information is given

27. A **majority** is a number greater than half of the total. What is the majority for the House of Representatives, at 435 voting members?

    (1) 222
    (2) 217
    (3) 218
    (4) 217.5
    (5) not enough information is given

28. Bess is planning a trip. She drives an average of 55 miles per hour. Her destination is 275 miles away. She wants to arrive by 4:00 P.M. and allow an extra hour for stops. By what time should she start driving?

    (1) 11:00 A.M.
    (2) 12:00 noon
    (3) 10:00 P.M.
    (4) 10:00 A.M.
    (5) not enough information is given

29. Hwa is buying four items at a store priced at $4.99, $2.49, $.98, and $6.29. Each item is subject to 4% sales tax. If he pays with a $20 bill, how much change should he receive?

    (1) $4.66
    (2) $15.34
    (3) $5.25
    (4) $14.75
    (5) $0.59

30. Lanelle found the pair of jeans she wants at five different stores. The original price of the jeans at each store is $35. Which of the following will give Norma the best deal on the jeans?

(1) 25% off

(2) $\frac{1}{3}$ off

(3) pay 70% of the original price

(4) $10 off

(5) not enough information is given

31. Alfredo is planning to invest some money in order to earn some interest. The annual interest rate is 5%. With which of the following investments will he earn the most money?

(1) $3,000 for 2 years

(2) $4,000 for 1 year

(3) $3,500 for 18 months

(4) $2,000 for 3 years

(5) $2,500 for $2\frac{1}{2}$ years

32. The model below represents what number?

(1) 80%

(2) 0.8

(3) $\frac{80}{100}$

(4) $\frac{4}{5}$

(5) all of the above

33. Which fraction below is the greatest?

(1) $\frac{3}{5}$

(2) $\frac{4}{7}$

(3) $\frac{5}{9}$

(4) $\frac{2}{3}$

(5) $\frac{7}{11}$

34. Deborah is framing a 4-inch by 6-inch rectangular photograph with some narrow ribbon. How much ribbon does she need?

(1) 24 inches
(2) 20 inches
(3) 12 inches
(4) 16 inches
(5) 36 inches

35. Deborah added a border all around her 4-inch by 6-inch photograph. The border is 3 inches wide. What is the area of the photograph and its border?

(1) 33 square inches
(2) 9 square inches
(3) 120 square inches
(4) 44 inches
(5) not enough information is given

36. Edward is making a dog kennel along one side of his garage. He wants it to be in the shape of a rectangle, with three sides fenced and one side the wall of the garage. See the diagram below. He wants to use all 30 feet of fencing he bought. Which of the following dimensions will result in the greatest area for the kennel?

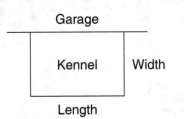

(1) length = 8 ft
(2) width = 8 ft
(3) length = 10 ft
(4) width = 9 ft
(5) width = 6 ft

37. A recipe calls for $2\frac{3}{4}$ cups of flour. How much flour will you use if you double the recipe?

(1) $4\frac{1}{2}$ cups
(2) $4\frac{3}{4}$ cups
(3) $5\frac{1}{2}$ cups
(4) 5 cups
(5) $6\frac{1}{2}$ cups

38. What is the perimeter of a rectangle if the length is two times the width?

(1) 2 units
(2) 2 square units
(3) 4 units
(4) 4 square units
(5) not enough information is given

ANSWERS ARE ON PAGE 309.

6 Data Analysis and Probability

MEAN, MEDIAN, MODE, AND RANGE

Data is information that is collected and analyzed. It is often, but not always, numerical. Statisticians use many different methods for collecting and analyzing data. Two important characteristics of a set of data are its center and its spread. The *center* of a data set can be described by three different measures: mean, median, and mode. One of these measures might be more appropriate than another for a given data set. The *spread* of a data set can be described by its range. Here are some definitions of these measures.

- The *mean* is the average value of a data set.

- The *median* is the middle value of a data set listed in order from least to greatest.

- The *mode* is the item that occurs most often in a data set.

- The *range* is the difference between the greatest and least items of a data set.

The examples show how to find these measures. They use Robin's Running Data, given below.

EXAMPLE 1   **Robin's Running Data**

Robin is training for a 5-kilometer race. Each day she runs 5 kilometers and records her time to the nearest minute. Here is the data she collected one week: 20, 24, 22, 22, 21, 20, 25.

Refer to Robin's Running Data. Find the mean.

STEP 1   Find the sum of all the items in the data set.

20 + 24 + 22 + 22 + 21 + 20 + 25 = 154

STEP 2   Count the number of items in the data set.

7 items

STEP 3　Divide the sum by the number of items in the data set.

$154 \div 7 = 22$

The mean is 22 minutes.

SUMMARY FOR FINDING THE MEAN

To find the mean:
1) Add all the items in the data set.
2) Divide by the number of items.

EXAMPLE 2　Refer to Robin's Running Data. Find the median.

STEP 1　List items in order from least to greatest.

20, 20, 21, 22, 22, 24, 25

STEP 2　Count the number of items in the data set.

7 items

STEP 3　If the number of items is odd, identify the middle value in the ordered list.

The middle value is 22.

The median is 22 minutes.

　　　Sometimes there is an even number of items in a data set. In this case, the median is the average of the two middle values.

EXAMPLE 3　Find the median of this data: 20, 24, 22, 22, 21, 20.

STEP 1　List items in order from least to greatest.

20, 20, 21, 22, 22, 24

STEP 2　Count the number of items in the data set.

6 items

STEP 3　If the number of items is even, identify the two middle values in the ordered list.

The two middle values are 21 and 22.

STEP 4　Find the average (mean) of the two middle values.

$21 + 22 = 43; 43 \div 2 = 21.5$

The median is 21.5.

SUMMARY FOR FINDING THE MEDIAN
To find the median: **1)** List all the items in the data set in order from least to greatest. **2)** Find the middle value. **3)** If there is an even number of items, find the average of the two middle values.

EXAMPLE 4   Refer to Robin's Running Data. Find the mode(s), if any.

STEP 1   Group items in the data set that are the same.

20, 20   21   22, 22   24   25

STEP 2   Find the item that occurs most often. A set of data might have one mode, more than one mode, or no modes.

The items 20 and 22 both occur most often (twice).

The modes are 20 minutes and 22 minutes.

SUMMARY FOR FINDING THE MODE
To find the mode: **1)** Group items in the data set that are the same. **2)** Find the item that occurs most often. A set of data might have one mode, more than one mode, or no modes.

EXAMPLE 5   Refer to Robin's Running Data. Find the range.

STEP 1   Identify the item with the greatest value.

25

STEP 2   Identify the item with the least value.

20

STEP 3   Subtract the item with least value from the item with greatest value.

$25 - 20 = 5$

The range is 5 minutes.

SUMMARY FOR FINDING THE RANGE
To find the range: Subtract the item with the least value from the item with the greatest value.

EXERCISE 1

Directions: Refer to Barbara's Running Data. Find each measure. Round to the nearest minute, if necessary.

> **Barbara's Running Data**
>
> Barbara is training for a 10-kilometer race. Each day she runs 10 kilometers and records her time to the nearest minute. Here is the data she collected one week: 42, 41, 45, 40, 46, 42, 44.

1. Mean

3. Mode

2. Median

4. Range

Directions: Find the measure for the given data.

5. Find the median.

House prices: $85,000; $108,000; $95,500; $120,000; $105,000; $99,900; $124,000

6. Find the mode(s), if any.

Favorite water sport: swimming, skiing, scuba diving, swimming, skiing, fishing, rafting, skiing, sailing

7. Find the mean.

High temperatures (°F) for February in Milwaukee: 10, 12, 30, 38, 22, 6, 2, 0, 0, 18, 22, 25, 16, 33, 40, 38, 32, 35, 10, 8, 5, 5, 9, 12, 15, 21, 30, 19

8. Find the mode(s), if any.

Number of siblings in a family: 2, 1, 4, 3, 1, 2, 1, 3, 3, 2, 4, 2

9. Find the range.

Ages of employees in a department: 24, 40, 58, 22, 33, 35, 29, 28, 64, 48

10. Find the median.

Shoe sizes of women: 7, $6\frac{1}{2}$, $8\frac{1}{2}$, 9, 10, 5, 7, 8

11. Find the mean.

Test scores: 75%, 72%, 88%, 90%, 85%, 100%, 77%, 86%

12. Find the range.

Prices for a new toaster: $39.99; $60; $24.50; $54.99; $64.99; $45; $41.49

Directions: Solve each problem.

13. Garry's bank statement listed his electronic withdrawals for the month: $40, $80, $100, $20, $50, $60, $20, $80, $60, $40, $30, $100, $60. What amount does he withdraw most often?

14. Employees of a small company have the following salaries: $24,000; $15,000; $100,000; $30,000; $12,000. Find the average salary and the median salary. Why do you think there is such a big difference in the two?

15. On March 31 in San Diego, a meteorologist reported 60°F as the high temperature for the day for the first time during March. The meteorologist also reported 60°F as the median high temperature for San Diego for the month. On how many March days in San Diego was the high temperature lower than 60°F?

16. Tim collected data on his height (to the nearest inch) and that of four of his friends, but he lost the data. Tim was the tallest, measuring 72 inches. Also, no two friends had the same height. Tim had calculated the following measures: median = 68, mean = 68, range = 7. Figure out what the original data was.

17. The age range for players on a soccer team is 10 years. The youngest player is 15 years old. What is the age of the oldest player?

18. Bill's test scores are 70%, 85%, 78%, and 80%. What score must Bill get on his next test in order to have an 80% average?

Directions: Choose the best answer.

19. Which best describes *median*?

    (1) average
    (2) most frequent
    (3) middle
    (4) difference

20. Which best describes *range*?

    (1) average
    (2) most frequent
    (3) middle
    (4) difference

21. Which best describes *mode*?

    (1) average
    (2) most frequent
    (3) middle
    (4) difference

22. Which best describes *mean*?

    (1) average
    (2) most frequent
    (3) middle
    (4) difference

ANSWERS ARE ON PAGE 309.

BAR GRAPHS

Data can be displayed in many different ways. A ***graph*** gives a visual picture of the data. With a graph you can often "see" things about the data that are difficult to see by looking only at the numbers.

A ***bar graph*** can help you make visual comparisons among numerical data. A bar graph is made up of rectangular bars that extend upward or lengthwise. The height of each bar corresponds to one number in the data. The higher the bar, the greater the number.

An example of a bar graph is given in Figure 1. This bar graph displays all the data given in Table 1.

Table 1   **Figure 1**

AVERAGE MONTHLY TEMPERATURES IN ANCHORAGE, ALASKA

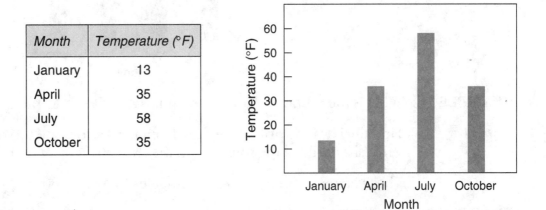

Month	Temperature (°F)
January	13
April	35
July	58
October	35

The table and the graph provide the same information, but the graph makes comparisons quick and easy. For example, you can see that April and October have the same average monthly temperature because their bars are the same height.

Here are some things to notice about the bar graph in Figure 1. This information will help you to read, interpret, and draw bar graphs.

• Along the ***horizontal axis***, the bottom of the graph, the months being compared are listed: January, April, July, and October.

• Along the ***vertical axis***, the left side of the graph, numbers representing temperatures from 10°F to 60°F are listed.

• The top of each bar aligns with the correct number on the vertical axis. In this graph, a bar for each of the four months gives the average temperature for the month.

The next three examples show how to read a bar graph to answer questions about the data displayed. The examples are based on Figure 2.

Figure 2

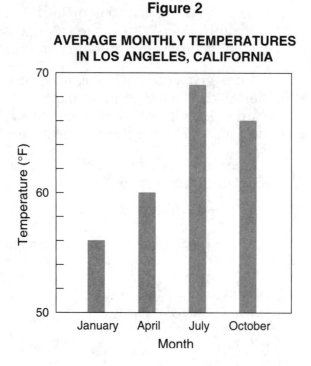

AVERAGE MONTHLY TEMPERATURES IN LOS ANGELES, CALIFORNIA

EXAMPLE 1   What is the average temperature in Los Angeles in April?

Find the bar for April. Trace a horizontal line from the top of this bar to the vertical axis. Read the number on the axis: 60.

The average temperature in Los Angeles in April is 60°F.

EXAMPLE 2   In what month is the average temperature in Los Angeles 69°F?

Since 69 does not appear on the vertical axis, determine that each mark represents 2 degrees. Trace a horizontal line from where 69 would be (halfway between 70 and the mark directly below it) to the top of a bar. Read the month for that bar: July.

The average temperature in Los Angeles is 69°F in July.

> **TIP:** When the number you are working with does not appear on an axis, determine the amount covered between marks and find its approximate location.

EXAMPLE 3   What is the range of average monthly temperatures in Los Angeles?

STEP 1   Read from the graph the lowest temperature, shown by the lowest bar: 56°F. Read from the graph the highest temperature, shown by the highest bar: 69°F.

STEP 2   Subtract to find the range: 69°F − 56°F = 13°F.

SUMMARY FOR READING A BAR GRAPH

To read a bar graph:

1) Find the bar that displays the information you seek.

2) Trace a line from the top of the bar to the vertical axis.

3) Read the number on the axis. (Or, do the opposite. Find the number, then the bar.)

EXERCISE 2

Directions: Use Figure 3 to answer each question.

Figure 3

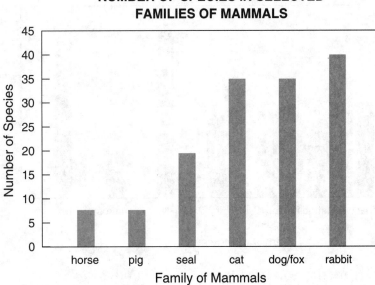

NUMBER OF SPECIES IN SELECTED FAMILIES OF MAMMALS

1. How many species are there in the horse family?   8

2. Which family of mammals has almost 20 species?   seal

3. Which family has about the same number of species as the cat family? *dog/fox*

4. How many species are there in the dog/fox family? *35*

5. Which two families have the fewest number of species? *horse, pig*

6. How many more species are there in the rabbit family than in the seal family? *20*

7. Which family has about twice as many species as the seal family? *rabbit*

8. How many times more species are there in the rabbit family than in the pig family?

5x

Directions: Refer to Figure 4 to answer each question.

Figure 4

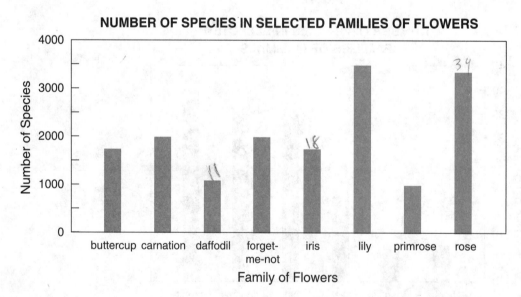

9. How many species are there in the forget-me-not family? *2000*

10. Which family of flowers has 1,100 species? *daff*

11. Which family has 2,500 more species than the primrose family? *lily*

12. Which family has about the same number of species as the daffodil family? *prim*

13. List the families in order from least number of species to greatest number of species; then find the median number of species for these families.

14. What is the average number of species for these families?

15. Which four families have about 2,000 species?

16. The sunflower family has 25,000 species. How many more is this than the lily family?

ANSWERS ARE ON PAGE 310.

⎓ PRE-GED Practice ⎓
EXERCISE 3

Directions: Refer to Figures 1–4 on pages 191–194. Choose the best answer.

1. Which statement is NOT true?

 (1) The carnation family and the forget-me-not family have about the same number of species.
 (2) The buttercup and iris families combined have about the same number of species as the lily family.
 (3) The primrose and daffodil families combined have about the same number of species as the carnation family.
 (4) The rose family has about twice as many species as the daffodil family.
 (5) The iris family has about half as many species as the lily family.

2. What is the average monthly temperature in Los Angeles in October?

 (1) 64°F
 (2) 66°F
 (3) 69°F
 (4) 56°F
 (5) 35°F

3. How much warmer is Los Angeles than Anchorage in July, on average?

 (1) 11°F
 (2) –11°F
 (3) 43°F
 (4) 58°F
 (5) 69°F

4. Which statement about Figure 2 is NOT true?

   (1) The average April temperature in Los Angeles is 60°F.
   (2) The average October temperature in Los Angeles is lower than the average July temperature.
   (3) In Los Angeles, the January temperature is lower than 58°F.
   (4) In Los Angeles, the January temperature usually is not lower than 50°F.
   (5) The average July temperature equals the sum of the average temperatures for January and April.

5. For which month does Anchorage record the coldest average temperature?

   (1) January
   (2) February
   (3) March
   (4) April
   (5) not enough information is given

6. Which statement is NOT true?

   (1) The seal family has more species than the pig family.
   (2) The rabbit family has more species than each of the other families given.
   (3) The dog/fox family has more species than the cat family.
   (4) The horse family has fewer species than the cat family.
   (5) The pig family and the horse family have the same number of species.

7. Which families of flowers have fewer than 1,500 species?

   (1) buttercup and rose
   (2) daffodil and primrose
   (3) carnation and iris
   (4) forget-me-not and lily
   (5) none of the above

8. Which families of mammals have more than 30 species?

   (1) horse, pig, and seal
   (2) pig, cat, and rabbit
   (3) horse, seal, and cat
   (4) cat, dog/fox, and rabbit
   (5) all of the above

ANSWERS ARE ON PAGE 310.

DRAWING BAR GRAPHS

Drawing a bar graph is another important skill to learn. Remember that a bar graph can help you make comparisons among numerical data. The lengths of the bars must be different enough so that someone reading the graph can quickly "see" the differences and make the important comparisons.

EXAMPLE   In the 1994 Winter Olympics, the U.S. won 6 gold, 5 silver, and 2 bronze medals. Draw a bar graph to display this data.

STEP 1   Draw a horizontal axis. Along the axis, write the types of medals: Gold, Silver, and Bronze. Label the axis: Type of Medal.

STEP 2   Draw a vertical axis. Along the axis, write numbers that at least cover the range of the data. Label the axis: Number of Medals.

STEP 3   For each type of medal, draw a bar that shows the number of medals won. The heights of the bars should match the data. Shade the bars.

STEP 4   Give the bar graph a title: Medals Won by the U.S. in the 1994 Winter Olympics.

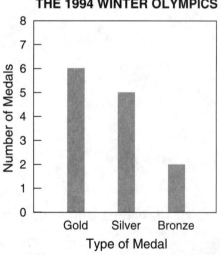

MEDALS WON BY THE U.S. IN THE 1994 WINTER OLYMPICS

SUMMARY FOR DRAWING BAR GRAPHS

To create a bar graph:

1) Draw and label horizontal and vertical axes.

2) Draw and shade bars to display the data.

3) Give the graph a title.

EXERCISE 4

Directions: Refer to the data in the table below to draw the bar graphs described.

Country	Gold Medals	Silver Medals	Bronze Medals	Total Medals
Top Medal Winners in the 1994 Winter Olympics, Lillehammer, Norway				
Norway	10	11	5	26
Germany	9	7	8	24
Russia	11	8	4	23
Italy	7	5	8	20
United States	6	5	2	13
Canada	3	6	4	13
Switzerland	3	4	2	9
Austria	2	3	4	9
South Korea	4	1	1	6
Finland	0	1	5	6

1. Draw a bar graph that displays the types and numbers of medals won by Norway.

2. Draw a bar graph that displays the number of gold medals won by the top five countries listed in the table.

3. Draw a bar graph that displays the types and numbers of medals won by the United States.

4. Draw a bar graph that displays the total number of medals won by the countries listed in the table.

5. Draw your own bar graph, displaying some of the data given in the table.

ANSWERS ARE ON PAGE 310.

LINE GRAPHS

A *line graph* can help you see patterns and trends in data. A line graph is made up of points that are connected by line segments. Line graphs are often used to display data over a period of time.

An example of a line graph is given in Figure 5. This line graph displays all the data given in Table 2.

Table 2

Figure 5

STEIN ROE STOCK FUND, NOVEMBER 21, 1984–1994

Year	Price of One Share
1984	$13.63
1985	$16.74
1986	$19.87
1987	$16.64
1988	$13.91
1989	$18.68
1990	$ 8.14
1991	$23.01
1992	$26.29
1993	$25.33
1994	$23.58

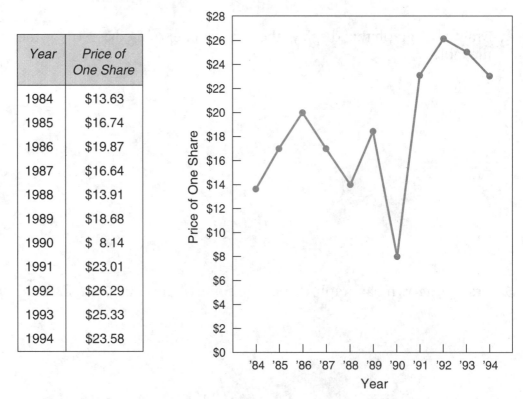

The table and the graph provide the same information, but the graph shows, visually, the dramatic decrease in the price in 1990 and the increase in 1991.

Like bar graphs, line graphs have a horizontal and vertical axis.

- In Figure 5, along the *horizontal axis*, the years refer to annual dates from November 21, 1984 to November 21, 1994.

- Along the *vertical axis*, numbers that fall within the range of the data represent the price of one share of the Stein Roe Stock Fund. Prices range from about $8 to about $27.

- In the body of the graph, the *points* display the data. Points connected by *line segments* show how the price changes (increases or decreases) from year to year.

The next three examples show how to read a line graph to answer questions about the data displayed. The examples are based on Figure 6.

Figure 6

EXAMPLE 1 If you invest $10,000 at an 8% annual interest rate, what will be its value in 25 years?

Find 25 years on the horizontal axis. Find the point directly above 25. Trace a line across to the vertical axis. Read the number: about $68,000.

In 25 years, the value of the money will be about $68,000.

EXAMPLE 2 If you invest $10,000 at an 8% annual interest rate, how long will it take for your money to be worth $40,000?

Find $40,000 on the vertical axis. Trace directly across to the graph. Where you intersect the line graph, draw a point. From this point, trace down to the horizontal axis. Read the number: about 18.

It will take about 18 years for the money to be worth $40,000.

Sometimes you can make predictions from a line graph. Look for a pattern or a trend in the line, and extend it to make the prediction.

EXAMPLE 3   If you invest $10,000 at an 8% annual interest rate, estimate the value of the money in 40 years.

Extend the horizontal axis across to 40 years. Extend the vertical axis up to at least $200,000, and list more values along the axis. Now notice the upward trend in the data, shown by the line. Also, each line segment is steeper than the one before it. Extend the line graph, following this pattern. On the line graph, draw a point for 40 years. From this point, trace across to the vertical axis to determine the estimated value of money at 40 years.

In 40 years, the value of the money will be about $200,000.

SUMMARY FOR READING A LINE GRAPH

To read a line graph:

1) Find the given information on the horizontal axis.

2) Directly above, find the point on the line graph.

3) Trace a line across to the vertical axis.

4) Read the number. (Or, do the opposite. Start with the vertical axis, trace to the line graph, and read the number from the horizontal axis.)

EXERCISE 5

Directions: Refer to Figure 7 to answer each question.

Figure   7

HOURLY TEMPERATURES IN GREAT FALLS, MONTANA ON NOVEMBER 21, 1994

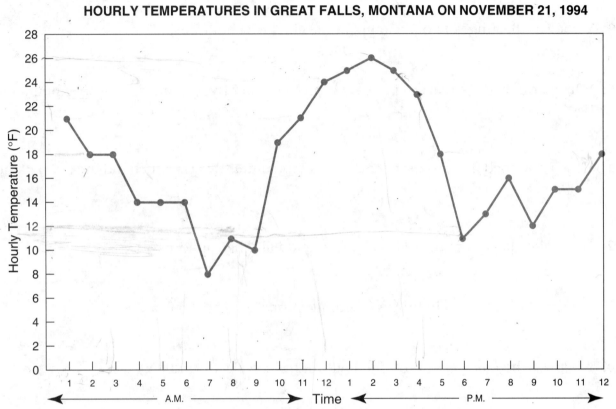

1. What was the temperature in Great Falls at 4:00 P.M.?

2. At what time was the hourly temperature 12°F?

3. At what time was the hourly temperature the highest? What was the temperature?

4. At what time was the hourly temperature the lowest? What was the temperature?

5. At what four times was the hourly temperature 18°F?

6. At what time was the hourly temperature the same as it was at 8:00 A.M.?

7. Was the temperature higher at 6:00 A.M. or at 6:00 P.M.?

8. What was the median hourly temperature for the 24-hour period?

9. What was the range of hourly temperatures in the 24-hour period?

10. Which hour had the greatest increase in temperature? By how much did the temperature rise?

11. Which hour had the greatest decrease in temperature? By how much did the temperature drop?

12. How much lower was the temperature at midnight than at noon?

13. What was the range of hourly temperatures from 7:00 A.M. to noon?

14. What was the range of hourly temperatures from 2:00 P.M. to 5:00 P.M.?

15. During five consecutive hours, the hourly temperatures rose. What was the temperature rise during that period?

ANSWERS ARE ON PAGE 311.

PRE-GED Practice
EXERCISE 6

Directions: Choose the best answer.

1. Refer to Figure 5. Which statement is NOT shown by the graph?

   (1) The price in 1992 is about twice the price in 1984.
   (2) The prices in 1985 and 1987 are about the same.
   (3) The year of greatest increase during this 10-year period was from 1990 to 1991.
   (4) The price has never been higher than about $26.
   (5) The lowest price in this 10-year period is about $8.

2. Refer to Figure 6. If you invest $10,000 at an 8% annual interest rate, what will be the value of the money in 35 years?

   (1) about $110,000
   (2) about $130,000
   (3) about $150,000
   (4) about $170,000
   (5) not enough information is given

3. Refer to Figure 6. If you invested $10,000 at 8% annual interest rate, and the current value of your money is $70,000, how many years ago did you invest the money?

   (1) 10 years ago
   (2) 15 years ago
   (3) 20 years ago
   (4) 25 years ago
   (5) 30 years ago

4. Refer to Figure 7. Which statement is NOT true?

   (1) The hourly temperature decreased more times than it increased.
   (2) The hourly temperature stayed the same four times.
   (3) The hourly temperature decreased by 3°F one time.
   (4) The hourly temperature increased by 3°F five times.
   (5) The hourly temperature changed by 2°F three times.

5. Refer to Figure 7. Sunset was at about 5:00 P.M., and sunrise was at about 7:30 A.M. Which statement is NOT true?

   (1) The temperature dropped from sunrise until mid-afternoon.
   (2) The temperature dropped dramatically at sunset.
   (3) The temperature did not drop in the afternoon until sunset.
   (4) The temperature dropped during the early morning hours until sunrise.
   (5) The temperature at sunset and midnight was about the same.

6. Refer to Figure 7. Which statement is true?

   (1) The graph shows 48 temperature readings.
   (2) The hourly temperature was never lower than 10°F.
   (3) The hourly temperature was never higher than 24°F.
   (4) The temperature changed by the same number of degrees each hour.
   (5) none of the above

ANSWERS ARE ON PAGE 311.

DRAWING LINE GRAPHS

EXAMPLE Table 3 gives the price of one share of the Stein Roe Special Fund on November 21 for ten years. Draw a line graph to display this data.

Table 3

Year	Price
1984	$14.39
1985	$17.38
1986	$20.03
1987	$15.55
1988	$14.46
1989	$20.20
1990	$16.45
1991	$19.08
1992	$22.23
1993	$24.89
1994	$23.10

STEP 1 Draw a horizontal axis. Along the axis, write the years: 1984 to 1994. Label the axis: Date (November 21 each year).

STEP 2 Draw a vertical axis. Along the axis, write numbers that at least cover the range of the data. Label the axis: Price of One Share.

STEP 3 For each year, draw a point that shows the approximate price of one share. Connect the points with line segments.

STEP 4   Give the line graph a title: Stein Roe Special Fund, November 21, 1984–1994.

STEIN ROE SPECIAL FUND, NOVEMBER 21, 1984–1994

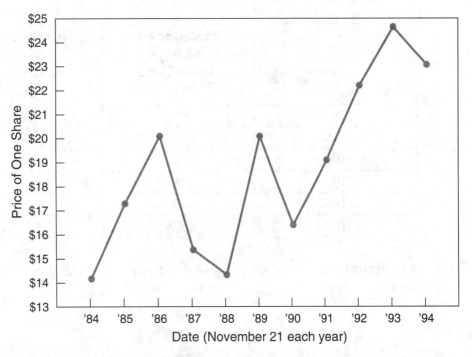

SUMMARY FOR DRAWING LINE GRAPHS

To draw a line graph:

1) Draw and label horizontal and vertical axes.

2) Draw points to display the data.

3) Connect the points with line segments.

4) Give the graph a title.

EXERCISE 7

Directions: The table below gives data on households in the United States. Use the data to draw the line graphs described.

Year	Number of People per Household	Number of Households (millions)
1930	4.11	30
1940	3.67	35
1950	3.37	44
1960	3.33	53
1970	3.14	63
1980	2.76	81
1990	2.63	93

1. Draw a line graph that shows the number of people per U.S. household over the 60-year period from 1930 to 1990.

2. Draw a line graph that shows the number of households (in millions) in the United States over the 60-year period from 1930 to 1990.

Directions: The table below gives consumer data for the United States. Use the data to draw the line graphs described.

Year	Consumer Price Index	Purchasing Power of the Dollar
1985	323.4	$.31
1986	325.7	$.31
1987	340.2	$.29
1988	357.9	$.28
1989	371.1	$.27
1990	399.4	$.25
1991	404.7	$.25
1992	416.3	$.24
1993	423.1	$.24

3. Draw a line graph that displays the Consumer Price Index in the United States from 1985 to 1993.

4. Draw a line graph that displays the Purchasing Power of the Dollar in the United States from 1985 to 1993.

ANSWERS ARE ON PAGE 311.

CIRCLE GRAPHS

A *circle graph* shows parts of a whole. The circle is the whole, or 100%. The circle is divided into parts, and all the parts add up to 100%. So circle graphs are often used to display data given as percents.

An example of a circle graph is given in Figure 8. This circle graph displays all the data given in Table 4. The graph shows that air exhaled by the human body contains parts of nitrogen, oxygen, carbon dioxide, and water. It also shows the size of each part. For example, nitrogen has the largest part of the circle (75%) because nitrogen is the largest part of exhaled air (75%).

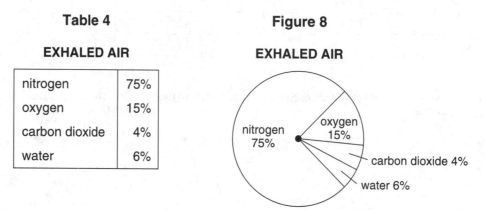

Table 4

EXHALED AIR

nitrogen	75%
oxygen	15%
carbon dioxide	4%
water	6%

Figure 8

EXHALED AIR

The next five examples show how to read a circle graph to answer questions about the data displayed. The examples are based on Figure 8 above.

EXAMPLE 1   What percent of exhaled air is oxygen?

Find oxygen in the circle graph. Read the percent: 15%.

Exhaled air is 15% oxygen.

EXAMPLE 2   What makes up 6% of exhaled air?

Find 6% in the circle graph. Read the label: water.

Water makes up 6% of exhaled air.

EXAMPLE 3   What fraction of exhaled air is nitrogen?

Find nitrogen in the circle graph. Read the percent: 75%.

Write 75% as a fraction: $\frac{75}{100} = \frac{75 \div 25}{100 \div 25} = \frac{3}{4}$

Exhaled air is $\frac{3}{4}$ nitrogen.

EXAMPLE 4   List the parts of exhaled air in order from least to greatest.

Write the percents given in the circle graph in order from least to greatest: 4%, 6%, 15%, 75%.

Write the parts in order from least to greatest: 4%, carbon dioxide; 6%, water; 15%, oxygen; 75%, nitrogen.

The list is: carbon dioxide, water, oxygen, nitrogen.

EXAMPLE 5   Suppose the amount of exhaled air is 760 millimeters of Mercury (mmHg). Find the amount of carbon dioxide in the exhaled air.

Find carbon dioxide in the circle graph. Read the percent: 4%.

Write a proportion: $\frac{\text{part}}{\text{whole}} = \frac{\%}{100}$.

$$\frac{h}{760} = \frac{4}{100}$$

Multiply to find the cross products, and divide:
$760 \times 4 \div 100 \approx 30$

The amount of carbon dioxide in the exhaled air is about 30 mmHg.

SUMMARY FOR READING A CIRCLE GRAPH

To read a circle graph:

1) Find the category you seek, and read the percent.

2) Or, do the opposite: Find the percent you seek, and read the category.

EXERCISE 8

Directions: Figure 9 shows the portion of miles of general coastline of each of the states along the U.S. Pacific coastline. Refer to this data to answer each question.

Figure 9

U.S. PACIFIC COASTLINE

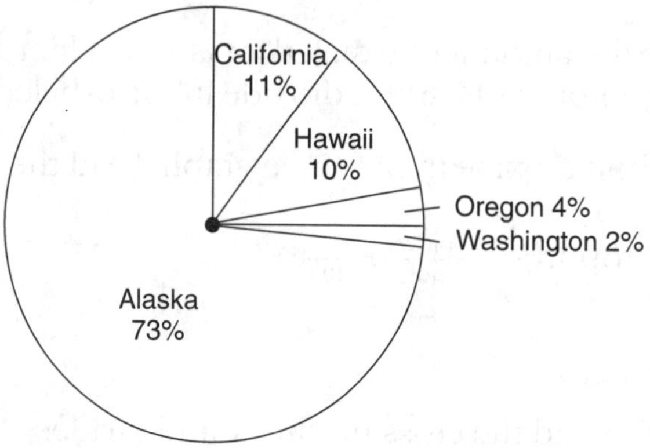

1. What percent of the U.S. Pacific coastline lies in Oregon?

2. Which state makes up 11% of the U.S. Pacific coastline?

3. Which state makes up almost $\frac{3}{4}$ of the U.S. Pacific coastline?

4. What fraction of the U.S. Pacific coastline lies in Hawaii?

5. How many states make up part of the U.S. Pacific coastline?

6. What percent of the U.S. Pacific coastline lies in the lower 48 states?

7. Which state has twice as much U.S. Pacific coastline as Washington?

8. The U.S. Pacific coastline is 7,623 miles long. Find the approximate length of the coastline in each state.

Directions: Exit polls were conducted on Election Day 1994 for "How Americans voted in the race for the House (of Representatives)." The circle graphs in Figure 10 display some of the data collected. Refer to them to answer each question.

Figure 10

HOW AMERICANS VOTED IN THE RACE FOR THE HOUSE, 1994

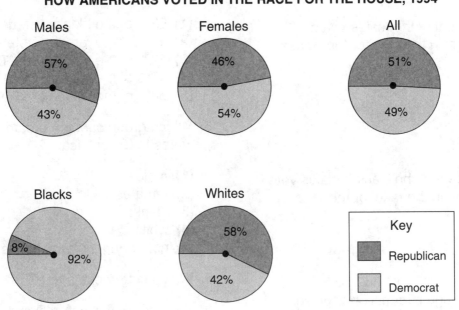

9. Which group showed the most support for Democrats? What percent of this group voted Democratic?

10. Which group showed the most support for Republicans? What percent of this group voted Republican?

11. Was the race between the Republicans and Democrats closer with the males or with the females?

12. Did the Democrats or the Republicans receive more votes? Which data did you use to answer this question?

ANSWERS ARE ON PAGES 311–312.

PRE-GED Practice
EXERCISE 9

Directions: Refer to Figure 10. Choose the best answer.

1. What percent of the males voted Democratic in the race for the House?

   (1) 43%
   (2) 57%
   (3) 92%
   (4) 42%
   (5) 49%

2. What percent of the black females voted Republican in the race for the House?

   (1) 46%
   (2) 8%
   (3) 54%
   (4) 38%
   (5) not enough information is given

3. A total of 10,210 voters participated in the exit poll. How many of these voters did not vote Republican?

   (1) 51% of voters
   (2) 5003 voters
   (3) 49% of voters
   (4) 5207 voters
   (5) not enough information is given

4. Which of the following is not shown by Figure 10?

   (1) 92% of the blacks voted Democratic.
   (2) 46% of the females voted Republican.
   (3) 49% of the voters voted Democratic.
   (4) 43% of the males voted Democratic.
   (5) 58% of the whites are Republicans.

5. Which group cast the greatest number of votes for Republicans?

   (1) males
   (2) females
   (3) blacks
   (4) whites
   (5) not enough information is given

6. Which statement is true?

   (1) More males voted Republican than voted Democrat.
   (2) More females voted Democrat than voted Republican.
   (3) More blacks voted Democrat than voted Republican.
   (4) More whites voted Republican than voted Democrat.
   (5) all of the above

ANSWERS ARE ON PAGE 312.

DRAWING CIRCLE GRAPHS

To draw a circle graph, you need to use some geometry skills. Recall that a ***central angle*** of a circle is an angle formed at the center. Figure 11 shows a central angle of a circle. To divide a circle graph into parts, you need to find the central angle for each part. The sum of all the central angles of a circle is 360°.

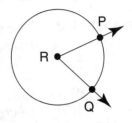

Central Angle PRQ

EXAMPLE 1   Data from an exit poll taken on Election Day 1994 is as follows: In the race for the House of Representatives, non-high school graduates voted 40% Republican and 60% Democratic. Draw a circle graph to display this data.

STEP 1   Calculate the central angle for each part. To do this, write the percent as a decimal and multiply by 360°. Round to the nearest degree, if necessary. Check the sum of the central angles (360°).

40% Republican: 0.40 × 360° = 144°
60% Democratic: 0.60 × 360° = 216°

Sum of central angles: 144° + 216° = 360°

STEP 2   Use a compass to draw a circle. Draw a point at the center of the circle. Use a protractor to draw each central angle.

STEP 3   Label each part of the circle graph with a name and a percent. Give the circle graph a title.

**NON-HIGH SCHOOL GRADUATES'
VOTES FOR THE HOUSE, 1994**

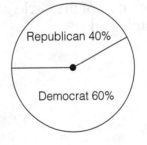

Sometimes data is given as numbers instead of percents. To draw the circle graph, you calculate a percent for each part.

EXAMPLE 2 The entire coastline of the United States is 12,383 miles long. It includes these four coasts: Atlantic, 2,069 miles; Gulf of Mexico, 1,631 miles; Pacific, 7,623 miles; Arctic, 1,060 miles. Draw a circle graph to display this data.

STEP 1 Calculate the percent for each part. Round to the nearest percent, if necessary. Check the sum of the percents (100%).

Atlantic: 2,069 ÷ 12,383 ≈ 0.17 = 17%
Gulf: 1,631 ÷ 12,383 ≈ 0.13 = 13%
Pacific: 7,623 ÷ 12,383 ≈ 0.62 = 62%
Arctic: 1,060 ÷ 12,383 ≈ 0.09 = 9%

Sum of the percents: 17% + 13% + 62% + 9% = 101%
The sum should be 100%, so adjust either by rounding Pacific to 61% or Arctic to 8%.

STEP 2 Calculate the central angle for each part. To do this, write the percent as a decimal and multiply by 360°. Round to the nearest degree, if necessary. Check the sum of the central angles (360°).

Atlantic: 0.17 × 360° ≈ 61°
Gulf: 0.13 × 360° ≈ 47°
Pacific: 0.61 × 360° ≈ 220°
Arctic: 0.09 × 360° ≈ 32°

Sum of the central angles: 61° + 47° + 220° + 32° = 360°

STEP 3 Use a compass to draw a circle. Draw a point at the center of the circle. Use a protractor to draw each central angle.

STEP 4 Label each part of the circle graph with a name and a percent. Give the circle graph a title.

U.S. COASTLINE

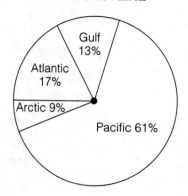

SUMMARY FOR DRAWING CIRCLE GRAPHS

To draw a circle graph:

1) Calculate the percent for each part, if necessary. The sum of the percents should be 100%.

2) Calculate the central angle for each part. The sum of the central angles should be 360°.

3) Draw a circle, mark the center, and draw each central angle.

4) Label each part and give the graph a title.

EXERCISE 10

1. On November 8, 1994, California voters passed Proposition 187 by a vote of 59% to 41%. This action bars illegal immigrants from receiving many state benefits. Draw a circle graph to display this data. Give the graph a title.

2. A telephone poll of 800 adult Americans was taken after Election Day 1994. The question asked was, "Now that the Republicans control Congress, is this a new era of government in Washington, or will there be a continuation of politics as usual?" The response was as follows: Politics as usual, 63%; New era, 32%; Not sure, 5%. Draw a circle graph that displays this data. Give the graph a title.

3. The U.S. House of Representatives, voted into office on November 8, 1994, includes 230 Republicans, 204 Democrats, and 1 Independent. Draw a circle graph that displays this data.

4. The coastline of the Gulf coast of the United States is 1,631 miles long. The five states bordering the Gulf coast, along with their respective miles of coastline, are shown below. Draw a circle graph that displays this data.

State	Coastline (miles)
Florida	770
Alabama	53
Mississippi	44
Louisiana	397
Texas	367

ANSWERS ARE ON PAGE 312.

PROBABILITY

Probability is the chance of something happening. It does not guarantee that something will happen, but it gives a measure of how likely it is that something will happen. For example, when a meteorologist reports an 80% chance of rain, the meteorologist is giving the probability of rain. It may rain, or it may not rain. But it is more likely to rain (80% chance) than not to rain (20% chance). If it were equally likely to rain as not to rain, the probability would be 50%.

When outcomes are equally likely, you can calculate the probability of an event using the fraction below.

$$\text{Probability of an event} = \frac{\text{number of favorable outcomes}}{\text{total number of possible outcomes}}$$

EXAMPLE 1   A number cube has faces numbered 1–6. When you roll a cube, what is the probability of rolling a 4?

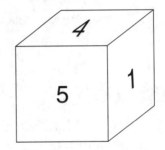

STEP 1   Find the total number of possible outcomes.

There are 6 different faces, so the total number of possible outcomes is 6.

STEP 2   Find the number of favorable outcomes.

The favorable outcome in this case is that the number cube lands on the face numbered 4, so there is 1 favorable outcome.

STEP 3   Calculate the probability.

$$\frac{\text{favorable outcomes}}{\text{total outcomes}} = \frac{1}{6}$$

The probability of rolling a 4 is $\frac{1}{6}$.

EXAMPLE 2   When you roll a cube, what is the probability of rolling an even number?

STEP 1   Find the total number of possible outcomes.

There are 6 different faces, so the total number of possible outcomes is 6.

STEP 2   Find the number of favorable outcomes.

The favorable outcome in this case is that the cube lands on 2, 4, or 6. There are 3 different favorable outcomes.

STEP 3   Calculate the probability.

$$\frac{\text{favorable outcomes}}{\text{total outcomes}} = \frac{3}{6} = \frac{1}{2}$$

The probability of rolling an even number is $\frac{1}{2}$.

You can express a probability as a fraction, a decimal, or a percent. Always write the fraction in lowest terms. The highest a probability can be is 1, or 100%. The lowest a probability can be is 0, or 0%.

EXAMPLE 3   What is the probability that the sun will set in the west the next time it sets?

The sun always sets in the west, so the probability is $\frac{1}{1}$, or 1, or 100%.

EXAMPLE 4   What is the probability that the sun will set in the east the next time it sets?

The sun never sets in the east, so the probability is $\frac{0}{1}$, or 0, or 0%.

EXERCISE 11

Directions: Solve each problem. Write each probability as a fraction, a decimal, and a percent. Refer to Figure 11 for numbers 1–4.

1. What is the probability of spinning $10?

Figure 11

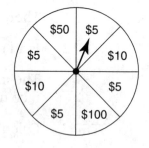

2. What is the probability of spinning at *least* $10?

3. Which two amounts of money are the least likely to be spun?

4. Which amount of money has a 50% probability of being spun?

5. When you flip a coin, what is the probability of flipping "heads"?

6. When you flip a coin, what is the probability of flipping "heads" or "tails"?

7. A standard deck of cards has 52 cards, including 4 Kings, 4 Queens, and 4 Jacks. When you draw one card, what is the probability of drawing a King?

8. When you roll a number cube, what is the probability of rolling a 4?

9. A meteorologist reports a 10% chance of rain. What is the probability of no rain?

10. A winning number appears on one of 10,000 baseball programs. If you buy a program, what are your chances of getting the winning number?

11. The Lopez family draws names for holiday presents. Each of the 10 family members puts their own name into a hat. What is the probability that someone will draw his own name?

12. One hundred raffle tickets are sold. The holder of the winning ticket will win a new car. If you buy five tickets for $3, what is the probability that you will win the new car?

13. A bag contains the following colored jelly beans: 10 red, 7 green, and 1 black. You pick one jelly bean without looking. What is the probability the jelly bean is red?

14. A bag contains the following colored jelly beans: 10 red, 7 green, and 1 black. You pick one jelly bean without looking. What is the probability the jelly bean is yellow?

ANSWERS ARE ON PAGE 312.

PRE-GED Practice
EXERCISE 12

Directions: Choose the best answer.

1. Suppose you roll a number cube. Which outcome is most likely?

   (1) an odd number
   (2) a number less than 5
   (3) 6
   (4) 1 or 2
   (5) a number greater than 3

2. A hat contains 26 small pieces of paper labeled with a letter from the alphabet. The letters are equally likely to be drawn. Suppose you draw one letter from the hat. Which outcome is least likely?

   (1) a vowel
   (2) a consonant
   (3) a letter in the second half of the alphabet
   (4) the first letter of your first name
   (5) A or Z

3. Which event has probability equal to 1?

   (1) Tuesday will immediately follow Wednesday.
   (2) Tuesday will be a rainy day.
   (3) Wednesday will not be a rainy day.
   (4) Wednesday will immediately follow Tuesday.
   (5) Tuesday and Wednesday will be rainy days.

4. Which event has probability closest to 0?

   (1) You will win a lottery.
   (2) You will sleep.
   (3) You will spend some money.
   (4) You will earn some money.
   (5) You will drink some water.

5. Which of the following is NOT a possible value for the probability of an event?

   (1) 0
   (2) $\frac{1}{2}$
   (3) $\frac{100}{101}$
   (4) 1
   (5) 1.21

6. Which of the following best describes an event that has 0 probability?

   (1) The event cannot happen.
   (2) The event may happen.
   (3) The event has already happened.
   (4) The event will happen regularly.
   (5) not enough information is given

ANSWERS ARE ON PAGE 312.

FAVORABLE OUTCOMES

Sometimes it is helpful to make a table or draw a tree diagram when finding the number of favorable outcomes. With either method, you generate a list of all the possible outcomes. Then you can see which of these are favorable and find the probability you seek.

EXAMPLE 1 Suppose you flip two coins. What is the probability of flipping two heads?

STEP 1 One way to solve this problem is to make a table. Let H = head, and let T = tail. The two possibilities for one coin are given in the top row: H and T. The two possibilities for the other coin are given in the left column: H and T.

	H	T
H		
T		

STEP 2 Complete the table. This gives all the possible outcomes.

	H	T
H	HH	HT
T	TH	TT

STEP 3 Find the total number of possible outcomes.

The possible outcomes are HH, HT, TH, and TT. There are 4 possible outcomes.

STEP 4 Find the number of favorable outcomes.

The favorable outcome is HH. There is 1 favorable outcome.

STEP 5 Calculate the probability.

$$\frac{\text{favorable outcomes}}{\text{total outcomes}} = \frac{1}{4} = 0.25 = 25\%$$

When you flip two coins, the probability of flipping two heads is $\frac{1}{4}$, or 0.25, or 25%.

EXAMPLE 2   Suppose you flip three coins. What is the probability of flipping exactly two heads?

STEP 1   One way to solve this problem is to draw a tree diagram. Let H = head, and let T = tail. The two possibilities for a coin are H and T. Each branch of the tree leads to a possible outcome.

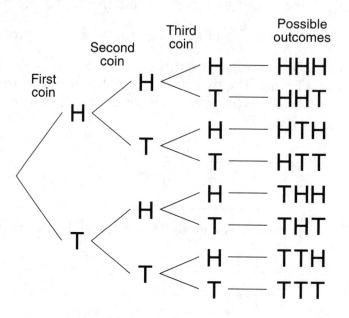

STEP 2   Find the total number of possible outcomes.

The possible outcomes are HHH, HHT, HTH, HTT, THH, THT, TTH, and TTT. There are 8 possible outcomes.

STEP 3   Find the number of favorable outcomes.

The favorable outcomes are HHT, HTH, and THH. There are 3 favorable outcomes.

STEP 4   Calculate the probability.

$$\frac{\text{favorable outcomes}}{\text{total outcomes}} = \frac{3}{8} = 0.375 = 37.5\%$$

When you flip three coins, the probability of flipping two heads is $\frac{3}{8}$, or 0.375, or 37.5%.

EXERCISE 13

Directions: The table below gives all possible outcomes for rolling two number cubes. Complete the table, then refer to it for numbers 1–6.

	1	2	3	4	5	6
1	1, 1	1, 2	1, 3	1, 4		
2	2, 1	2, 2				
3	3, 1					
4	4, 1					
5						
6						

1. How many possible outcomes are there?

2. Often when you roll two number cubes, you add the two numbers to find the sum. How many different sums are possible?

3. List the three favorable outcomes for rolling a sum of 4. What is the probability of rolling a sum of 4?

4. What is the probability of rolling a sum of 8?

5. Which sum is most likely to be rolled?

6. What is the probability of rolling "doubles" (the two cubes have the same number)?

Directions: The tree diagram below gives all possible outcomes for three children in a family, with B = boy and G = girl. Assume boy and girl are equally likely outcomes. Complete the tree diagram, then refer to it for numbers 7–14.

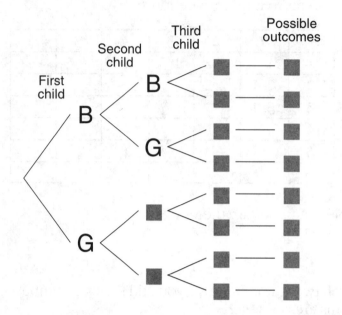

7. List all possible outcomes for three children in a family.

8. What is the probability of three girls?

9. What is the probability of two girls and one boy, in any order?

10. What is the probability of two girls and one boy, in that order?

11. What is the probability of no girls?

12. What is the probability of all girls or all boys?

13. List all favorable outcomes for one girl and two boys.

14. What is the probability of having a boy, then a girl, then a boy?

Directions: Choose the best answer.

15. Suppose you flip some coins. Which event has the lowest probability?

(1) Flip 1 head.
(2) Flip 2 heads in a row.
(3) Flip 3 heads in a row.
(4) Flip 4 heads in a row.
(5) Flip 5 heads in a row.

16. Suppose you roll two number cubes. Which outcome is most likely?

(1) Sum of 12
(2) Sum of 7
(3) Doubles
(4) At least one 6
(5) (1,5) or (5,1)

ANSWERS ARE ON PAGE 313.

DEPENDENT PROBABILITY

Sometimes a probability depends upon a previous outcome. Two events are **dependent** if the outcome of one depends on the outcome of the other. Two events are **independent** if the outcome of one does not depend on the outcome of the other. Here are some examples.

EXAMPLE 1 Suppose you flip a coin, then you flip it again. Are the two events dependent or independent? Explain.

These two events are independent. The second flip does not depend on the outcome of the first flip. With each flip, "heads" and "tails" are equally likely outcomes.

EXAMPLE 2 Suppose you have some black socks and some blue socks loose in a drawer. You close your eyes, grab one sock, and put it on your foot. Then you grab another sock, hoping it matches the one on your foot. Are the two events dependent or independent? Explain.

These two events are dependent. The outcome of the second sock drawn depends on the outcome of the first sock drawn. If the first sock you draw is blue, there is one less blue sock in the drawer.

EXAMPLE 3 Color blindness is a genetic trait that occurs more often in males than in females. Are color blindness and gender dependent or independent events? Explain.

They are dependent events. The outcome of one event (colorblindness) depends on the outcome of the other event (gender). A male is more likely to be colorblind than a female.

The next two examples illustrate the difference between independent and dependent probability.

EXAMPLE 4   A standard deck has 52 cards, including 4 aces. You draw one ace from the deck and keep it in your hand. What is the probability of drawing another ace?

STEP 1   Find the total number of possible outcomes.

There are 52 cards total, but you have already drawn one card. There are only 51 cards left to draw from. The total number of possible outcomes is 51.

STEP 2   Find the number of favorable outcomes.

The favorable outcome is that you draw another ace. There are 4 aces total, but you have already drawn one ace. There are only 3 aces left to draw from. The number of favorable outcomes is 3.

STEP 3   Calculate the probability.

$$\frac{\text{favorable outcomes}}{\text{total outcomes}} = \frac{3}{51} = \frac{1}{17} \approx 6\%$$

The probability of drawing another ace is $\frac{1}{17}$, or about 6%.

EXAMPLE 5   In a 52-card deck, there are 4 aces. You draw one ace from the deck and put it back into the deck. What is the probability of drawing another ace?

STEP 1   Find the total number of possible outcomes.

There are 52 cards total, so the total number of possible outcomes is 52.

STEP 2   Find the number of favorable outcomes.

The favorable outcome is that you draw another ace. There are 4 aces total, so the number of favorable outcomes is 4.

STEP 3   Calculate the probability.

$$\frac{\text{favorable outcomes}}{\text{total outcomes}} = \frac{4}{52} = \frac{1}{13} \approx 8\%$$

The probability of drawing another ace is $\frac{1}{13}$, or about 8%.

EXERCISE 14

Directions: Solve each problem. Write each probability as a fraction, a decimal, and a percent. State if the problem involves *dependent* or *independent* events.

1. In a 52-card deck, there are 12 face cards. You draw a face card from the deck and keep it in your hand. What is the probability of drawing another face card?

2. A 52-card deck has 12 face cards. You draw one face card from the deck and put it back into the deck. What is the probability of drawing another face card?

3. Suppose you have a daughter. What is the probability that your next child will be a daughter?

4. Suppose you have a daughter. What is the probability that your next child will be a son?

5. Suppose you have 10 socks loose in a drawer. Four of the socks are blue and six are black. You grab a black sock, put it on your foot, then grab another sock. What is the probability the two socks will be the same color?

6. Suppose you have 10 socks loose in a drawer. Four of the socks are blue and six are black. You grab a black sock, put it back in the drawer because you want a blue sock, then grab another sock. What is the probability the second sock you draw is blue?

Directions: Choose the best answer.

7. Which two events are independent?

    (1) draw a card and keep it, draw another card
    (2) roll a number cube and keep it, roll another number cube
    (3) draw a name from a hat and keep it, draw another name
    (4) grab a sock from the dryer, grab a second sock
    (5) plant a tulip bulb, grow a tulip

8. Which two events are dependent?

    (1) spin a spinner, spin it again
    (2) flip a dime, flip a nickel
    (3) rain today, rain tomorrow
    (4) draw a card and put it back, draw another card
    (5) have a son, have another child

ANSWERS ARE ON PAGE 313.

DATA ANALYSIS AND PROBABILITY REVIEW

Directions: In Questions 1–18, solve each problem. Write each probability as a fraction, a decimal, and a percent. Show your work to the right.

Table 5

Names and Ages of Employees

Name	Age	Name	Age
Tyson	28	Jade	22
Tat	37	Lin	40
Heidi	19	Rosa	63
Carlos	51	Chung	40
Pedro	40	Luisa	25
Carmen	31		

1. Refer to Table 5. Find the mean age of the employees.

2. Refer to Table 5. Find the median age of the employees.

3. Refer to Table 5. Find the mode(s), if any.

4. Refer to Table 5. Find the age range of the employees.

Figure 12

NEWSPAPER EMPLOYEES

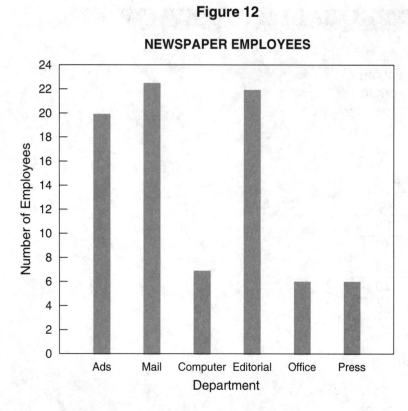

5. Refer to Figure 12. How many newspaper employees are there in the computer department?

6. Refer to Figure 12. Which departments have at least 20 employees?

Table 6

Number of Species in Selected Families of Birds

Family of Birds	Number of Species
Parrots	243
Pheasants	214
Finches	153
Ducks	140
Larks	75
Falcons	60

7. Draw a bar graph that displays the data given in Table 6.

Figure 13

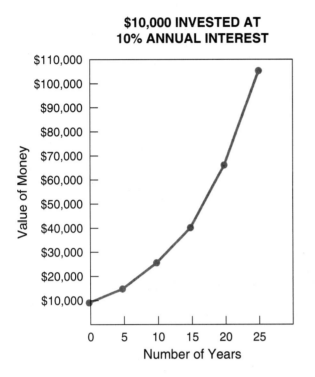

**$10,000 INVESTED AT
10% ANNUAL INTEREST**

8. Refer to Figure 13. If you invest $10,000 at a 10% annual interest rate, what will be the value of the money in 10 years?

9. Refer to Figure 13. If you invest $10,000 at a 10% annual interest rate, how long will it take for the money to be worth $80,000?

Table 7

**Daily Low Temperature
for One Week**

Day	Temp. (°F)
Sunday	20
Monday	16
Tuesday	14
Wednesday	10
Thursday	10
Friday	15
Saturday	19

10. Draw a line graph that displays the data given in Table 7.

Figure 14

THE WONG FAMILY BUDGET

11. Refer to Figure 14. Which budget item costs twice as much as the amount of money the Wongs put into savings?

12. Refer to Figure 14. If the Wongs' total monthly budget is $2,000, how much money do they spend on rent?

13. Blood is made up of 55% plasma and 45% cells. Draw a circle graph that displays this data.

14. When you roll a number cube, what is the probability of rolling an odd number?

Figure 15

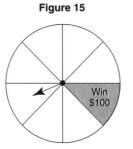

15. Refer to Figure 15. If you spin the spinner once, what is the probability of winning $100?

16. List all possible gender outcomes for two children in a family. Let B = boy, and let G = girl.

17. When you roll two number cubes, what is the probability of a sum of 3?

18. Each letter of the alphabet is written on a piece of paper and put into a hat. You will keep drawing letters from the hat until you get "Z". The first letter you draw is "A". What is the probability that the next letter you draw is "Z"?

Directions: Questions 19–32 include applications of whole numbers, decimals, fractions, measurement, geometry, ratios, proportions, percents, data analysis, and probability. Choose the correct answer to each problem. Remember the problem-solving skills you have learned.

19. The ratio of males to females at a party is 1 to 4. There is a total of 20 people at the party. How many are female?

   (1) 4
   (2) 15
   (3) 12
   (4) 16
   (5) 5

20. Which figure described has the greatest area?

   (1) a rectangle whose length is 6 meters and width is 9 meters
   (2) a circle whose radius is 4 meters
   (3) a square whose side is 7 meters
   (4) a rectangle whose length is 5 meters and width is 10 meters
   (5) a circle whose diameter is 7 meters

21. How many cups are in 10 gallons?

   (1) 80 cups
   (2) 160 cups
   (3) 320 cups
   (4) 100 cups
   (5) 18 cups

22. Tim flipped a quarter and got heads. He's ready to flip it again. What statement best describes what will happen?

   (1) He has a better chance of getting tails because he just got heads.
   (2) He has a better chance of getting heads because that's usually what he gets.
   (3) He has a 50% chance of getting heads and a 50% chance of getting tails.
   (4) He has a 50% chance of getting either heads or tails.
   (5) There is no way of knowing what the chances are for getting heads or tails.

23. Which is the best buy for donuts?

   (1) 2 for $.69
   (2) 5 for $2
   (3) $.35 each
   (4) 4 for $1.50
   (5) 3 for $1

24. Which of the following is a set of equivalent numbers?

   (1) $\frac{8}{10}$, 8%, 0.08

   (2) 0.8, $\frac{4}{5}$, 8%

   (3) 80%, $\frac{80}{100}$, 0.08

   (4) $\frac{4}{5}$, 80%, 0.8

   (5) 8%, $\frac{8}{100}$, 0.8

25. Whitney wants to graph the price of a U.S. postage stamp for the last 20 years. What type of graph would work the best?

   (1) bar graph
   (2) line graph
   (3) circle graph
   (4) tree diagram
   (5) any of the above

26. The average height of the starting lineup of a women's basketball team is 5 feet 10 inches. Which set of heights is possible for the women?

    (1) 5 feet 5 inches, 5 feet 6 inches, 6 feet, 6 feet 2 inches, 5 feet 10 inches
    (2) 6 feet, 6 feet, 5 feet 8 inches, 5 feet 7 inches, 5 feet 11 inches
    (3) 5 feet 4 inches, 5 feet 6 inches, 5 feet 11 inches, 6 feet, 6 feet 1 inch
    (4) 6 feet 1 inch, 5 feet 9 inches, 5 feet 9 inches, 5 feet 5 inches, 5 feet 10 inches
    (5) 6 feet 2 inches, 6 feet, 6 feet, 5 feet 7 inches, 5 feet 8 inches

27. Which set of data has a range equal to its median?

    (1) 0, 4, 7, 6, 8, 5
    (2) 7, 10, 5, 4, 12, 10
    (3) 2, 8, 5, 10, 8, 6
    (4) 3, 8, 7, 8, 10, 2
    (5) 4, 9, 9, 9, 7, 1

28. The E.J. Brach Company produced 1.8 billion pieces of candy corn for Halloween 1994. This was enough candy for every child under 12 in the U.S. to have 36 pieces. According to this data, how many children under 12 are there in the United States?

    (1) about 64.8 billion
    (2) about 50 million
    (3) about 21.6 billion
    (4) about 150,000,000
    (5) about 64.8 million

29. Suppose you are playing cards with a friend, using a standard deck of 52 cards. Each player has 7 cards, you have 1 ace, and you know that your friend does not have an ace. The rest of the deck is in the draw pile. What is the probability that the next card you draw will be an ace?

    (1) about 8%
    (2) about 3%
    (3) about 6%
    (4) about 7%
    (5) about 2%

30. Fingernails grow about $1\frac{1}{2}$ inches per year. At this rate, how much have the fingernails of a 48-year-old grown?

    (1) 6 inches
    (2) 2 feet
    (3) 32 inches
    (4) 6 feet
    (5) 70 inches

31. A scale drawing of a new storage shed is shown below. The scale for the drawing is 1 centimeter : 2 meters. Which proportion would you solve to find the actual length of the longer side of the shed?

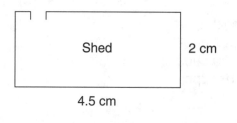

    Shed   2 cm

    4.5 cm

    (1) $\dfrac{1\ cm}{2\ m} = \dfrac{2\ cm}{h}$

    (2) $\dfrac{1\ cm}{h} = \dfrac{2\ m}{4.5\ cm}$

    (3) $\dfrac{1\ cm}{4.5\ cm} = \dfrac{h}{2\ m}$

    (4) $\dfrac{4.5\ cm}{h} = \dfrac{2\ m}{1\ cm}$

    (5) $\dfrac{1\ cm}{2\ m} = \dfrac{4.5\ cm}{h}$

32. Gerrard has a lump sum of money to invest. With which investment will Gerrard earn the most money?

(1) 8% for 2 years
(2) 3% for 8 years
(3) 5% for 5 years
(4) 12% for 1 year
(5) The amount to be invested must be known.

33. Which two numbers are equivalent?

(1) .333 . . . and $\frac{3}{10}$

(2) $\frac{5}{6}$ and .565656 . . .

(3) 0.222 and $\frac{2}{9}$

(4) .750 and $66\frac{2}{3}$

(5) none of the above

34. Which pair of fractions has a sum that is greater than 1?

(1) $\frac{1}{3}$ + $\frac{1}{6}$

(2) $\frac{1}{2}$ + $\frac{1}{10}$

(3) $\frac{3}{7}$ + $\frac{4}{9}$

(4) $\frac{2}{5}$ + $\frac{4}{10}$

(5) $\frac{3}{5}$ + $\frac{4}{7}$

35. Which pair of decimals has a difference that is less than 1?

(1) 3.75 and 4.85
(2) 5.032 and 4.001
(3) 1.219 and 0.315
(4) 11.5 and 12.6
(5) not enough information is given

ANSWERS ARE ON PAGE 313.

7 Basic Algebra Concepts

EXPONENTS AND SQUARE ROOTS

In the expression 2^4, 2 is called the **base**, and 4 is called the **exponent**. To find the value, you multiply the base times itself the number of times indicated by the exponent. The expression 2^4 is the same as the product of $2 \times 2 \times 2 \times 2 = 16$.

EXAMPLE 1 Find the value of 3^5.

STEP 1 Identify the base and the exponent.

Base: 3
Exponent: 5

STEP 2 Write the base as many times as the exponent indicates.

$3 \times 3 \times 3 \times 3 \times 3$

STEP 3 Multiply.

$3 \times 3 \times 3 \times 3 \times 3 = 243$

The value of 3^5 is 243.

EXAMPLE 2 Find the value of 1^3.

STEP 1 Identify the base and the exponent.

Base: 1
Exponent: 3

STEP 2 Write the base as many times as the exponent indicates.

$1 \times 1 \times 1$

STEP 3 Multiply.

$1 \times 1 \times 1 = 1$
The value of 1^3 is 1.

EXAMPLE 3   Find the value of 9^1.

STEP 1   Identify the base and the exponent.

Base: 9
Exponent: 1

STEP 2   Write the base as many times as the exponent indicates.

9

Notice that you do not need to multiply, because 9 is written just once.

The value of 9^1 is 9.

SUMMARY FOR FINDING THE VALUE OF EXPRESSIONS WITH EXPONENTS

To find the value of expressions with exponents:

1) Identify the base and the exponent.

2) Write the base as many times as the exponent indicates.

3) Multiply.

To find the value of an expression that has 0 as an exponent, use the following tip.

TIP: When the exponent is 0, the value of the expression is 1.

EXAMPLE 4   Find the value of 9^0.

STEP 1   Identify and base and the exponent.

Base: 9
Exponent: 0

STEP 2   Use the tip above.

The exponent is 0, so the value of the expression is 1.

The value of 9^0 is 1.

The expression 7^2 is sometimes called "7 squared" or "the square of 7." The exponent $\underline{2}$ indicates that the base is squared. Recall that 7^2 is the same as 7×7, so the value of 7^2 is 49.

The expression $\sqrt{49}$ is read, "the square root of 49." Finding the square root of a number is the opposite of finding the square of a number. A number's square root is the one number that, multiplied by itself, will yield the square.

EXAMPLE 5   Find the value of $\sqrt{49}$.

STEP 1   Think: "What number multiplied by itself is 49?"

$$h \times h = 49$$
$$7 \times 7 = 49$$

STEP 2   Write the square root.

$$\sqrt{49} = 7$$

The value of $\sqrt{49}$ is 7.

EXAMPLE 6   Find the value of $\sqrt{100}$.

STEP 1   Think: "What number multiplied by itself is 100?"

$$h \times h = 100$$
$$10 \times 10 = 100$$

STEP 2   Write the square root.

$$\sqrt{100} = 10$$

The value of $\sqrt{100}$ is 10.

SUMMARY FOR FINDING A SQUARE ROOT

1) Think: "What number multiplied by itself is the number found under the square root symbol?"

2) Write the square root.

3) Many square roots are memorized as part of the multiplication facts.

EXERCISE 1

Directions: Find the value of each of the following.

1. 6^3

2. 9^2

3. 10^1

4. 7^4

5. 12^0

6. 4^5

7. 3^4

8. 2^6

9. 8^0

10. 1^7

11. 7^3

12. 0^6

13. $\sqrt{25}$

14. $\sqrt{144}$

15. $\sqrt{0}$

16. $\sqrt{1}$

17. $\sqrt{36}$

18. $\sqrt{16}$

19. $\sqrt{64}$

20. $\sqrt{9}$

Directions: Complete each table.

21.

Number	Square
1	$1^2 =$
2	$2^2 =$
3	
4	
5	
6	
7	
8	
9	
10	
11	
12	
13	
14	
15	
20	

22.

Number	Square Root
1	$\sqrt{1} =$
4	$\sqrt{4} =$
9	
16	
25	
36	
49	
64	
81	
100	
121	
144	
169	
196	
225	
400	

Directions: Solve each problem.

23. Each side of a square is 8 meters long. Find the area of the square.

24. A square has area 225 square meters. Find the length of each side of the square.

25. The value of $\sqrt{20}$ lies between what two consecutive whole numbers?

26. The value of $\sqrt{150}$ lies between what two consecutive whole numbers?

27. What whole number is between $\sqrt{60}$ and $\sqrt{70}$?

ANSWERS ARE ON PAGE 314.

PRE-GED Practice
EXERCISE 2

Directions: Choose the best answer.

1. Which of the following is the same as 4^5?

   (1) $5 \times 5 \times 5 \times 5$
   (2) $4 \times 4 \times 4 \times 4 \times 4$
   (3) 4×5
   (4) 5×4
   (5) 5^4

2. Which of the following is not the same as 2^8?

   (1) $2 \times 2 \times 2 \times 2 \times 2 \times 2 \times 2 \times 2$
   (2) 256
   (3) 8×8
   (4) 4^4
   (5) 16^2

3. If the square root of a number is 9, what is the number?

   (1) 3
   (2) $\sqrt{81}$
   (3) $\sqrt{9}$
   (4) $\sqrt{3}$
   (5) 81

4. If the square of a number is 25, what is the number?

   (1) 5
   (2) 625
   (3) 5^2
   (4) $\sqrt{5}$
   (5) 25^2

5. Evaluate $(1 + 2 + 3)^2$

   (1) 14
   (2) 123
   (3) 36
   (4) 12
   (5) 32

6. Evaluate $\sqrt{17^2 - 15^2}$

   (1) 4
   (2) 8
   (3) 64
   (4) 255
   (5) none of the above

7. What is the difference between 5^2 and 6^2?

   (1) 1
   (2) 61
   (3) 121
   (4) 7^2
   (5) 11

8. What is the sum of $\sqrt{49}$ and $\sqrt{64}$?

   (1) $\sqrt{113}$
   (2) 15
   (3) 56
   (4) $\sqrt{15}$
   (5) 1

ANSWERS ARE ON PAGE 315.

ARITHMETIC EXPRESSIONS

An arithmetic expression often includes more than one operation. When finding the value of an arithmetic expression, you need to know the proper order to perform the operations. For example, the expression $8 - 4 \times 2$ suggests two possible ways to solve the problem. Working from left to right, you would subtract first and get $8 - 4 = 4$; $4 \times 2 = 8$, an incorrect answer. But if you multiply first, you would get $4 \times 2 = 8$; $8 - 8 = 0$, the correct answer.

Use the following set of rules whenever you find the value of an arithmetic expression.

SUMMARY FOR ORDER OF OPERATIONS

To find the value of an arithmetic expression, follow these steps in the order indicated. If an expression includes more than one operation of the same type, work from left to right.

1) Do operations within parentheses.

2) Do exponents and square roots.

3) Do multiplication and division.

4) Do addition and subtraction.

EXAMPLE 1   Find the value of the expression $5 \times (6 - 2) \div 2 - 2^3$.

STEP 1   Do operations within parentheses.

$5 \times 4 \div 2 - 2^3$

STEP 2   Do exponents and square roots.

$5 \times 4 \div 2 - 8$

STEP 3   Do multiplication and division. Work from left to right.

$20 \div 2 - 8$
$10 - 8$

STEP 4   Do addition and subtraction.

2

The value of the expression is 2.

If an expression does not include all the operations listed in the rules, just skip a step and go on to the next step.

EXAMPLE 2   Find the value of the expression $3 \times 4 - (8 + 1)$

STEP 1   Do operations within parentheses.

$3 \times 4 - 9$

STEP 2   Do exponents and square roots.

(There are none, so skip this step.)

STEP 3   Do multiplication and division.

$12 - 9$

STEP 4   Do addition and subtraction.

3

The value of the expression is 3.

If an expression includes a set of parentheses inside another set, work from the inside to the outside.

EXAMPLE 3   Find the value of the expression $100 - [2 \times (9 - 2)] \times \sqrt{9}$.

STEP 1   Do operations within parentheses.

$100 - [2 \times 7] \times \sqrt{9}$
$100 - 14 \times \sqrt{9}$

STEP 2   Do exponents and square roots.

$100 - 14 \times 3$

STEP 3   Do multiplication and division.

$100 - 42$

STEP 4   Do addition and subtraction.

58

The value of the expression is 58.

EXERCISE 3

Directions: Find the value of each of the following.

1. $(12 + 4) \div (1 + 7)$

9. $(2^3 + 3^3) \div 7$

2. $3^2 + 6^2 \div 3$

10. $13 + 6 \times 2 \div 4 - 9$

3. $\sqrt{25} + 6 \times 4 - 10$

11. $3 \times (10 - 4) \div 9 + 4^2$

4. $[(30 - 8) \div 2] + 5$

12. $9 \times 8^0 + (6 - 1)$

5. $24 \div (1^5 + 5)$

13. $60 - [25 - (13 - 4)]$

6. $100 \div 5 - 3 \times 4$

14. $\sqrt{100} \div 5 + 3 \times 6$

7. $[3 \times (11 - 4)] - 16$

15. $(5 + 7) \div (12 - 8) \div 3$

8. $(\sqrt{49} - 1) \div 2$

16. $5 \times 8 \div 2 \times 1 \div 10$

ANSWERS ARE ON PAGE 315.

═ PRE-GED Practice ═
EXERCISE 4

Directions: Choose the best answer.

1. Which has the greatest value?

   (1) $10 \times (4 - 1) + 5$
   (2) $10 \times 4 - 1 + 5$
   (3) $10 \times (4 - 1 + 5)$
   (4) $10 \times 4 - (1 + 5)$
   (5) $(10 \times 4 - 1) + 5$

2. Which has the least value?

   (1) $3^2 + 6 \times 4 - 2$
   (2) $(3^2 + 6) \times (4 - 2)$
   (3) $(3^2 + 6) \times 4 - 2$
   (4) $3^2 + (6 \times 4) - 2$
   (5) $3^2 + 6 \times (4 - 2)$

3. What is the value of the expression $14 - 2^3 + 6 \times 2$?

   (1) 20
   (2) 18
   (3) 28
   (4) 24
   (5) 14

4. Which expression does not have the same value as the expression $40 + 12 \div 6$?

   (1) $6 + 4 \times 3 + 12$
   (2) $(3 \times 7) \times 2$
   (3) $\sqrt{36} \times (6 + 1)$
   (4) $15 \times (3 + 2) - 33$
   (5) $4 \times 8 + 2 \times 5$

5. Which expression has the same value as $(5) \times (8 - 2) \div (4)$?

   (1) $(5 \times 8) - (2 \div 4)$
   (2) $5 \times 8 - 2 \div 4$
   (3) $5 \times (8 - 2) \div 4$
   (4) $(5 \times 8) - 2 \div (4)$
   (5) not enough information is given

6. Which expression has the greatest value?

   (1) $1 + 2 + 3 + 4$
   (2) $1 \times 2 \times 3 \times 4$
   (3) $(1 + 2) \times (3 + 4)$
   (4) $1 + 2 \times 3 + 4$
   (5) $(1 \times 2) + (3 \times 4)$

7. Which expression has the least value?

   (1) $5^2 + 4^2$
   (2) $5 \times 2 + 4 \times 2$
   (3) $(5 + 4)^2$
   (4) $5 \times 2 \times 4 \times 2$
   (5) All have the same value.

8. Which two expressions are equal?

   (1) $3^2 + 4^2$ and 5^2
   (2) $10^2 - 8^2$ and 6^2
   (3) $8^2 + 15^2$ and 17^2
   (4) $13^2 - 12^2$ and 5^2
   (5) all of the above

ANSWERS ARE ON PAGE 316.

VARIABLES AND SIMPLE EQUATIONS

An **equation** is a statement that two amounts are equal. In algebra, an equation usually has at least one variable. A **variable** is a letter used to represent an unknown amount. A **solution** to an equation is the value of the variable that makes the equation a true statement.

EXAMPLE 1   Is 8 a solution to the equation $n + 7 = 15$?

STEP 1   Substitute the value for the variable in the equation. In this case, substitute 8 for n.

$$8 + 7 = 15$$

STEP 2   Decide whether or not the equation is a true statement.

$8 + 7 = 15$ is a true statement.

Yes, 8 is a solution.

EXAMPLE 2   Is 8 a solution to the equation $\frac{x}{3} = 5$?

STEP 1   Substitute the value for the variable in the equation. In this case, substitute 8 for x.

$$\frac{8}{3} = 5$$

STEP 2   Decide whether or not the equation is a true statement.

$\frac{8}{3} = 5$ is not a true statement, because $\frac{8}{3} \neq 5$.

No, 8 is not a solution.

To solve an equation, you can use the **inverse operations** listed below:

- The inverse of addition is subtraction.

- The inverse of subtraction is addition.

- The inverse of multiplication is division.

- The inverse of division is multiplication.

EXAMPLE 3   Solve the equation $y + 4 = 21$.

STEP 1   Identify the operation used in the equation.

There is a plus sign, so the operation is addition.

STEP 2   Identify the inverse operation.

The inverse of addition is subtraction.

STEP 3 Use the inverse operation to solve the equation. In this case, subtract 4 from the numbers on each side of the equal sign.

$$\begin{array}{r} y + 4 = 21 \\ -\ 4 \quad -4 \\ \hline y \quad = 17 \end{array}$$

STEP 4 Check the solution, as in Examples 1 and 2.

$17 + 4 = 21$ is a true statement.

The solution is 17. Write $y = 17$.

EXAMPLE 4 Solve the equation $3a = 24$.

STEP 1 Identify the operation used in the equation.

$3a$ means $3 \times a$, so the operation is multiplication.

STEP 2 Identify the inverse operation.

The inverse of multiplication is division.

STEP 3 Use the inverse operation to solve the equation. In this case, divide the numbers on each side of the equal sign by 3.

$$3a = 24$$
$$\frac{3a}{3} = \frac{24}{3}$$
$$a = 8$$

STEP 4 Check the solution, as in Examples 1 and 2.

$3 \times 8 = 24$ is a true statement.

The solution is 8. Write $a = 8$.

EXAMPLE 5 Solve the equation $x - 8 = 18$.

STEP 1 Identify the operation used in the equation.

There is a minus sign, so the operation is subtraction.

STEP 2 Identify the inverse operation.

The inverse of subtraction is addition.

STEP 3 Use the inverse operation to solve the equation. In this case, add 8 to the numbers on each side of the equal sign.

$$\begin{array}{r} x - 8 = 18 \\ +8 \quad +8 \\ \hline x \quad = 26 \end{array}$$

STEP 4   Check the solution, as in Examples 1 and 2.

$26 - 8 = 18$ is a true statement.

The solution is 26. Write $x = 26$.

EXAMPLE 6   Solve the equation $\frac{z}{6} = 5$.

STEP 1   Identify the operation used in the equation.

$\frac{z}{6}$ means $z \div 6$, so the operation is division.

STEP 2   Identify the inverse operation.

The inverse of division is multiplication.

STEP 3   Use the inverse operation to solve the equation. In this case, multiply the numbers on each side of the equal sign by 6.

$$\frac{z}{6} = 5$$

$$\frac{z}{6} \times 6 = 5 \times 6$$

$$z = 30$$

STEP 4   Check the solution, as in Examples 1 and 2.

$\frac{30}{6} = 5$ is a true statement.

The solution is 30. Write $z = 30$.

SUMMARY FOR SOLVING SIMPLE EQUATIONS

To solve a simple equation, follow these steps:

1) Identify the operation used in the equation.

2) Identify the inverse operation.

3) Use the inverse operation to solve the equation. Whatever operation you perform on one side of the equal sign, do the same on the other side.

4) Check the solution by substituting the answer for the variable in the equation, and see if the equation is true.

EXERCISE 5

Directions: Is the value given for the variable a solution to the equation? Write *yes* or *no*.

1. $9y = 27; y = 3$

2. $x + 3 = 7; x = 10$

3. $n - 14 = 10; n = 24$

4. $4z = 32; z = 8$

5. $\frac{x}{2} = 11; x = 22$

6. $\frac{a}{5} = 20; a = 4$

Directions: Solve each equation.

7. $5y = 35$

8. $n - 1 = 10$

9. $y + 20 = 21$

10. $\frac{z}{3} = 2$

11. $8n = 32$

12. $n + 1 = 8$

13. $\frac{x}{4} = 9$

14. $a - 17 = 11$

15. $z - 4 = 5$

16. $10a = 200$

17. $\frac{y}{2} = 16$

18. $x + 9 = 19$

19. $a + 3 = 37$

20. $9z = 54$

21. $y - 8 = 6$

22. $\frac{a}{7} = 1$

23. $x - 15 = 3$

24. $2x = 50$

25. $\frac{n}{6} = 6$

26. $z + 14 = 23$

Directions: Choose the best answer.

27. Which equation has 3 as the solution?

    (1) $2x = 9$
    (2) $8x = 30$
    (3) $4x = 12$
    (4) $3x = 15$
    (5) $5x = 18$

28. Which equation does not have 6 as the solution?

    (1) $y + 6 = 12$
    (2) $y + 10 = 16$
    (3) $y - 2 = 4$
    (4) $y - 6 = 12$
    (5) $y + 5 = 11$

ANSWERS ARE ON PAGE 316.

FORMULAS AND PROBLEM SOLVING

A *formula* is an equation with more than one variable. It is an equation that is always true. It is a useful tool for solving problems. To use a formula, you substitute into the equation all the values you know, then solve for the value you do not know.

EXAMPLE 1   The formula for distance is: rate × time, or $d = rt$.

distance = 200 miles; time = 4 hours; rate = _____

STEP 1   Write the formula you will use.

$d = rt$

STEP 2   Identify the values you know and the value you do not know.

Values you know: $d = 200$, and $t = 4$
Value you do not know: r

STEP 3   Substitute into the formula all the values you know.

$200 = r \times 4$

STEP 4   Solve for the value you do not know.

The equation $200 = r \times 4$ is the same as the equation $4r = 200$.
To solve, divide the numbers on each side of the equal sign by 4.

$$\frac{4r}{4} = \frac{200}{4}$$

$$r = 50$$

The rate is 50 miles per hour.

You can use formulas to solve many word problems. Here are some formulas and two examples.

Interest = principal × rate × time $(i = prt)$
Distance = rate × time $(d = rt)$
Total cost = number of units × cost per unit $(c = nr)$
Fahrenheit temperature = 1.8 × Celsius temperature + 32
    $(F = 1.8C + 32)$
Batting average = number of hits ÷ number of times at bat
    $(a = \frac{h}{n})$

EXAMPLE 2   Mei bought 3 rolls of film for $10.50. How much did each roll of film cost?

STEP 1   Write the formula you will use.

$c = nr$

STEP 2   Identify the values you know and the value you do not know.

Values you know: $c = \$10.50$, and $n = 3$
Value you do not know: r

STEP 3   Substitute into the formula all the values you know.

$\$10.50 = 3r$

STEP 4   Solve for the value you do not know.

$\$10.50 = 3r$ is the same as $3r = \$10.50$.

$$\frac{3r}{3} = \frac{\$10.50}{3}$$

$$r = \$3.50$$

Each roll of film cost $3.50.

EXAMPLE 3   If the Celsius temperature is 14°, what is the equivalent Fahrenheit temperature?

STEP 1   Write the formula you will use.

$F = 1.8C + 32$

STEP 2   Identify the values you know and the value you do not know.

Value you know: $C = 14$
Value you do not know: F

STEP 3   Substitute into the formula all the values you know.

$F = 1.8 \times 14 + 32$

STEP 4   Solve for the value you do not know.

$$F = 1.8 \times 14 + 32$$
$$= 25.2 + 32$$
$$= 57.2°$$

The Fahrenheit temperature is 57.2°.

SUMMARY FOR SOLVING PROBLEMS USING A FORMULA

To solve problems using a formula:

1) Write the formula you will use.

2) Identify the values you know and the value you do not know.

3) Substitute into the formula all the values you know.

4) Solve for the value you do not know.

EXERCISE 6

Directions: Use the formula given, and find the unknown value.

1. Formula: $c = nr$
total cost = $28
price per item = $7
number of items = _____

4. Formula: $F = 1.8C + 32$
Celsius temperature = 10
Fahrenheit temperature = _____

2. Formula: $i = prt$
interest = $360
rate = 6%
time = 3 years
principal = _____

5. Formula: $d = rt$
distance = 100 miles
time = 1 hour 45 minutes
rate = _____

3. Formula: $a = \frac{h}{n}$
batting average = 0.300
number of times at bat = 50
number of hits = _____

6. Formula: $i = prt$
principal = $10,000
rate = 8%
time = 5 years
interest = _____

Directions: Solve each problem.

7. Patty bought 4 tires at $37.99 each. What was the total cost of the tires?

8. Raffi earned $80 in interest by investing $1,000 for 2 years. What was the interest rate?

9. If the Celsius temperature is 30, what is the equivalent Fahrenheit temperature?

10. If Angelo drives 55 miles per hour for 6 hours, how far will he have driven?

11. During the softball season, Tasha had 12 hits in 40 times at bat. What was her batting average?

12. How long will it take to drive 300 miles at an average of 60 miles per hour?

13. Saul's batting average is 0.380. In the next 5 times at bat, about how many hits would you expect Saul to make?

14. Peder bought 12 gallons of gasoline for $14.94. What was the price per gallon of the gasoline?

15. Maria invested $5,000 at a 5% interest rate. She earned $750 in interest. For how long was the money invested?

16. In one hour, the temperature dropped from 20°C to 15°C. How much was the drop in temperature (in °F)?

ANSWERS ARE ON PAGE 316.

THE COORDINATE PLANE

A **coordinate plane** is formed by two number lines perpendicular to each other at 0. The horizontal number line is called the **x-axis**, and the vertical number line is called the **y-axis**. The point where the two lines meet is called the **origin**. See Figure 1 below.

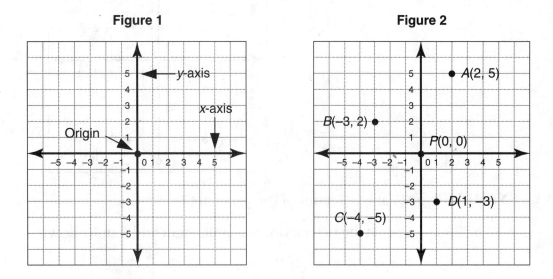

Figure 1   **Figure 2**

A point in the coordinate plane is named by two coordinates, an **x-coordinate** and a **y-coordinate**. Together the coordinates form an **ordered pair**. The pair is *ordered* because the *order* of the two coordinates matters. The x-coordinate is always first in the pair, and the y-coordinate is always second. The ordered pair tells exactly where the point lies in the coordinate plane.

Figure 2 above shows five points in the coordinate plane. Point P is the origin, which has ordered pair (0, 0). The x-coordinate tells how far the point is—right or left—from the origin. The y-coordinate tells how far the point is—up or down—from the origin. Point A has ordered pair (2, 5), which means that point A is 2 units right and 5 units up from the origin. Point B is at (–3, 2), or 3 units left and 2 units up from the origin. Point C is at (–4, –5), or 4 units left and 5 units down from the origin. Point D is at (1, –3), or 1 unit right and 3 units down from the origin.

TIP: A positive coordinate is *right* or *up* from the origin, while a negative coordinate is *left* or *down* from the origin.

Figure 3 below shows some points graphed on a coordinate plane. Use Figure 3 for the examples that follow.

Figure 3

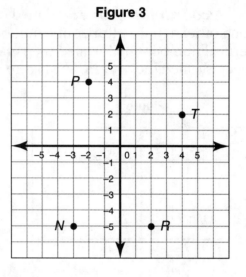

EXAMPLE 1 What is the letter of the point at $(2, -5)$?

STEP 1 Start at the origin. Count 2 units right and 5 units down.

STEP 2 Identify the point: R.

The point at $(2, -5)$ is R.

EXAMPLE 2 What is the ordered pair for point T?

STEP 1 Start at the origin. Count the number of units to the right until T is directly above: 4. Count the number of units up to T: 2.

STEP 2 Write the ordered pair: (4 right, 2 up) = $(4, 2)$.

The ordered pair for point T is $(4, 2)$.

EXAMPLE 3 What is the ordered pair for point N?

STEP 1 Start at the origin. Count the number of units to the left until N is directly below: 3. Count the number of units down to N: 5.

STEP 2 Write the ordered pair: (3 left, 5 down) = $(-3, -5)$

The ordered pair for point N is $(-3, -5)$.

EXERCISE 7

Directions: Refer to Figure 4. Write the letter of the point at each ordered pair.

1. $(3, -2)$

2. $(8, 5)$

3. $(-9, -4)$

4. $(8, -4)$

5. $(-3, 6)$

6. $(9, 2)$

7. $(-6, -5)$

8. $(-4, 2)$

Figure 4

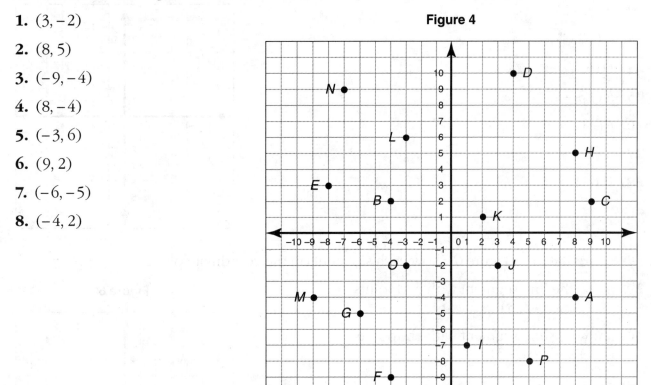

Directions: Refer to Figure 4. Write the ordered pair for each point.

9. K **11.** E **13.** I **15.** N

10. O **12.** D **14.** P **16.** F

Directions: Refer to Figure 4.

17. Which points have a positive *x*-coordinate and a positive *y*-coordinate?

18. Which points have a negative *x*-coordinate and a negative *y*-coordinate?

19. Which points have a positive *x*-coordinate and a negative *y*-coordinate?

20. Which points have a negative *x*-coordinate and a positive *y*-coordinate?

Directions: Refer to Figure 5. Graph each point on the coordinate plane.

21. *A* (1, 1)

22. *B* (4, −2)

23. *C* (−2, 3)

24. *D* (5, 4)

25. *E* (−3, −2)

26. *F* (−1, 4)

27. *G* (2, −5)

28. *H* (−4, −4)

Figure 5

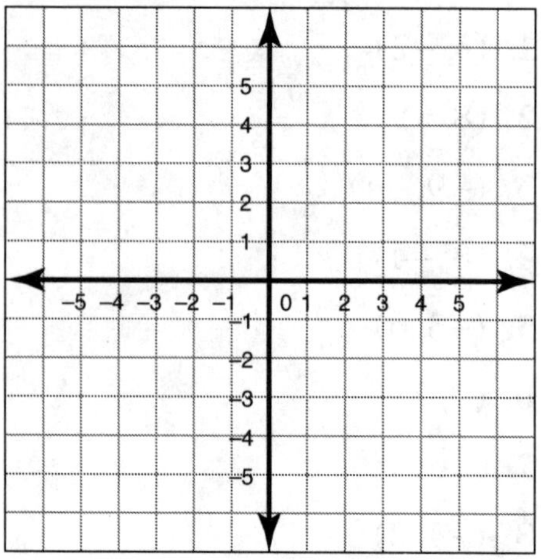

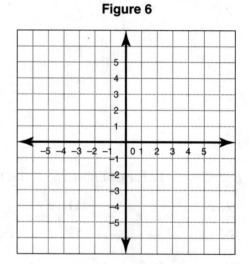

Directions: Refer to Figure 6. Show each segment on the coordinate plane.

29. Show the line segment with endpoints (4, 2) and (−3, 5).

30. Show the line segment with endpoints (4, 0) and (−4, −3).

Figure 6

ANSWERS ARE ON PAGE 317.

Directions: Use the space to the right to graph the points below; then choose the best answer.

1. Graph each point on a coordinate plane: (2, 5), (2, 2), and (7, 2). Connect the points in the order given. If these three points, along with a fourth point, form a rectangle, what is the fourth point?

(1) (5, 7)
(2) (5, 3)
(3) (7, 3)
(4) (7, 5)
(5) (3, 5)

2. Graph each point on a coordinate plane: (−1, −1), (−1, 3), and (−5, 3). Connect the points in the order given. If these three points, along with a fourth point, form a square, what is the fourth point?

(1) (−1, −5)
(2) (−5, −1)
(3) (−5, 1)
(4) (−4, −1)
(5) (5, −1)

ANSWERS ARE ON PAGE 317.

SLOPE OF A LINE

Slope is a measure of how "steep" a line is. The slope of a line can be positive, negative, zero, or undefined. Figures 6–8 show the graphs of many lines, labeled with their slopes. Notice that lines with *positive* slope go *up* from left to right. Lines with *negative* slope go *down* from left to right. Lines with zero slope are horizontal, and lines with undefined slope are vertical.

Figure 6   **Figure 7**   **Figure 8**

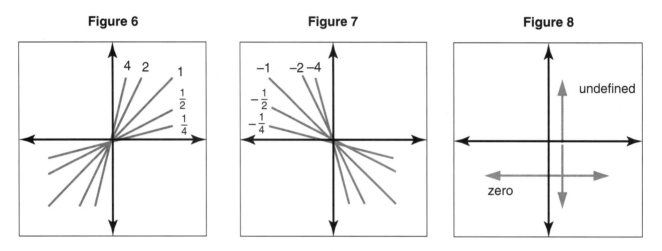

There are several ways to find the slope of a line. One way is to think of slope as a ratio of the vertical change in y to the corresponding horizontal change in x. When a line is graphed on a coordinate plane, you can count the vertical change and the horizontal change, then find the slope. See Examples 1 and 2.

EXAMPLE 1   Find the slope of the line graphed in Figure 9.

Figure 9

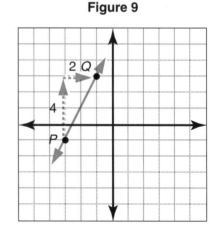

STEP 1   Start at point P. To get to point Q, count up 4 units and right 2 units. So the vertical change is 4, and the horizontal change is 2.

STEP 2   Write the ratio $\frac{\text{vertical change}}{\text{horizontal change}}$.

$$\frac{4}{2} = \frac{2}{1} = 2$$

The slope of the line is 2.

EXAMPLE 2   Find the slope of the line through the points $P(2, 5)$ and $Q(4, -1)$.

STEP 1   Graph the points on a coordinate plane. Draw a line through the points.

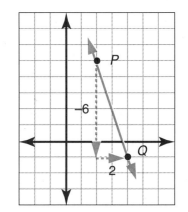

STEP 2   Start at point P. To get to point Q, count down 6 units and right 2 units. So the vertical change is -6, and the horizontal change is 2.

STEP 3   Write the ratio $\frac{\text{vertical change}}{\text{horizontal change}}$.

$$\frac{-6}{2} = \frac{-3}{1} = -3$$

The slope of the line is -3.

You can also use a formula to find the slope of a line. The **_slope formula_** is: slope $= \frac{y_2 - y_1}{x_2 - x_1}$, where (x_1, y_1) and (x_2, y_2) are the ordered pairs of two points on the line. So the formula is a ratio of the difference in y-coordinates to the difference in x-coordinates. To use the formula, you need the coordinates of two points on the line.

EXAMPLE 3   Find the slope of the line through the points $P(1, 3)$ and $Q(4, 3)$.

STEP 1   Decide which point is (x_1, y_1), and which point is (x_2, y_2). It does not matter what you decide, but it does matter that you stay with your decision while you calculate the slope.

Let $P(1, 3) = (x_1, y_1)$, and let $Q(4, 3) = (x_2, y_2)$.

STEP 2   Subtract the y-coordinates: $y_2 - y_1 = 3 - 3 = 0$

STEP 3   Subtract the x-coordinates: $x_2 - x_1 = 4 - 1 = 3$

STEP 4   Use the formula.

$$\text{slope} = \frac{y_2 - y_1}{x_2 - x_1} = \frac{0}{3} = 0$$

The slope of the line is 0.

SUMMARY FOR FINDING THE SLOPE OF A LINE

To find the slope of a line, use one of these two methods:

1) Identify two points on the graph of the line. Going from one point to the other, count the vertical change and the horizontal change.

2) Write the ratio $\frac{\text{vertical change}}{\text{horizontal change}}$.

3) Use the formula: slope $= \frac{y_2 - y_1}{x_2 - x_1}$, where (x_1, y_1) and (x_2, y_2) are the ordered pairs of two points on the line.

EXERCISE 9

Directions: Find the slope of the line graphed on each coordinate plane.

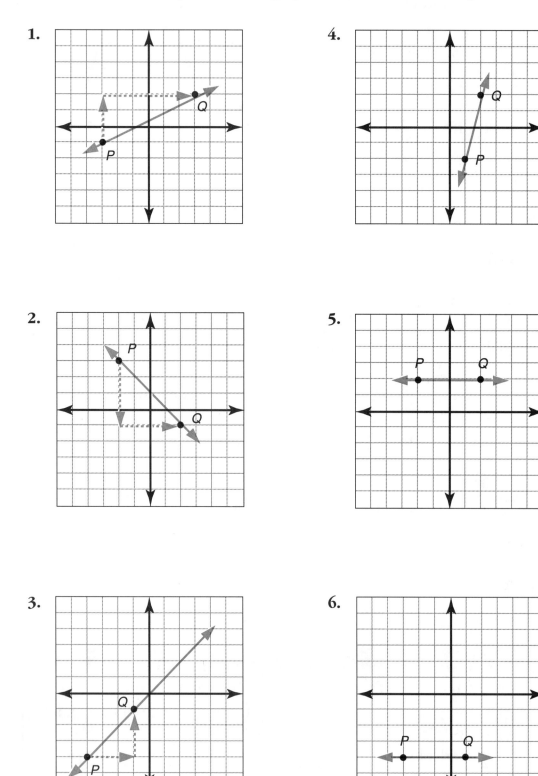

Directions: Graph the two points on the coordinate plane. Draw a line through the points. Find the slope of the line.

7. $A\ (0, 0)$ and $B\ (2, -4)$

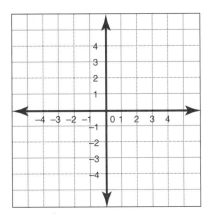

10. $A\ (2, 1)$ and $B\ (-2, 2)$

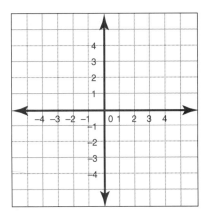

8. $A\ (1, 1)$ and $B\ (3, 2)$

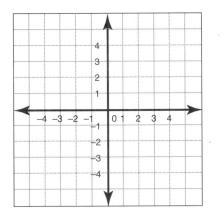

11. $A\ (4, -1)$ and $B\ (3, 3)$

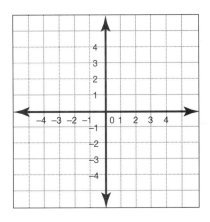

9. $A\ (-4, -3)$ and $B\ (-2, 3)$

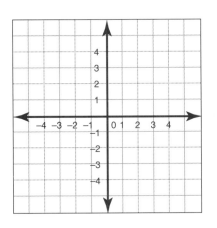

12. $A\ (-3, -2)$ and $B\ (3, 2)$

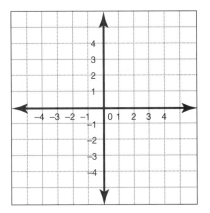

Directions: Find the slope of the line through the given points. Use the slope formula.

13. $P(1, 6)$ and $Q(3, 9)$

18. $P(-8, -2)$ and $Q(0, 0)$

14. $P(4, 4)$ and $Q(-1, -1)$

19. $P(-9, -7)$ and $Q(3, -7)$

15. $P(-2, 10)$ and $Q(3, 5)$

20. $P(1, 2)$ and $Q(4, -4)$

16. $P(5, -2)$ and $Q(-1, 2)$

21. $P(0, 0)$ and $Q(-4, 3)$

17. $P(6, 1)$ and $Q(6, 6)$

22. $P(-2, 6)$ and $Q(0, 0)$

ANSWERS ARE ON PAGES 317–318.

PRE-GED Practice
EXERCISE 10

Directions: Refer to Figure 10. Choose the best answer.

Figure 10

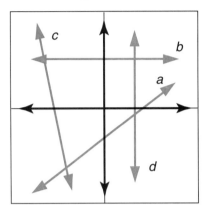

1. The slope of line *a* is

   (1) positive
   (2) negative
   (3) zero
   (4) undefined
   (5) unknown

2. The slope of line *b* is

   (1) positive
   (2) negative
   (3) zero
   (4) undefined
   (5) unknown

3. The slope of line *c* is

   (1) positive
   (2) negative
   (3) zero
   (4) undefined
   (5) unknown

4. The slope of line *d* is

   (1) positive
   (2) negative
   (3) zero
   (4) undefined
   (5) unknown

5. For the point at which lines *a* and *b* meet,

   (1) the *x*-coordinate is positive and the *y*-coordinate is positive
   (2) the *x*-coordinate is negative and the *y*-coordinate is positive
   (3) the *x*-coordinate is negative and the *y*-coordinate is negative
   (4) the *x*-coordinate is positive and the *y*-coordinate is negative
   (5) unknown

6. For the point at which lines *b* and *c* meet,

   (1) the *x*-coordinate is positive and the *y*-coordinate is positive
   (2) the *x*-coordinate is negative and the *y*-coordinate is positive
   (3) the *x*-coordinate is negative and the *y*-coordinate is negative
   (4) the *x*-coordinate is positive and the *y*-coordinate is negative
   (5) unknown

7. For the point at which lines *a* and *d* meet,

   (1) the *x*-coordinate is positive and the *y*-coordinate is positive
   (2) the *x*-coordinate is negative and the *y*-coordinate is positive
   (3) the *x*-coordinate is negative and the *y*-coordinate is negative
   (4) the *x*-coordinate is positive and the *y*-coordinate is negative
   (5) unknown

8. For the point at which lines *a* and *c* meet,

   (1) the *x*-coordinate is positive and the *y*-coordinate is positive
   (2) the *x*-coordinate is negative and the *y*-coordinate is positive
   (3) the *x*-coordinate is negative and the *y*-coordinate is negative
   (4) the *x*-coordinate is positive and the *y*-coordinate is negative
   (5) unknown

BASIC ALGEBRA CONCEPTS REVIEW

Directions: For Questions 1–20, solve each problem. Show your work to the right.

1. Find the value of $\sqrt{25}$.

2. Is 3 a solution to the equation $\frac{m}{8} = 24$?

3. Solve: $y - 7 = 4$

4. Use the formula $F = 1.8C + 32$. If $C = 9$, then $F =$ _____

5. Find the value of 8^0.

6. Find the value of $3^2 + 6 \times 2 - 15$.

7. How much money must you invest to earn $900 interest in 3 years with an 8% interest rate? (Use the formula $i = prt$.)

8. Solve: $3z = 33$

9. Find the value of 2^5.

10. Use the formula $d = rt$. If distance $= 250$ miles, and rate $= 50$ miles per hour, then time $=$ _____

11. Solve: $\frac{x}{2} = 15$

12. Find the value of $(4 + 5) \times (6 - 3)$.

13. Is 5 a solution to the equation $4a = 20$?

14. Find the value of $\sqrt{64}$.

15. A dozen large eggs cost $1.09. What is the cost of each egg? (Use the formula $c = nr$, if you wish.)

16. Solve: $n + 19 = 27$

17. Find the slope of the line through the points $A\,(-2, 8)$ and $B\,(1, 2)$.

Figure 11

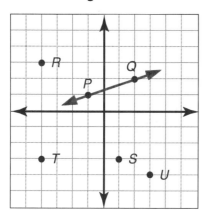

18. Refer to Figure 11. What is the letter of the point at $(-4, 3)$?

19. Refer to Figure 11. What is the ordered pair for point S?

20. Refer to Figure 11. What is the slope of the line through points P and Q?

Directions: Questions 21–36 include applications of whole numbers, decimals, fractions, measurement, geometry, ratios, proportions, percents, data analysis, probability, and algebra. Choose the correct answer to each problem. Remember the problem-solving skills you have learned.

21. Ralph got $10 worth of unleaded gasoline priced at $1.347 per gallon. How many gallons did Ralph get?

    (1) about 8
    (2) about 13
    (3) about 14
    (4) about 10
    (5) about 7

22. Rosie has a piece of fabric 45 inches wide. For a quilt she is making, Rosie needs to cut as many strips as possible. Each strip will be 2 inches wide after sewing, and Rosie will allow $\frac{1}{4}$ inch on each side of a strip for seams. How many strips can she cut from the fabric?

    (1) 22 strips
    (2) 23 strips
    (3) 18 strips
    (4) 20 strips
    (5) not enough information is given

23. Zaida's current annual salary is $18,000. Next month, a 4% raise will become effective. At that time, what will be Zaida's monthly salary?

    (1) $720
    (2) $1,560
    (3) $18,720
    (4) $1,500
    (5) $6,000

24. The blood that circulates in the human body accounts for about 7% of body weight. About what percent of body weight is not accounted for by blood?

    (1) 7%
    (2) 70%
    (3) 93%
    (4) 3%
    (5) not enough information is given

25. Suppose you receive a "recipe club" letter in the mail. You are to send a copy of the letter to 6 of your friends, then each friend sends a copy of the letter to 6 of their other friends. Each of your friends and each of their friends sends you a favorite recipe. How many recipes will you receive?

(1) 6 recipes
(2) 12 recipes
(3) 18 recipes
(4) 36 recipes
(5) 216 recipes

26. A baby is gaining weight at a rate of about an ounce a day. How much will the baby gain in a month?

(1) about 1 pound
(2) about 2 pounds
(3) about 3 pounds
(4) about 4 pounds
(5) about 16 pounds

27. The ratio of white keys to black keys on a piano is $\frac{13}{9}$. There are 36 black keys on a piano. How many black keys and white keys are there altogether?

(1) 61 keys
(2) 88 keys
(3) 52 keys
(4) 58 keys
(5) not enough information is given

28. Five homes recently sold in a neighborhood at these prices: $109,000; $85,500; $74,000; $99,900; $115,000. Which of the following statements are true of this data?

(1) The range is $41,000.
(2) The median is $99,900.
(3) There are no modes.
(4) The mean is $96,680.
(5) All of the statements above are true.

29. Which of the following has the greatest value?

(1) 200^1
(2) 5^4
(3) 1^{200}
(4) 2^{10}
(5) 20^2

30. A book club advertises "8 books for $1.99." In small print, you read, "plus shipping and handling," which is $4.95. You also read, ". . . when you agree to take 4 more shipments of 2 books each!" These shipments will be sent every 4 weeks for only $4.99 per book, plus $2.95 shipping and handling. If you join the club, which of the statements are true?

(1) You will spend $58.66 for 16 books.
(2) You will spend $16.75 on shipping and handling alone.
(3) You will end up with at least 16 books.
(4) You will pay about $3.67 per book, including shipping and handling.
(5) All of the statements above are true.

31. Geraldo has $20 worth of nickels. How many nickels does Geraldo have?

(1) 100 nickels
(2) 1,000 nickels
(3) 400 nickels
(4) 40 nickels
(5) 800 nickels

32. If you graph the three given points on a coordinate plane, then connect the points in the order given, which set of points does not form a right angle?

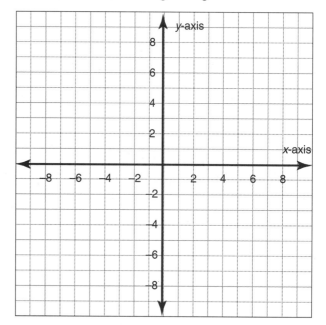

(1) (3, 7), (3, 3), (8, 3)
(2) (−4, −1), (−4, −5), (−6, −5)
(3) (1, −3), (−2, −3), (−2, 2)
(4) (−5, 5), (0, 0), (2, 2)
(5) (4, −1), (4, −6), (8, −1)

33. The ratio of males to females at a meeting was 2 : 3, with 12 men and 18 women. Later, another man and woman joined the meeting. Which of the following statements is true about the ratio now?

(1) The ratio of men to women stayed the same, since one of each joined the meeting.

(2) The ratio of men to women is 3 : 4.

(3) The ratio of men to women is 2 : 3.

(4) The ratio of men to women is 13 : 19.

(5) The ratio of women to men is 13 : 19.

34. A store advertised, "Buy one sweater, and get the second for half price!" Assuming you buy 2 sweaters, this is the same as which of the following deals?

(1) 50% off

(2) 25% off

(3) $\frac{1}{3}$ off

(4) 2 for the price of 3

(5) 3 for the price of 4

35. Thad has 8 feet of wire. He will use the wire to make a frame for a wreath. He will make two circles, leaving 5 inches between the circles for branches. See Figure 12. He wants to make as big a wreath as possible with the amount of wire he has. What should be the radii of the two circles he makes with the wire?

Figure 12

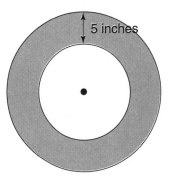

(1) 3 inches and 8 inches

(2) 4 inches and 9 inches

(3) 5 inches and 10 inches

(4) 6 inches and 11 inches

(5) 7 inches and 12 inches

36. Which of the following is most likely to happen?

(1) You flip 2 quarters and get 2 "heads."

(2) You draw 1 card from a standard deck of 52 cards, and get 1 King.

(3) You draw 2 cards from a standard deck of 52 cards, and get 2 Kings.

(4) You roll 2 number cubes and get 2 "2's".

(5) You roll 1 number cube and get "2."

ANSWERS ARE ON PAGE 318.

Post-Test

This Post-Test consists of 56 multiple-choice questions. It should give you a good idea of how well you learned the mathematics and problem-solving skills you studied in this book. You should take the Post-Test only after you have completed all the chapters.

Record your answers on the grid on page 276. Choose the best of five answer choices by filling in the corresponding circle on the answer grid.

Using the Evaluation Chart on pages 288–289, circle the number of each question that you missed to determine which skills you might need to review before you move on to Contemporary Books' *GED Test 5: Mathematics, Preparation for the High School Equivalency Examination.*

1 ① ② ③ ④ ⑤   15 ① ② ③ ④ ⑤   29 ① ② ③ ④ ⑤   43 ① ② ③ ④ ⑤

2 ① ② ③ ④ ⑤   16 ① ② ③ ④ ⑤   30 ① ② ③ ④ ⑤   44 ① ② ③ ④ ⑤

3 ① ② ③ ④ ⑤   17 ① ② ③ ④ ⑤   31 ① ② ③ ④ ⑤   45 ① ② ③ ④ ⑤

4 ① ② ③ ④ ⑤   18 ① ② ③ ④ ⑤   32 ① ② ③ ④ ⑤   46 ① ② ③ ④ ⑤

5 ① ② ③ ④ ⑤   19 ① ② ③ ④ ⑤   33 ① ② ③ ④ ⑤   47 ① ② ③ ④ ⑤

6 ① ② ③ ④ ⑤   20 ① ② ③ ④ ⑤   34 ① ② ③ ④ ⑤   48 ① ② ③ ④ ⑤

7 ① ② ③ ④ ⑤   21 ① ② ③ ④ ⑤   35 ① ② ③ ④ ⑤   49 ① ② ③ ④ ⑤

8 ① ② ③ ④ ⑤   22 ① ② ③ ④ ⑤   36 ① ② ③ ④ ⑤   50 ① ② ③ ④ ⑤

9 ① ② ③ ④ ⑤   23 ① ② ③ ④ ⑤   37 ① ② ③ ④ ⑤   51 ① ② ③ ④ ⑤

10 ① ② ③ ④ ⑤   24 ① ② ③ ④ ⑤   38 ① ② ③ ④ ⑤   52 ① ② ③ ④ ⑤

11 ① ② ③ ④ ⑤   25 ① ② ③ ④ ⑤   39 ① ② ③ ④ ⑤   53 ① ② ③ ④ ⑤

12 ① ② ③ ④ ⑤   26 ① ② ③ ④ ⑤   40 ① ② ③ ④ ⑤   54 ① ② ③ ④ ⑤

13 ① ② ③ ④ ⑤   27 ① ② ③ ④ ⑤   41 ① ② ③ ④ ⑤   55 ① ② ③ ④ ⑤

14 ① ② ③ ④ ⑤   28 ① ② ③ ④ ⑤   42 ① ② ③ ④ ⑤   56 ① ② ③ ④ ⑤

Direction: Solve each problem.

1. As of January 1, 1995, the cost of mailing a first-class letter is 32¢ for the first ounce and 23¢ for each additional ounce, up to 12 ounces. At this rate, how much does it cost to mail a first-class letter that weighs 4 ounces?

   (1) $1.01
   (2) $.92
   (3) $1.24
   (4) $1.19
   (5) $1.28

2. Which three statements are true?

   Opposite sides of a rectangle:
   A. are perpendicular
   B. are parallel
   C. are the same length
   D. are usually not the same length
   E. intersect
   F. never intersect

   (1) A, C, and F
   (2) A, D, and E
   (3) B, C, and F
   (4) B, C, and E
   (5) A, C, and E

3. Anita lives in Wyoming, which has a general state sales tax on purchases made. If Anita buys a car for $18,000, how much money will she pay in sales tax?

   (1) $900
   (2) $180
   (3) $1,800
   (4) $1,080
   (5) not enough information is given

4. Between which two consecutive whole numbers does $\sqrt{51}$ lie?

   (1) $\sqrt{50}$ and $\sqrt{52}$
   (2) 5 and 11
   (3) 5 and 6
   (4) 7 and 8
   (5) 25 and 26

5. A stick of butter is the same as 8 tablespoons, or $\frac{1}{2}$ cup. A cookie recipe calls for $\frac{3}{4}$ cup butter. How much butter is this?

   (1) $\frac{3}{8}$ stick
   (2) $1\frac{1}{2}$ stick
   (3) 12 tablespoons
   (4) (1) and (3) are both correct
   (5) (2) and (3) are both correct

6. Which of the following whole numbers is the greatest?

   (1) sixty-eight thousand sixty-eight
   (2) sixty-eight thousand eighty-six
   (3) eighty-six thousand eight
   (4) eighty-six thousand sixty
   (5) eighty-six thousand six

7. Which of the following arithmetic expressions will solve the proportion $\frac{5}{9} = \frac{40}{\_\_}$?

   (1) $5 \times 9 \div 40$
   (2) $5 \times 40 \div 9$
   (3) $9 \times 40 \div 5$
   (4) $9 \times 5 \div 40$
   (5) $40 \times 5 \div 9$

8. Which of the following lists the lengths from least to greatest?

   A. 840 centimeters
   B. 6 meters
   C. 2,842 millimeters
   D. 0.005 kilometers

   (1) C, A, B, D
   (2) C, D, B, A
   (3) D, C, B, A
   (4) B, C, A, D
   (5) A, B, D, C

9. There are five children in the Peregrino family. Two of the children have curly hair. What percent of the children in the Peregrino family DO NOT have curly hair?

(1) 60%
(2) 40%
(3) 6%
(4) 4%
(5) not enough information is given

10. What is the slope of the line passing through points P and Q ?

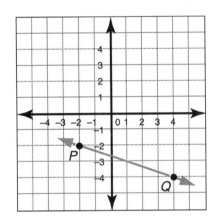

(1) 3
(2) −3
(3) $\frac{1}{3}$
(4) $-\frac{1}{3}$
(5) none of the above

11. The volume of a cube is 216 cubic inches. Find the length of one side.

(1) about 15 inches
(2) 6 inches
(3) about 6 inches
(4) 72 inches
(5) not enough information is given

12. What is the probability that a family with three children has three girls? (Assume that "boy" and "girl" are equally likely.)

(1) $\frac{1}{3}$
(2) $\frac{1}{9}$
(3) $\frac{1}{6}$
(4) $\frac{1}{27}$
(5) $\frac{1}{8}$

13. One week, Raoul worked from 7:00 P.M. to 11:00 P.M., Monday through Friday. His hourly wage is $7.50. On Saturday, he worked from 8:00 A.M. to 2:00 P.M., earning one-and-a-half times his hourly wage. He did not work on Sunday. How much money did Raoul earn that week?

(1) $217.50
(2) $172.50
(3) $236.25
(4) $204
(5) $159

Table 1

Height (inches)	Desirable Weight (pounds)	
	Men	Women
58		102
60		107
62	123	113
64	130	120
66	136	128
68	145	136
70	154	144
72	162	152
74	171	
76	181	

14. Refer to Table 1. What is the desirable weight for a male who is 6 feet 2 inches tall?

    (1) 123 pounds
    (2) 113 pounds
    (3) 171 pounds
    (4) 162 pounds
    (5) none of the above

15. Refer to Table 1. Which statement is true?

    (1) For a given height, a woman's desirable weight is usually 10 pounds less than a man's desirable weight.
    (2) For women at least 64 inches tall, a gain of an inch in height allows a gain of about 4 pounds in weight.
    (3) The desirable weight for a male who is 5 feet 5 inches is about 133 pounds.
    (4) The desirable weight for a female who is 74 inches tall is about 160 pounds.
    (5) All of the statements are true.

16. Refer to Table 1. If a woman weighs 136 pounds, and her weight is considered desirable for her height, how tall is she?

    (1) 5 feet 6 inches
    (2) 5 feet 8 inches
    (3) 66 inches
    (4) both (1) and (3) are correct
    (5) both (2) and (3) are correct

17. Which of the following lists four fractions in order from least to greatest?

    (1) $\frac{7}{12}, \frac{7}{13}, \frac{7}{14}, \frac{7}{15}$
    (2) $\frac{10}{3}, \frac{9}{3}, \frac{8}{3}, \frac{7}{3}$
    (3) $\frac{1}{10}, \frac{1}{9}, \frac{1}{8}, \frac{1}{7}$
    (4) $\frac{4}{5}, \frac{3}{5}, \frac{2}{5}, \frac{1}{5}$
    (5) $\frac{1}{2}, \frac{1}{3}, \frac{1}{4}, \frac{1}{5}$

18. Which of the following amounts of money has the greatest value?

    (1) eighteen quarters
    (2) fifty-two dimes
    (3) a five-dollar bill
    (4) one hundred nine pennies
    (5) sixty-four nickels

19. The perimeter of a square is 28 inches. Find the area of the square.

    (1) 49 square inches
    (2) 14 square inches
    (3) $\sqrt{28}$ square inches
    (4) 56 square inches
    (5) none of the above

20. Jack and Jill expect about 100 guests at their wedding reception. How many tables should they rent, if each table seats 8 guests?

    (1) 12
    (2) 12.5
    (3) $12\frac{1}{2}$
    (4) 13
    (5) 14

21. The following sign appears in front of an airport parking lot. If you park your car in the lot on Monday, January 2, at 7:00 A.M. and return on Wednesday, January 11, at 12:00 noon, how much money do you owe?

Parking Lot Rates
$1.50 per hour
Not to exceed $15 per day
Not to exceed $75 per week

(1) $150
(2) $114
(3) $154.50
(4) $112.50
(5) $120

22. The ratio of black keys to white keys on a standard piano is 9 : 13. There are 88 keys altogether. How many keys on a standard piano are black?

(1) 36
(2) 75
(3) 9
(4) 52
(5) not enough information is given

23. Which is least likely to happen?

(1) Flipping a coin and getting "heads."
(2) Drawing an ace from a standard deck of 52 cards.
(3) Drawing a face card from a standard deck of 52 cards.
(4) Rolling a number cube and getting a "4."
(5) Rolling two number cubes and getting a sum of 5.

24. If you fold a piece of notebook paper in half six times, how many rectangles of the same size are formed by the folding?

(1) 12
(2) 24
(3) 32
(4) 36
(5) 64

25. The acreage of Yellowstone National Park is 2,219,784.68. Round this to the nearest thousand acres.

(1) 2,000,000
(2) 2,200,000
(3) 2,220,000
(4) 2,219,000
(5) 2,219,800

26. Which equation does not have the solution $x = 7$?

(1) $x - 8 = 15$
(2) $x + 10 = 17$
(3) $\frac{x}{7} = 1$
(4) $9x = 63$
(5) $\sqrt{49} = x$

27. Which of the following statements is not true?

A. The amount of surface covered by a rectangle is its area.
B. The distance around a triangle is its perimeter.
C. The distance around a circle is its circumference.
D. The amount of space inside a cube is its area.
E. The area of a circle depends on its radius or diameter.

(1) A
(2) B
(3) C
(4) D
(5) E

POST-TEST

28. On January 1, 1995, the cost of a first-class stamp was increased from 29¢ to 32¢. Twenty stamps are sold in a book. Which of the following expressions describes the increased cost of a book of stamps?

   A. ($.32 − $.29) × 20
   B. 20 × $.32 − 20 × $.29

   (1) A
   (2) B
   (3) Either A or B
   (4) neither A nor B
   (5) none of the above

29. In a survey, 45% of the people responded "yes," while the rest responded "no." How many people responded "no"?

   (1) 55
   (2) 45
   (3) more than 45
   (4) at least 55
   (5) not enough information is given

30. Which of the following is a set of equivalent numbers?

   (1) 5%, $\frac{1}{5}$, 0.5

   (2) 10%, $\frac{1}{10}$, 0.10

   (3) 60%, $\frac{1}{60}$, 0.6

   (4) 1%, $\frac{1}{100}$, 0.1

   (5) 32%, $\frac{32}{100}$, 32

31. The median age of a set of eleven employees is 36. The employee who figured out the median age will not reveal his/her own age. The ages of the other ten employees are as follows: 32, 35, 24, 50, 29, 45, 36, 38, 25, 36. Which of the following ages is not possible for the eleventh employee?

   (1) 36
   (2) 30
   (3) 60
   (4) 48
   (5) 40

32. Eric lives in Massachusetts. He wishes to call Daniel in Hawaii. The time in Massachusetts is 5 hours later than the time in Hawaii. At what time should Eric make the call if he wishes to reach Daniel at 1:00 P.M.?

   (1) 8:00 A.M.
   (2) 9:00 A.M.
   (3) 5:00 P.M.
   (4) 6:00 P.M.
   (5) 6:00 A.M.

33. Karina is making a quilt. One quilt block is shown below. The shaded areas represent the darker fabric. Karina will sew together 12 of these quilt blocks to make the quilt. What fraction of the quilt is made of the darker fabric?

   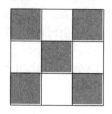

   (1) $\frac{5}{12}$

   (2) $\frac{5}{9}$

   (3) $\frac{2}{3}$

   (4) almost $\frac{1}{2}$

   (5) not enough information is given

34. A bag contains 15 yellow and blue marbles. The probability of randomly drawing a blue marble is $\frac{1}{3}$. How many yellow marbles are in the bag?

(1) 10
(2) 3
(3) 5
(4) 12
(5) not enough information is given

35. Chang gets a paycheck biweekly (every two weeks), while Leah gets a paycheck twice each month. Which of the following statements is not true?

(1) Leah and Chang get the same number of paychecks in a year.
(2) Leah gets 24 paychecks each year.
(3) Twice a year, Chang gets 3 paychecks in a month.
(4) Chang gets 2 more paychecks a year than Leah gets.
(5) Leah gets the same number of paychecks each month.

36. Which is the best buy for soda pop?

(1) a 12-pack of 12-oz cans for $4.99
(2) a 6-pack of 12-oz cans for $2.79
(3) a case (24 cans) of 12-oz cans for $10
(4) 75¢ for a 12-oz can
(5) 79¢ for a 16-oz bottle

37. Michael makes about 60% of the free throws he attempts in basketball practice. Of the next 25 free throws he attempts in practice, how many would you expect Michael to make?

(1) 19
(2) 10
(3) 20
(4) 15
(5) There is no way of knowing how many free throws to expect Michael to make.

38. Sonia is building a fence for a rectangular area of her yard. She wants to use all 80 feet of fencing she bought. She will place a post every 5 feet, including one at each corner. Which of the following dimensions will not work for the rectangular area she will fence?

(1) 5 feet by 35 feet
(2) 10 feet by 30 feet
(3) 15 feet by 25 feet
(4) 20 feet by 20 feet
(5) 40 feet by 2 feet

39. What does the expression 6^3 mean?

(1) 3 x 3 x 3 x 3 x 3 x 3
(2) 6 x 3
(3) 6 + 6 + 6
(4) 6 x 6 x 6
(5) all of the above

40. Which of the following points is 5 units from $P(3, 1)$?

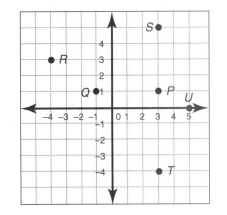

(1) $S(3, 5)$
(2) $T(3, -4)$
(3) $R(-4, 3)$
(4) $Q(-1, 1)$
(5) $U(5, 0)$

Table 2

Human Activity	Quarts of blood pumped per minute	Number of heart beats per minute
rest	5–6	60–80
mild exercise	7–8	100–120
strenuous exercise	30	up to 200

41. Refer to Table 2. How many times does an average person's heart beat while sleeping for 8 hours?

    (1) 28,800
    (2) 38,400
    (3) 33,600
    (4) 2,640
    (5) 560

42. Refer to Table 2. What type of activity is someone doing if the person's heart pumps between 7 and 8 gallons of blood per minute?

    (1) rest
    (2) mild exercise
    (3) strenuous exercise
    (4) an exercise level between "mild" and "strenuous"
    (5) any of the above

43. Refer to Table 2. How many more quarts of blood does your heart pump if you exercise strenuously, rather than mildly, for a half hour?

    (1) about 2,500
    (2) 80 to 100
    (3) 22 to 23
    (4) about 675
    (5) none of the above

44. Which of the following is true of statements A and B?

    A. A rectangle has four right angles.
    B. If a square has a 2-inch side, all of its sides are 2 inches long.

    (1) **A** is never true.
    (2) **A** is always true.
    (3) **B** is always true.
    (4) **A** and **B** are never true.
    (5) **A** and **B** are always true.

45. Which investment will earn the greatest amount of interest? (Use the formula $i = prt$.)

    (1) $1,000 at 8% for 2 years
    (2) $500 at 12% for 1 year
    (3) $2,000 at 6% for 6 months
    (4) $1,000 at 5% for 4 years
    (5) $500 at 3% for 10 years

46. Thiu runs 3 miles in 25 minutes. Kai runs an 8-minute mile. Lin runs $7\frac{1}{2}$ miles per hour. Which statement is true?

    (1) Thiu runs the fastest.
    (2) Kai runs the fastest.
    (3) Lin runs the fastest.
    (4) Thiu runs faster than Kai.
    (5) Lin and Kai run at the same rate.

47. A square has the same area as a rectangle that measures 4 feet by 16 feet. What is the length of a side of the square?

    (1) 32 feet
    (2) 8 feet
    (3) $\sqrt{40}$ feet
    (4) 20 feet
    (5) 64 feet

Figure 1

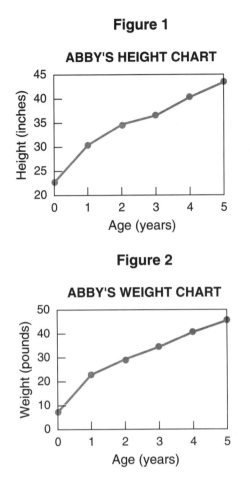

ABBY'S HEIGHT CHART

Figure 2

ABBY'S WEIGHT CHART

48. Refer to Figures 1 and 2. How tall was Abby when she was 2 years old?

(1) about 28 inches
(2) about 35 inches
(3) about 24 inches
(4) about 38 inches
(5) about 30 inches

49. Refer to Figures 1 and 2. How much did Abby weigh when she was about 40 inches tall?

(1) about 40 pounds
(2) about 35 pounds
(3) about 44 pounds
(4) about 30 pounds
(5) not enough information is given

50. Refer to Figures 1 and 2. In her first 5 years, how much overall weight did Abby gain?

(1) about 21 pounds
(2) about 43 pounds
(3) about 32 pounds
(4) about 44 pounds
(5) about 36 pounds

51. Refer to Figures 1 and 2. Which statement is true?

(1) Abby's height increased fastest during her first year.
(2) Abby's weight increased fastest during her first year.
(3) Abby's height and weight both increased fastest during her first year.
(4) Abby's height increased at a constant rate since birth.
(5) Abby's weight increased at a constant rate since birth.

52. Maria asked 100 people, "What's your favorite color—blue, red, or yellow?" The results were as follows: 44 blue, 30 red, and 26 yellow. Maria wants to draw a circle graph to display this data. What will be the measure of the central angle for the part of the circle that represents "red" as a favorite color?

(1) 108°
(2) 30°
(3) 54°
(4) 300°
(5) 150°

53. The high temperatures during a week in January in Bismarck, North Dakota were 10°F, 15°F, 9°F, 0°F, 5°F, 21°F, and 18°F. What was the average high temperature for the week?

(1) 10°F
(2) about 10°F
(3) 11°F
(4) about 11°F
(5) 13°F

54. A circle has a circumference of 22 centimeters. Which dimension is possible
for the circle? (Use the formula $C = \pi \times$ diameter, with $\pi \approx \frac{22}{7}$.)

(1) radius = 7 centimeters
(2) diameter = 7 centimeters
(3) radius = 14 centimeters
(4) diameter = 14 centimeters
(5) Both (1) and (4) are correct.

55. Which ratio will not form a proportion with the ratio "1 to 4"?

(1) 2 to 8
(2) 4 to 1
(3) 0.5 to 2
(4) 5 to 20
(5) 10 to 40

56. Which of the following is equal to 100%?

(1) 100
(2) 0.01
(3) 1
(4) 0.1
(5) 10

ANSWERS ARE ON PAGE 287.

Post-Test Answer Key

1. **(1)**; $\$.32 + 3(\$.23) = \$.32 + \$.69 = \$1.01$
2. **(3)**; Opposite sides of a rectangle are parallel, are the same length, and never intersect.
3. **(5)**; You need to know the sales tax rate in order to solve the problem.
4. **(4)**; $\sqrt{51}$ lies between $\sqrt{49} = 7$ and $\sqrt{64} = 8$
5. **(5)**; $\frac{3}{4}$ cup $= \frac{1}{2}$ cup $+ \frac{1}{4}$ cup $= 1$ stick $+ \frac{1}{2}$ stick $= 1\frac{1}{2}$ sticks; $\frac{3}{4}$ cup $= \frac{1}{2}$ cup $+ \frac{1}{4}$ cup $= 8$ tablespoons $+ 4$ tablespoons $= 12$ tablespoons
6. **(4)**; (1) 68,068; (2) 68,086; (3) 86,008; (4) 86,060; (5) 86,006
7. **(3)**; $9 \times 40 \div 5 = 72$; $\frac{5}{9} = \frac{40}{72}$; $5 \times 72 = 9 \times 40$
8. **(2)**; A. 840 cm = 8.4 m; B. 6 m; C. 2,842 mm = 2.8 m; D. 0.005 km = 5 m; Order: C, D, B, A
9. **(1)**; 3 of the 5 children do not have curly hair; $\frac{3}{5} = 60\%$
10. **(4)**; slope $= \frac{\text{vertical change}}{\text{horizontal change}} = \frac{-2}{6} = -\frac{1}{3}$
11. **(2)**; Volume $= 6 \times 6 \times 6 = 216$; side $= 6$
12. **(5)**; Let B = boy, G = girl. Eight possible outcomes: BBB, BBG, BGB, GBB, GGB, GBG, BGG, GGG. One favorable outcome: GGG. Probability $= \frac{\text{favorable outcomes}}{\text{possible outcomes}} = \frac{1}{8}$
13. **(1)**; $(4 \times 5 \times \$7.50) + (6 \times \$7.50 \times 1.5) = \$150 + \$67.50 = \$217.50$
14. **(3)**; 6 feet 2 inches $= (6 \times 12) + 2 = 74$ inches
15. **(5)**
16. **(2)**; 68 inches $= (5 \times 12) + 8 = 5$ feet 8 inches
17. **(3)**
18. **(2)**; (1) $18 \times \$.25 = \$4.50$; (2) $52 \times \$.10 = \$5.20$; (3) $\$5.00$; (4) $\$1.09$; (5) $64 \times \$.05 = \$3.20$
19. **(1)**; $28 \div 4 = 7$; Area $= 7 \times 7 = 49$
20. **(4)**; $100 \div 8 = 12.5$ or $12\frac{1}{2}$; rent 13
21. **(4)**; from Jan. 2, 7:00 A.M. to Jan. 9, 7:00 A.M. is 1 week = $\$75$; from Jan. 9, 7:00 A.M. to Jan. 11, 7:00 A.M. is 2 days, and $2 \times \$15 = \$30$; Jan. 11, 7:00 A.M. to 12:00 Noon is 5 hours, and $5 \times \$1.50 = \$7.50$; $\$75 + \$30 + \$7.50 = \$112.50$
22. **(1)**; $\frac{\text{black}}{\text{total}} = \frac{\text{black}}{\text{black + white}} = \frac{9}{9 + 13} = \frac{9}{22}$; $\frac{9}{22} = \frac{b}{88}$; $b = \frac{88 \cdot 9}{22} = 36$
23. **(2)**; (1) probability $= \frac{1}{2} = 50\%$; (2) probability $= \frac{4}{52} \approx 8\%$; (3) probability $= \frac{12}{52} \approx 23\%$; (4) probability $= \frac{1}{6} \approx 17\%$; (5) probability $= \frac{4}{36} \approx 11\%$
24. **(5)**; $2^6 = 2 \times 2 \times 2 \times 2 \times 2 \times 2 = 64$
25. **(3)**; $7 > 5$, so round the thousands' place up; 9 rounds up to 10, so 19 rounds up to 20.
26. **(1)**; $7 - 8 \neq 15$
27. **(4)**; The amount of space inside a cube is its volume, not its area.
28. **(3)**
29. **(5)**; You need to know how many people responded in order to solve the problem.
30. **(2)**; $10\% = \frac{10}{100} = \frac{1}{10} = 0.1 = 0.10$
31. **(2)**; List the 10 ages in order from least to greatest: 24, 25, 29, 32, 35, 36, 36, 38, 45, 50; Since 36 is the median, 36 must be the 6th age when the missing age is listed. If the person was younger than 36, then the median age would be less than 36 so the missing age must be at least 36. It cannot be 30.
32. **(4)**; 5 hours later than 1:00 P.M. is 6:00 P.M.
33. **(2)**; 5 of the 9 squares are shaded in each quilt block, so $\frac{5}{9}$ of the quilt is made of the darker fabric.
34. **(1)**; $\frac{1}{3} = \frac{5}{15}$, so there are 5 blue marbles; 15 total − 5 blue = 10 yellow
35. **(1)**; Leah: 12 months $\times$ 2 = 24 paychecks each year; Chang: 52 weeks $\div$ 2 = 26 paychecks each year.
36. **(1)**; (1) $\$4.99 \div 12 \approx \$.416$/can; (2) $\$2.79 \div 6 \approx \$.47$/can; (3) $\$10.00 \div 24 \approx \$.417$/can; (4) $\$.75$/can; (5) $\$.79$/bottle. (1) is the best buy for a can, so compare this with (5). (1) $\$.42 \div 12$ oz $\approx \$.04$/oz; (5) $\$.79 \div 16$ oz $\approx \$.05$/oz; (1) is the better buy.
37. **(4)**; 60% of $25 = 0.60 \times 25 = 15$
38. **(5)**; (1) $5 + 35 + 5 + 35 = 80$; (2) $10 + 30 + 10 + 30 = 80$; (3) $15 + 25 + 15 + 25 = 80$; (4) $20 + 20 + 20 + 20$; (5) $40 + 2 + 40 + 2 = 84$. By drawing diagrams, you can see that each of the first four sets of dimensions allows a post at each corner and every 5 ft.

39. (4)
40. (2)

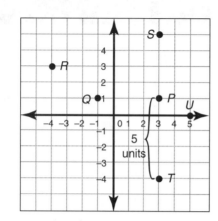

41. (3); 70 beats/minute × 60 minutes/hour × 8 hours = 33,600 beats
42. (3); 7.5 gallons × 4 = 30 quarts; strenuous
43. (4); 30 − 7.5 = 22.5; 22.5 quarts/minute × 30 minutes = 675 quarts
44. (5)
45. (4); (1) $1,000 × 0.08 × 2 = $160; (2) $500 × 0.12 × 1 = $60; (3) $2,000 × 0.06 × 0.5 = $60; (4) $1,000 × 0.05 × 4 = $200; (5) $500 × 0.03 × 10 = $150
46. (5); Thiu: 3 miles/25 minutes × 60 minutes/hour = 7.2 miles/hour; Kai: 1 mile/8 minutes × 60 minutes/hour = 7.5 miles/hour; Lin: 7.5 miles/hour

47. (2); Area of the rectangle = 4 × 16 = 64; Area of the square = 64 = 8 × 8, so side = 8.
48. (2); Use Figure 1, find 2 years, then find the height, about 35 inches.
49. (1); Use Figure 1, find 40 inches, then find her age, about 4 years. Then use Figure 2, find 4 years, then find her weight, about 40 pounds.
50. (5); Weight at age 5, about 44 pounds; Weight at birth, about 8 pounds; 44 − 8 = 36
51. (3)
52. (1); $\frac{30}{100}$ × 360 = 108
53. (4); 10 + 15 + 9 + 0 + 5 + 21 + 18 = 78; 78 ÷ 7 ≈ 11
54. (2); Circumference = π × diameter; 22 cm = $\frac{22}{7}$ × diameter = $\frac{22}{7}$ × 7; diameter = 7 cm; radius = 7 ÷ 2 = 3.5 cm
55. (2); $\frac{1}{4}$ ≠ $\frac{4}{1}$
56. (3); 100% = $\frac{100}{100}$ = $\frac{1}{1}$ = 1

Post-Test Evaluation Chart

On the following chart, circle the number of any problem you got wrong. After each problem you will see the name of the section (or sections) where you can find the skills you need to solve the problem. When a problem involves more than one skill, the sections are separated by a slash (/).

Problem	Section	Starting Page
	Whole Numbers and Problem Solving	
1, 3, 25	Estimation	32
6	Place Value	11
13	Problem-Solving Strategies/Multiple-Step Problems	35/40
14, 15, 16, 32, 35	Problem-Solving Strategies	35
20, 41, 42, 43	The Basic Operations/Problem-Solving Strategies	13/35

Problem	Section	Starting Page
18 21	**Decimals** Comparing Decimals Solving Problems Involving Decimals	47 64
33 5, 17 13	**Fractions and Mixed Numbers** The Meaning of Fractions and Mixed Numbers Comparing and Ordering Fractions Multiplying Fractions and Mixed Numbers	69 81 98
2, 27, 44 8 11 19 24 38, 47, 54	**Measurement and Geometry** Geometric Definitions Metric Units Perimeter and Circumference Area Geometric Definitions/Problem-Solving Strategies Perimeter, Circumference, Area, & Volume Problems	117 113 123 128 117/35 123
7 9, 30 22, 55 29 36, 46 37 56	**Ratios, Proportions, and Percents** Solving Proportions Common Percents, Fractions, and Decimals Ratios/Solving Proportions Percent Problems and Proportions Rates Percent of a Number Percents	158 166 149/158 175 152 168 161
12 23 31, 53 34 48, 49, 50, 51 52	**Data Analysis and Probability** Circle Graphs Probability/Favorable Outcomes Mean, Median, Mode, and Range Probability Line Graphs Drawing Circle Graphs	210 219 185 219 200 215
4, 39 10 26 28 40 45	**Basic Algebra Concepts** Exponents and Square Roots Slope of a Line Variables and Simple Equations Arithmetic Expressions The Coordinate Plane Formulas and Problem Solving	239 264 250 246 259 254

POST-TEST

Answer Key

CHAPTER 1: WHOLE NUMBER REVIEW AND PROBLEM SOLVING

EXERCISE 1

Page 12

1. 7 tens or 70
2. 9 million or 9,000,000
3. 5 ones or 5
4. 0 hundreds
5. 0 ten millions
6. 8 hundred thousands or 800,000
7. 1 thousand or 1,000
8. 6 hundred millions or 600,000,000
9. 20 thousands or 20,000
10. 5 billions or 5,000,000,000
11. 4 thousands or 4,000
12. 1 one or 1
13. 9 ten thousands or 90,000
14. 6 hundreds or 600
15. 6 tens or 60
16. 6 ones or 6

EXERCISE 2

Pages 13–14

1.

+	1	2	3	4	5	6	7	8	9	10
1	2	3	4	5	6	7	8	9	10	11
2	3	4	5	6	7	8	9	10	11	12
3	4	5	6	7	8	9	10	11	12	13
4	5	6	7	8	9	10	11	12	13	14
5	6	7	8	9	10	11	12	13	14	15
6	7	8	9	10	11	12	13	14	15	16
7	8	9	10	11	12	13	14	15	16	17
8	9	10	11	12	13	14	15	16	17	18
9	10	11	12	13	14	15	16	17	18	19
10	11	12	13	14	15	16	17	18	19	20

2.

×	1	2	3	4	5	6	7	8	9	10
1	1	2	3	4	5	6	7	8	9	10
2	2	4	6	8	10	12	14	16	18	20
3	3	6	9	12	15	18	21	24	27	30
4	4	8	12	16	20	24	28	32	36	40
5	5	10	15	20	25	30	35	40	45	50
6	6	12	18	24	30	36	42	48	54	60
7	7	14	21	28	35	42	49	56	63	70
8	8	16	24	32	40	48	56	64	72	80
9	9	18	27	36	45	54	63	72	81	90
10	10	20	30	40	50	60	70	80	90	100

3. 1,367

4. 10,335

$$
\begin{array}{r}
795 \\
\times\,13 \\
\hline
2385 \\
795 \\
\hline
10,335
\end{array}
$$

5. 8,176

$$
\begin{array}{r}
8,176 \\
9\overline{)73,584} \\
72 \\
\hline
15 \\
9 \\
\hline
68 \\
63 \\
\hline
54 \\
54 \\
\hline
0
\end{array}
$$

6. 22,419

7. 114,780

8. $3.31

$$
\begin{array}{r}
\$\,3.31 \\
25\overline{)\$82.75} \\
75 \\
\hline
77 \\
75 \\
\hline
25 \\
25 \\
\hline
0
\end{array}
$$

9. 380,991

10. 203,348

11. 5,427

12. 35,469

13. 2,254

$$
\begin{array}{r}
2254 \\
7\overline{)15,778} \\
14 \\
\hline
17 \\
14 \\
\hline
37 \\
35 \\
\hline
28 \\
28 \\
\hline
0
\end{array}
$$

14. 5,185

$$
\begin{array}{r}
305 \\
\times\,17 \\
\hline
2135 \\
305 \\
\hline
5,185
\end{array}
$$

EXERCISE 3
Pages 15–16

1. 9 tens, 7 ones
2. 8 thousands, 5 hundreds, 0 tens, 2 ones
3. 3 hundreds, 6 tens, 4 ones
4. 3 hundred thousands, 1 ten thousands, 6 thousands, 0 hundreds, 0 tens, 8 ones
5. 4 millions, 8 hundred thousands, 7 ten thousands, 0 thousands, 9 hundreds, 2 tens, 1 one
6. 7 billions, 9 hundred millions, 1 ten millions, 5 millions, 2 hundred thousands, 4 ten thousands, 3 thousands, 6 hundreds, 0 tens, 0 ones
7. 214
8. 69,436
9. 9,190,647
10. 4,809,190,002
11. 70,933,088
12. 50,310
13. 500,000 + 30,000 + 2,000 + 900 + 7
14. 4,000,000 + 600,000 + 5,000 + 800 + 70 + 3
15. 30,000 + 9,000 + 900 + 1

EXERCISE 4
Page 18

1. $4.15; $4
2. $28.60; $29
3. $13.95; $14
4. $2.25; $2
5. $10.40; $10
6. $11.67; $12
7. $56.47; $56

EXERCISE 5
Pages 20–22

1. c. hours of television per month
2. c. men and women finishing the class
3. b. federal, state, and city taxes
4. c. rent, electricity, car, and telephone expenses
5. three and four; 7 people (3 + 4)
6. 350 and three; 1,050 napkins (350 × 3)
7. $52.49, $23.50, $15; $90.99 (52.49 + $23.50 + $15)
8. two hours, one hour, 6 p.m.; 3 p.m. (3 hours earlier than 6 p.m.)
9. underline $425 a month, rent in a year; multiplication; $425 × 12 = $5100
10. underline twelve albums for $1.25 each; multiplication; 12 × $1.25 = $15.00
11. underline 8 cents per gallon, 26 cents per gallon, how much more; subtraction; 26¢ – 8¢ = 18¢
12. underline $70,300, risen $35,800; addition; $70,300 + $35,800 = $106,100
13. underline $525.46, 43 hours, hourly wage; division; $525.46 ÷ 43 = $12.22 per hour

14. underline over 5 million, over 11 times; multiplication; 5,000,000 × 11 = 55,000,000; over 55,000,000 female employees in 1990

EXERCISE 6
Pages 22–23

1. 36 in.
2. 32 oz
3. 2 yd
4. 4 pt
5. 12 qt
6. 6,000 lb
7. 360 sec
8. 4 lb
9. 9 ft
10. 2 ft 8 in.; 32 ÷ 12 = 2 R8
11. 2 lb 8 oz; 40 ÷ 16 = 2 R8
12. 2 hr 18 min; 138 ÷ 60 = 2 R18
13. 2 gal 1 qt; 9 ÷ 4 = 2 R1
14. 12 yd 2 ft; 38 ÷ 3 = 12 R2
15. 4 da 4 hr; 100 ÷ 24 = 4 R4
16. 5; 3; 0; 8
17. 9; 7; 3; 2; 1; 9; 4
18. 2; 8; 5; 3; 6
19. 3 hundreds or 300
20. 0 thousands
21. 0 hundred thousands
22. 9 hundred thousands
23. 13 ft 1 in.
24. 11 yd 1 ft
25. 9 gal
26. 12 lb 5 oz
27. 8 hr 6 min
28. 14 qt
29. 33 min 3 sec
30. 44 wks 3 d
31. 18 dollars 43 cents
32. 16 yrs 5 mos
33. 51 wks
34. 53 min

EXERCISE 7
Page 26

1. underline increasing $30, $415 now; $30 + $415 = $445
2. underline 2,975 pounds, 475 pounds, combined weight; 2,975 + 475 = 3,450 lb
3. underline Guillaume and three friends, $26.56, split equally; $26.56 ÷ 4 = $6.64
4. underline fifteen calls, twice; 15 × 2 = 30 service calls
5. underline $156 a year, monthly charge; $156 ÷ 12 = $13 per month
6. underline $1,500, pay back $985, left to pay; $1,500 – $985 = $515
7. underline $1.39 per gallon, 12 gallons cost; $1.39 × 12 = $16.68
8. underline pieces 8 inches long from a 96-inch board; 96 ÷ 8 = 12 pieces
9. underline 64,441,087 passengers, 51,943,567 passengers, How many more; 64,441,087 – 51,943,567 = 12,497,520
10. underline 127°F, 2°F, difference; 127 – 2 = 125°F

EXERCISE 8
Page 27

1. $19.78; $20
2. $31.26; $31
3. $53.82; $54
4. $40.12; $40
5. $74.75; $75
6. $13.61; $14
7. $99.99; $100
8. $.65; $1
9. more
10. shorter
11. lighter
12. faster
13. millimeter
14. milligram
15. milliliter
16. 15 meters
17. 8 liters
18. 22 kilograms
19. one-half meter
20. 10 liters
21. one-half pound

EXERCISE 9
Page 30

1. 79
2. 190
3. 5400
4. 46
5. 700
6. 152
7. 116
8. 71
9. 62
10. 32,000
11. 92
12. 4,000,000
13. 240,000
14. 40
15. 387
16. 136
17. 120 sq ft
18. 44 ft
19. 101 adults
20. 9 adults

EXERCISE 10
Page 31

1. 90,000 + 7,000 + 100 + 4
2. 7,000,000 + 500,000 + 6,000 + 100 + 30 + 8
3. 800,000 + 90,000 + 400 + 60 + 8
4. 5,000 + 200 + 80
5. 10,000 + 3,000 + 90
6. 6,000,000 + 600,000 + 10,000 + 4,000 + 200 + 30 + 1
7. 100,000 + 50,000 + 8,000 + 600 + 20

EXERCISE 11
Pages 33–34

1. 70; rounding
2. 350; rounding
3. 400; rounding
4. 130 if rounding (60 + 70) or 120 if front-end digits (50 + 70)
5. 1,200 if rounding to nearest hundred (300 + 300 + 600), 1,190 if rounding to nearest ten (280 + 320 + 590), 1,000 if front-end digits (200 + 300 + 500) or 1,200 if compatible numbers (280 + 320 + 600)
6. 5; compatible numbers (1,500 ÷ 300 = 5)
7. rounding: 6,000 (100 × 60); front-end digits: 4,500 (90 × 50); compatible numbers: 6,000 (100 × 60)

8. rounding: 5,000 (3,000 + 1,000 + 1,000 or 2,800 + 900 + 1,300); front-end digits: 3,900 (2,000 + 900 + 1,000); compatible numbers: 4,900 (2,700 + 900 + 1,300)
9. rounding: 30 (600 ÷ 20); front-end digits: 25 (500 ÷ 20); compatible numbers: 24 (600 ÷ 25) or 29 (580 ÷ 20) or 30 (600 ÷ 20)

EXERCISE 12
Page 35

1. about $400; rounding (700 – 300)
2. about 5,000 or 4,800 cans; rounding or compatible numbers (100 × 50 or 100 × 48)
3. about 40 miles per hour; rounding or compatible numbers (70 – 30)
4. about 550 or 500 feet high; rounding (400 + 150) or front-end digits (400 + 100)

EXERCISE 13
Pages 39–40

1. 10 handshakes; drawing a picture;

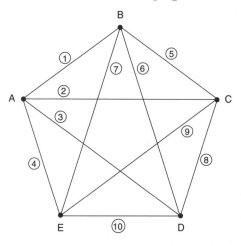

2. 1,173; guess and check; 642 + 531, 542 + 631, 632 + 541, or 641 + 532
3. Pittsburgh to Cleveland to St. Louis; using information from a table (492 + 115 = 607 miles)
4. Turtle C; drawing a picture;

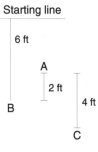

5. 543 and 6; guess and check (543 × 6 = 3,258; 643 × 5 = 3,215; 654 × 3 = 1,962)
6. 1990; using information from a table (417,179 cars)

7. 431 × 52; guess and check (22,412)
8. 20 times; drawing a picture

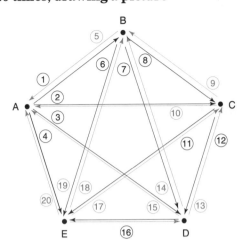

9. 86 and 75 or 85 and 76; guess and check
   (86 + 75 = 161; 87 + 65 = 152)
10. 5 miles; drawing a picture

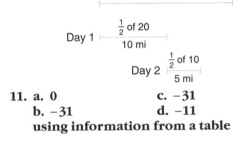

11. a. 0   c. −31
    b. −31   d. −11
    using information from a table

EXERCISE 14
Page 41

1. $5.10; (5 × $0.75) + (3 × $0.45) =
   $3.75 + $1.35 = $5.10
2. $7.33; $10 − (3 × $0.89) = $10 − $2.67 =
   $7.33
3. $131.50; (4 × $25) + (3 × $10.50) =
   $100 + $31.50 = $131.50
4. no; $11.25 + $15.50 + $10.75 = 37.50 and
   $37.50 is more than $35
5. no; $5.35 + $35.60 + $20 + $10 + $15 =
   $85.95 and $85.95 is more than $80
6. $197.50; (2 × $95) + (6 × $1.25) =
   $190 + $7.50 + $197.50
7. $25,400; $1,900 + $1,200 = $3,100;
   $28,500 − $3,100 = $25,400
8. Kiwi; 2 × $89 = $178, and $178 is less than
   $188
9. $10.25; $6.50 + $3.25 = $9.75;
   $20 − $9.75 = $10.25
10. Yes. $1.27 × 9 = $11.43

EXERCISE 15
Page 42

1. 24,461
2. 76,285;
```
    803
   × 95
   4015
  7227
 76,285
```
3. 321;
```
        321
   6)1,926
       18
       12
       12
        6
        6
        0
```
4. 605,629
5. 45,630;
```
   3,042
  ×   15
  15 210
  30 42
  45,630
```
6. 35;
```
        35
   24)840
       72
      120
      120
        0
```
7. 88,734
8. 52,014
9. 4,498
10. 713 R4
11. 88,632
12. 632,479
13. 1; 0; 6
14. 4; 2; 9; 6
15. 2; 7; 8; 6; 5
16. 4; 0; 6; 9; 1; 8
17. 0; 9; 7
18. 1; 6; 8; 7; 5
19. 8; 6; 5; 6; 4; 2; 2
20. 5; 5; 8; 0; 0; 2; 5; 0

WHOLE NUMBER AND PROBLEM SOLVING REVIEW
Page 43

1. 2 hundreds or 200
2. 6 ones or 6
3. 0 tens or 0
4. 8 ten thousands or 80,000
5. 6 thousands or 6,000
6. 4 millions or 4,000,000
7. about 400 (rounding) or 300 (front-end
   digits); 409; difference of 9
8. about 4,000 (rounding) or 3,000 (front-end
   digits); 3,914; difference of 86
9. about 1,000,000 (rounding) or 800,000
   (front-end digits); 1,078,170; difference of
   78,170
10. about 400 (compatible numbers or
    rounding); 385; difference of 15
11. about 920 (rounding); 933; difference of 13

12. about 4,000 (rounding) or 3,000 (front-end digits); 3,736; difference of 264
13. 1,956
14. 800,343
15. 1,403,001
16. 23,215
17. 5
18. 8
19. 8
20. 2 d, 8 hr

CHAPTER 2: DECIMALS

EXERCISE 1
Pages 48–49

1. 0.9	7. 0.821
2. 0.60 or 0.6	8. 0.05
3. 1.08	9. 0.007
4. 1.36	10. 6.048
5. 0.4	11. 9.81
6. 0.39	12. 23.105

13. Four and seven hundredths
14. Fifteen and thirty-eight hundredths
15. One hundred sixty-nine thousandths
16. Seven and two hundred five thousandths
17. Nine and one tenth
18. Twelve and eighty-six hundredths

19. 0.5 < 0.8	28. 3.2 < 4
20. 0.47 > 0.39	29. 0.99 > 0.954
21. 4.7 < 4.82	30. 8.09 < 8.9
22. 5.5 > 5.05	31. 6.50 < 6.57
23. .001 < .010	32. 1.33 > 1.303
24. 7.75 > .075	33. 9.08 < 9.9
25. 3.101 > 3.1	34. .03 < .25
26. 0.25 < 0.257	35. 99.9 > .999
27. 1.9 < 1.999	36. .503 > 0.5

EXERCISE 2
Page 50

1. $9.42; $9
2. $19.75; $20
3. $43.50; $44
4. $1.41; $1
5. $20.80; $21

EXERCISE 3
Page 52

1. 6; 5.9; 5.89	6. 29¢
2. 20; 20.5; 20.49	7. $68.54
3. 1; 1.0; 1.04	8. $0.82
4. 7; 6.7; 6.71	9. $3.74
5. $1.34	10. 54¢

11. 20 cents for 1 folder;
    100¢ ÷ 5 = 20¢
12. 9 cents for 1 pencil;
    49 ÷ 6 = 8 R1 → 9¢

13. 34 cents for 1 kiwi; $100¢ ÷ 3 = 33\frac{1}{3}¢$
14. **$3.17;**
    949 ÷ 3 = 316 R1 → 317¢ = $3.17
15. **$0.75;**
    899 ÷ 12 = 74 R11 → 75¢ = $0.75
16. **$.21 for 1 doughnut;**
    $2.52 ÷ 12 = $.21

EXERCISE 4
Page 53

1. 2.5 cm	2. 0.38 in.; 0.4 in.

3. $0.34; $3.99 ÷ 12 = $0.33 R3 → $0.34
4. $0.04; $0.40
   139 ÷ 10 = 13 R9 → 14¢ = $0.14,
   99 ÷ 10 = 9 R9 → 10¢ = $0.10,
   $0.14 − $0.10 = 14¢ − 10¢ = 4¢ = $0.04;
   $1.39 − $0.99 = 139¢ − 99¢ = 40¢ = $0.40

EXERCISE 5
Pages 55–56

1. $0.60; $0.10	2. $0.95; $0.25
0.10	0.25
0.10	0.05
0.05	0.05
0.05	0.05
0.05	0.05
0.05	0.05
0.05	0.05
0.05	0.05
$0.60	0.05
	0.05
	$0.95

3. $1.05; $0.10	4. $1.30; $0.25
0.10	0.25
0.10	0.25
0.10	0.10
0.10	0.10
0.10	0.05
0.10	0.05
0.10	0.05
0.25	0.05
$1.05	0.05
	0.05
	0.05
	0.05
	$1.30

5. 0.9	15. 6.3
6. $0.91	16. $2.14
7. 1.825	17. 7.6
8. 68.277	18. 32.46
9. 9.681	19. 3.978
10. 26.472	20. $7.37
11. 41.109	21. 5.502
12. 102.769	22. 8.768
13. 9.69	23. $21.28
14. 1,023.81	24. 362.241

EXERCISE 6
Pages 56–57

1. **18.88**
2. **1.3**
3. **$24.82**
4. **2.863**
5. **$5.62**
6. **105.255**
7. **10.7 percent**; $13.1 - 2.4 = 10.7$
8. **12.902 million**; $8.655 + 4.057 + 0.19 = 12.902$
9. **$1.27**
10. **$21.68**; $12.93 + $2 + $6.75 = $21.68

EXERCISE 7
Pages 59–60

1. **$2.30**; $23 \times $0.10 = $2.30
2. **$10.00**; $40 \times $0.25 = $10.00
3. **$3.50**; $350 \times $.01 = $3.50
4. **$3.75**; $75 \times $.05 = $3.75
5. **$0.90**; $18 \times $0.05 = $0.90
6. **$5.50**; $11 \times $0.50 = $5.50
7. **$1.10**; $11 \times $.10 = $1.10
8. **$4.00**; $8 \times $.50 = $4.00
9. **0.15**
10. **1.68**
11. **3.15**
12. **20.4**
13. **1.35**
14. **26.16**
15. **.325**
16. **7.245**
17. **1.457**
18. **1.1814**
19. **$39.15**
20. **2.0685**

EXERCISE 8
Pages 60–61

1. **24**
2. **1134.48**
3. **$103.50**
4. **36.12**
5. **$86.43**
6. **$.75**; $5.99 ÷ 8 = $.74 R7 → $.75
7. **$.90**; $2.69 ÷ 3 = $.89 R2 → $.90
8. **about 34 or 35 inches**; 40.8 inches (34 × 1.2)
9. **$1.164 or $1.17** (38.8¢ × 3)

EXERCISE 9
Pages 63–64

1. **$5.67**
2. **1.6**
3. **160**
4. **1.6**
5. **16**
6. **3**
7. **30**
8. **60**
9. **6**
10. **.09**
11. **700**
12. **4.9**
13. **4.8**
14. **23**
15. **8.1**
16. **70**
17. **160**
18. **.1959 in.**; 19.59 ÷ 100 = .1959
19. **about $.12 per ounce**;
    $1.67 ÷ 14 = $.11 R13 → $.12
20. **2.1 in.; 2.14 in.**

21. **7 tapes for $5.99**;
    3 for $4.99 → $4.99 ÷ 3 = $1.66 R1 → $1.67;
    7 for $5.99 → $5.99 ÷ 7 = $.85 R4 → $.86
22. **983,403 people**;
    789,704 + 193,699 = 983,403
23. **33.1 miles**; 6.2 + 26.9 = 33.1

DECIMALS REVIEW
Pages 65–67

1. **1**
2. **0.9**
3. **$58.95**; (5 × $10) + (7 × $1) + (6 × $.25) +
   (9 × $.05) = $50 + $7 + $1.50 + $.45 = $58.95
4. **98; 97.6; 97.64**
5. **$3.90**; $38.92 ÷ 10 = $3.892 → $3.90
6. **62.444**
7. **35.18**
8. **3.105**
9. **.5**
10. **500**
11. **(3)**; .382 − .328 = .054
12. **(5)**; $1.75 × 6 = $10.50
13. **(2)**; 23.2 ÷ 8 = 2.9
14. **(5)**
15. **(4)**
16. **(4)**
17. **(4)**; 28.5 × 17.4 = 495.9
18. **(1)**; .465 + .289 = .754, 1 − .754 = .246

CHAPTER 3: FRACTIONS AND MIXED NUMBERS

EXERCISE 1
Pages 72–73

1. **5**
2. $5\frac{1}{4}$
3. $5\frac{2}{3}$
4. $6\frac{3}{5}$
5. $6\frac{5}{6}$
6. $5\frac{3}{7}$
7. $9\frac{4}{9}$
8. $12\frac{3}{8}$
9. $9\frac{1}{3}$
10. $\frac{29}{8}$
11. $\frac{20}{3}$
12. $\frac{33}{8}$
13. $\frac{19}{4}$
14. $\frac{47}{6}$
15. $\frac{48}{5}$
16. $\frac{131}{12}$
17. $\frac{90}{10}$
18. $\frac{88}{7}$

19. **40 slices**
20. **more**; $\frac{17}{2} = 8\frac{1}{2}$ yards
21. **7,790,000**;
    23,350,000 − 15,560,000 = 7,790,000
22. **$9.46**; $37.84 ÷ 4 = $9.46
23. $2\frac{2}{3}$; $1\frac{1}{3} + 1\frac{1}{3} = 2\frac{2}{3}$
24. $3\frac{1}{7}$; $\frac{22}{7} = 3\frac{1}{7}$

EXERCISE 2
Pages 75–76

Samples are given for #1–4.

1. $\frac{6}{16}, \frac{9}{24}, \frac{12}{32}$

2. $\frac{2}{12}, \frac{3}{18}, \frac{4}{24}$

3. $\frac{14}{20}, \frac{21}{30}, \frac{28}{40}$

4. $\frac{22}{24}, \frac{33}{36}, \frac{44}{48}$

5. $3; \frac{3}{5}$ 8. $92; \frac{92}{100}$ 11. $48; \frac{48}{50}$

6. $1; \frac{1}{3}$ 9. $27; \frac{27}{30}$ 12. $22; \frac{22}{24}$

7. $7; \frac{7}{8}$ 10. $4; \frac{4}{7}$ 13. $9; \frac{9}{16}$

7. $28, 9; \frac{7}{9} \times \frac{4}{4} = \frac{28}{36};$
   $\frac{3}{12} \times \frac{3}{3} = \frac{9}{36}$

8. $3, 4; \frac{1}{2} \times \frac{3}{3} = \frac{3}{6}$
   $\frac{2}{3} \times \frac{2}{2} = \frac{4}{6}$

9. $25, 11; \frac{5}{6} \times \frac{5}{5} = \frac{25}{30};$
   $\frac{11}{30} = \frac{11}{30}$

10. $63, 38; \frac{7}{10} \times \frac{9}{9} = \frac{63}{90};$
    $\frac{19}{45} \times \frac{2}{2} = \frac{38}{90}$

11. $48, 65; \frac{8}{15} \times \frac{6}{6} = \frac{48}{90};$
    $\frac{13}{18} \times \frac{5}{5} = \frac{65}{90}$

12. $50, 27; \frac{5}{9} \times \frac{10}{10} = \frac{50}{90};$
    $\frac{3}{10} \times \frac{9}{9} = \frac{27}{90}$

13. $75, 42; \frac{15}{16} \times \frac{5}{5} = \frac{75}{80};$
    $\frac{21}{40} \times \frac{2}{2} = \frac{42}{80}$

14. $117, 76; \frac{13}{20} \times \frac{9}{9} = \frac{117}{180}; \frac{19}{45} \times \frac{4}{4} = \frac{76}{180}$

15. $136, 125; \frac{17}{25} \times \frac{8}{8} = \frac{136}{200};$
    $\frac{5}{8} \times \frac{25}{25} = \frac{125}{200}$

16. $4, 3; \frac{1}{15} \times \frac{4}{4} = \frac{4}{60}; \frac{1}{20} \times \frac{3}{3} = \frac{3}{60}$

EXERCISE 3
Page 78

1. .25   5. .66   9. .375
2. .875   6. .125   10. .7272 or .73
3. 2.75   7. .125   11. .467 or .47
4. .75   8. .425   12. .8

13. $\frac{7}{20}$ 17. $6\frac{13}{25}$ 21. $1\frac{37}{40}$

14. $\frac{17}{250}$ 18. $5\frac{47}{100}$ 22. $7\frac{1}{80}$

15. $\frac{3}{4}$ 19. $1\frac{39}{50}$ 23. $4\frac{23}{25}$

16. $2\frac{2}{5}$ 20. $9\frac{9}{200}$ 24. $8\frac{1}{2}$

EXERCISE 4
Page 80

1. 6: 6, 12, 18, 24, 30, 36, 42, 48, 54, 60; 5: 5, 10, 15, 20, 25, 30, 35, 40, 45, 50, 55, 60; common multiples: 30, 60

2. 8: 8, 16, 24, 32, 40, 48, 56, 64; 12: 12, 24, 36, 48; common multiples: 24, 48

3. 9: 9, 18, 27, 36, 45, 54, 63, 72; 36: 36, 72; common multiples: 36, 72

4. 7: 7, 14, 21, 28, 35, 42
   21: 21, 42; common multiples: 21, 42

5. $4, 3; \frac{1}{2} \times \frac{4}{4} = \frac{4}{8}; \frac{3}{8} = \frac{3}{8}$

6. $12, 5; \frac{4}{5} \times \frac{3}{3} = \frac{12}{15};$
   $\frac{1}{3} \times \frac{5}{5} = \frac{5}{15}$

EXERCISE 5
Page 83

1. $\frac{1}{4} > \frac{3}{16}$;

   $\frac{1}{4} \times \frac{4}{4} = \frac{4}{16}$ and

   $\frac{4}{16} > \frac{3}{16}$

2. $\frac{5}{8} < \frac{11}{16}$;

   $\frac{5}{8} \times \frac{2}{2} = \frac{10}{16}$ and

   $\frac{10}{16} < \frac{11}{16}$

3. $\frac{3}{4} < \frac{13}{16}$;

   $\frac{3}{4} \times \frac{4}{4} = \frac{12}{16}$ and

   $\frac{12}{16} < \frac{13}{16}$

4. $1\frac{1}{4} > 1\frac{1}{8}$;

   $1\frac{1}{4} = 1\frac{2}{8}$ and

   $1\frac{2}{8} > 1\frac{1}{8}$

5. $1\frac{4}{5} > \frac{8}{5}$;

   $1\frac{4}{5} = \frac{9}{5}$ and $\frac{9}{5} > \frac{8}{5}$

6. $\frac{16}{10} > \frac{6}{5}$;

   $\frac{6}{5} \times \frac{2}{2} = \frac{12}{10}$ and

   $\frac{16}{10} > \frac{12}{10}$

7. $\frac{3}{8} < \frac{3}{5}$;

   $\frac{3}{8} \times \frac{5}{5} = \frac{15}{40}$ and

   $\frac{3}{5} \times \frac{8}{8} = \frac{24}{40}$;

   $\frac{15}{40} < \frac{24}{40}$

8. $\frac{1}{4} > \frac{1}{6}$;

   $\frac{1}{4} \times \frac{3}{3} = \frac{3}{12}$ and

   $\frac{1}{6} \times \frac{2}{2} = \frac{2}{12}$;

   $\frac{3}{12} > \frac{2}{12}$

9. $\frac{5}{12} > \frac{1}{3}$;

   $\frac{1}{3} \times \frac{4}{4} = \frac{4}{12}$ and

   $\frac{5}{12} > \frac{4}{12}$

10. $\frac{13}{16} < \frac{7}{8}$;

    $\frac{7}{8} \times \frac{2}{2} = \frac{14}{16}$ and

    $\frac{13}{16} < \frac{14}{16}$

11. $\frac{7}{10} < \frac{7}{9}$;

    $\frac{7}{10} \times \frac{9}{9} = \frac{63}{90}$ and

    $\frac{7}{9} \times \frac{10}{10} = \frac{70}{90}$;

    $\frac{63}{90} < \frac{70}{90}$

12. $\frac{9}{10} < \frac{11}{12}$;

    $\frac{9}{10} \times \frac{6}{6} = \frac{54}{60}$ and

    $\frac{11}{12} \times \frac{5}{5} = \frac{55}{60}$;

    $\frac{54}{60} < \frac{55}{60}$

EXERCISE 6
Pages 86–87

1. $\frac{5}{6}$; $\frac{2}{6} + \frac{3}{6} = \frac{5}{6}$

2. $\frac{1}{2}$; $\frac{5}{8} - \frac{1}{8} = \frac{4}{8} = \frac{1}{2}$

3. $1\frac{2}{5}$; $\frac{4}{5} + \frac{3}{5} = \frac{7}{5} = 1\frac{2}{5}$

4. $\frac{3}{4}$; $\frac{11}{12} - \frac{2}{12} = \frac{9}{12} = \frac{3}{4}$

5. $1\frac{1}{5}$; $\frac{9}{10} + \frac{3}{10} = \frac{12}{10} = \frac{6}{5} = 1\frac{1}{5}$

6. $\frac{1}{2}$; $\frac{13}{16} - \frac{5}{16} = \frac{8}{16} = \frac{1}{2}$

7. $\frac{2}{3}$; $\frac{5}{12} + \frac{3}{12} = \frac{8}{12} = \frac{2}{3}$

8. $\frac{3}{4}$

   $\begin{array}{r} \frac{7}{8} \\ -\frac{1}{8} \\ \hline \frac{6}{8} = \frac{3}{4} \end{array}$

9. $\frac{3}{8}$

   $\begin{array}{r} \frac{9}{16} \\ -\frac{3}{16} \\ \hline \frac{6}{16} = \frac{3}{8} \end{array}$

10. $\frac{3}{5}$; $\frac{9}{10} - \frac{3}{10} = \frac{6}{10} = \frac{3}{5}$

11. $\frac{5}{8}$; $\frac{7}{16} + \frac{3}{16} = \frac{10}{16} = \frac{5}{8}$

12. $\frac{1}{3}$

$\frac{7}{18}$

$-\frac{1}{18}$

$\frac{6}{18} = \frac{1}{3}$

13. $1\frac{1}{2}$; $\frac{5}{8} + \frac{7}{8} = \frac{12}{8} = \frac{3}{2} = 1\frac{1}{2}$

14. 1

$\frac{11}{20}$

$+\frac{9}{20}$

$\frac{20}{20} = 1$

15. $\frac{1}{5}$; $\frac{14}{15} - \frac{11}{15} = \frac{3}{15} = \frac{1}{5}$

16. $1\frac{1}{3}$; $\frac{11}{12} + \frac{5}{12} = \frac{16}{12} = \frac{4}{3} = 1\frac{1}{3}$

17. $\frac{1}{5}$; $\frac{23}{25} - \frac{18}{25} = \frac{5}{25} = \frac{1}{5}$

18. $\frac{3}{10}$

$\frac{33}{50}$

$-\frac{18}{50}$

$\frac{15}{50} = \frac{3}{10}$

19. $1\frac{2}{3}$

$\frac{8}{9}$

$+\frac{7}{9}$

$\frac{15}{9} = \frac{5}{3} = 1\frac{2}{3}$

20. $\frac{13}{18}$; $\frac{31}{36} - \frac{5}{36} = \frac{26}{36} = \frac{13}{18}$

21. $1\frac{3}{10}$

$\frac{43}{100}$

$+\frac{87}{100}$

$\frac{130}{100} = \frac{13}{10} = 1\frac{3}{10}$

EXERCISE 7
Pages 90–91

1. $\frac{5}{6} - \frac{1}{2}$; $\frac{1}{3}$ $\quad \frac{5}{6} - \frac{1}{2} = \frac{5}{6} - \frac{3}{6} = \frac{2}{6} = \frac{1}{3}$

2. $\frac{3}{4} + \frac{7}{8}$; $1\frac{5}{8}$ $\quad \frac{3}{4} + \frac{7}{8} = \frac{6}{8} + \frac{7}{8} = \frac{13}{8} = 1\frac{5}{8}$

3. $\frac{7}{10} + \frac{1}{4}$; $\frac{19}{20}$ $\quad \frac{7}{10} + \frac{1}{4} = \frac{14}{20} + \frac{5}{20} = \frac{19}{20}$

4. $\frac{3}{4} - \frac{1}{3}$; $\frac{5}{12}$ $\quad \frac{3}{4} - \frac{1}{3} = \frac{9}{12} - \frac{4}{12} = \frac{5}{12}$

5. 3; $\frac{7}{15}$

$\frac{2}{3} = \frac{10}{15}$

$-\frac{1}{5} = \frac{3}{15}$

$\phantom{\frac{1}{5}=}\frac{7}{15}$

6. 6; $\frac{2}{3}$

$\frac{1}{6} = \frac{2}{12}$

$+\frac{1}{2} = \frac{6}{12}$

$\phantom{\frac{1}{2}=}\frac{8}{12} = \frac{2}{3}$

7. 3; 16; $\frac{19}{24}$

$\frac{1}{8} = \frac{3}{24}$

$+\frac{2}{3} = \frac{16}{24}$

$\phantom{\frac{2}{3}=}\frac{19}{24}$

8. 21; 12; $\frac{9}{28}$

$\frac{3}{4} = \frac{21}{28}$

$-\frac{3}{7} = \frac{12}{28}$

$\phantom{\frac{3}{7}=}\frac{9}{28}$

9. 9; 5; $\frac{2}{15}$

$\frac{3}{10} = \frac{9}{30}$

$-\frac{1}{6} = \frac{5}{30}$

$\phantom{\frac{1}{6}=}\frac{4}{30} = \frac{2}{15}$

10. 55, 16; $\frac{13}{20}$

$\frac{11}{12} = \frac{55}{60}$

$-\frac{4}{15} = \frac{16}{60}$

$\phantom{\frac{4}{15}=}\frac{39}{60} = \frac{13}{20}$

11. 8; 4; $\frac{15}{16}$

$\frac{3}{16} = \frac{3}{16}$

$\frac{1}{2} = \frac{8}{16}$

$+\frac{1}{4} = \frac{4}{16}$

$\phantom{\frac{1}{4}=}\frac{15}{16}$

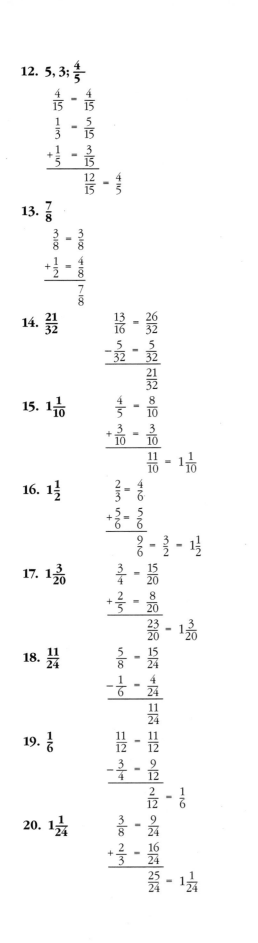

12. 5, 3; $\frac{4}{5}$

$$\frac{4}{15} = \frac{4}{15}$$
$$\frac{1}{3} = \frac{5}{15}$$
$$+\frac{1}{5} = \frac{3}{15}$$
$$\frac{12}{15} = \frac{4}{5}$$

13. $\frac{7}{8}$

$$\frac{3}{8} = \frac{3}{8}$$
$$+\frac{1}{2} = \frac{4}{8}$$
$$\frac{7}{8}$$

14. $\frac{21}{32}$

$$\frac{13}{16} = \frac{26}{32}$$
$$-\frac{5}{32} = \frac{5}{32}$$
$$\frac{21}{32}$$

15. $1\frac{1}{10}$

$$\frac{4}{5} = \frac{8}{10}$$
$$+\frac{3}{10} = \frac{3}{10}$$
$$\frac{11}{10} = 1\frac{1}{10}$$

16. $1\frac{1}{2}$

$$\frac{2}{3} = \frac{4}{6}$$
$$+\frac{5}{6} = \frac{5}{6}$$
$$\frac{9}{6} = \frac{3}{2} = 1\frac{1}{2}$$

17. $1\frac{3}{20}$

$$\frac{3}{4} = \frac{15}{20}$$
$$+\frac{2}{5} = \frac{8}{20}$$
$$\frac{23}{20} = 1\frac{3}{20}$$

18. $\frac{11}{24}$

$$\frac{5}{8} = \frac{15}{24}$$
$$-\frac{1}{6} = \frac{4}{24}$$
$$\frac{11}{24}$$

19. $\frac{1}{6}$

$$\frac{11}{12} = \frac{11}{12}$$
$$-\frac{3}{4} = \frac{9}{12}$$
$$\frac{2}{12} = \frac{1}{6}$$

20. $1\frac{1}{24}$

$$\frac{3}{8} = \frac{9}{24}$$
$$+\frac{2}{3} = \frac{16}{24}$$
$$\frac{25}{24} = 1\frac{1}{24}$$

21. $1\frac{13}{30}$

$$\frac{3}{5} = \frac{18}{30}$$
$$+\frac{5}{6} = \frac{25}{30}$$
$$\frac{43}{30} = 1\frac{13}{30}$$

22. $\frac{5}{36}$

$$\frac{8}{9} = \frac{32}{36}$$
$$-\frac{3}{4} = \frac{27}{36}$$
$$\frac{5}{36}$$

23. $\frac{2}{3}$

$$\frac{1}{12} = \frac{1}{12}$$
$$\frac{1}{3} = \frac{4}{12}$$
$$+\frac{1}{4} = \frac{3}{12}$$
$$\frac{8}{12} = \frac{2}{3}$$

24. $\frac{7}{48}$

$$\frac{13}{16} = \frac{39}{48}$$
$$-\frac{2}{3} = \frac{32}{48}$$
$$\frac{7}{48}$$

EXERCISE 8
Page 92

1. $\frac{47}{8}$

2. $5\frac{2}{5}$

3. sample answer:
$\frac{10}{12}, \frac{15}{18}, \frac{20}{24}$

4. .42; $5 \div 12 = .4166 \ldots$

5. $\frac{9}{125}$

6. $\frac{7}{10} = \frac{28}{40}; \frac{5}{8} = \frac{25}{40}$

7. $\frac{4}{5} > \frac{3}{4}$;
$\frac{4}{5} = \frac{16}{20}$ and $\frac{3}{4} = \frac{15}{20}; \frac{16}{20} > \frac{15}{20}$

8. $\frac{1}{16}$ inch thicker $\frac{11}{16} - \frac{5}{8} = \frac{11}{16} - \frac{10}{16} = \frac{1}{16}$

9. $1\frac{1}{2}$ inches $\frac{5}{8} + \frac{7}{8} = \frac{12}{8} = \frac{3}{2} = 1\frac{1}{2}$

10. Longer; $\frac{1}{32}$ inch $\frac{5}{16} - \frac{9}{32} = \frac{10}{32} - \frac{9}{32} = \frac{1}{32}$

EXERCISE 9
Pages 94–95

1. $8\frac{8}{10} = 8\frac{4}{5}$

2. $1\frac{1}{4}; 2\frac{2}{4}; 3\frac{3}{4}$

3. $3\frac{14}{16}; 4\frac{5}{16}; 7\frac{19}{16} = 8\frac{3}{16}$

4. $6\frac{10}{18}; 8\frac{15}{18}; 14\frac{25}{18} = 15\frac{7}{18}$

5. $7\frac{6}{9}; 5\frac{4}{9}; 12\frac{10}{9} = 13\frac{1}{9}$

6. $11\frac{10}{15}; 2\frac{12}{15}; 13\frac{22}{15} = 14\frac{7}{15}$

7. $13\frac{1}{24}; 8\frac{16}{24} + 4\frac{9}{24} = 12\frac{25}{24} = 13\frac{1}{24}$

8. $17\frac{11}{20}; 7\frac{16}{20} + 9\frac{15}{20} = 16\frac{31}{20} = 17\frac{11}{20}$

9. $10\frac{17}{24}; 5\frac{20}{24} + 4\frac{21}{24} = 9\frac{41}{24} = 10\frac{17}{24}$

10. $21\frac{17}{30}; 12\frac{27}{30} + 8\frac{20}{30} = 20\frac{47}{30} = 21\frac{17}{30}$

11. $20\frac{23}{60}; 9\frac{35}{60} + 10\frac{48}{60} = 19\frac{83}{60} = 20\frac{23}{60}$

12. $37\frac{51}{100};$
$20\frac{75}{100} + 16\frac{76}{100} = 36\frac{151}{100} = 37\frac{51}{100}$

EXERCISE 10
Pages 97–98

1. $5\frac{9}{10}; 3\frac{5}{10}; 2\frac{4}{10} = 2\frac{2}{5}$

2. $3\frac{2}{12} = 2\frac{14}{12}; 1\frac{9}{12} = 1\frac{9}{12}; 1\frac{5}{12}$

3. $9\frac{4}{12} = 8\frac{16}{12}; 6\frac{5}{12} = 6\frac{5}{12}; 2\frac{11}{12}$

4. $8\frac{9}{24} = 7\frac{33}{24}; 4\frac{20}{24} = 4\frac{20}{24}; 3\frac{13}{24}$

5. $4\frac{1}{20}; 10\frac{16}{20} - 6\frac{15}{20} = 4\frac{1}{20}$

6. $5\frac{43}{60}; 15\frac{18}{60} = 14\frac{78}{60}; 9\frac{35}{60} = 9\frac{35}{60}; 14\frac{78}{60} - 9\frac{35}{60} = 5\frac{43}{60}$

7. $\frac{7}{18}; 5\frac{3}{18} = 4\frac{21}{18}; 4\frac{14}{18} = 4\frac{14}{18}; 4\frac{21}{18} - 4\frac{14}{18} = \frac{7}{18}$

8. $5\frac{7}{25}; 13\frac{25}{25}; 13\frac{25}{25} - 8\frac{18}{25} = 5\frac{7}{25}$

9. $28\frac{11}{20};$
$39\frac{7}{20} = 38\frac{27}{20};$
$10\frac{16}{20};$
$38\frac{27}{20} - 10\frac{16}{20} = 28\frac{11}{20}$

10. $3\frac{47}{105}; 20\frac{12}{105} = 19\frac{117}{105}; 16\frac{70}{105} = 16\frac{70}{105};$
$19\frac{117}{105} - 16\frac{70}{105} = 3\frac{47}{105}$

11. $5\frac{7}{24}$ **pounds;**
$1\frac{1}{4} + 2\frac{3}{8} + 1\frac{2}{3} = 1\frac{6}{24} + 2\frac{9}{24} + 1\frac{16}{24} =$
$4\frac{31}{24} = 5\frac{7}{24}$

12. **about $60; $64;** $2 \times 100 \times \$.30 = \$60;$
$2 \times 100 \times \$.32 = \$64$

13. **Michael Stulze; 18 ft** $2\frac{13}{16}$ **in.;** 71 ft $2\frac{1}{2}$ in. –
52 ft $11\frac{11}{16}$ in. = 71 ft $2\frac{8}{16}$ in. – 52 ft $11\frac{11}{16}$ in. =
71 ft $1\frac{24}{16}$ in. – 52 ft $11\frac{11}{16}$ in. = 70 ft $13\frac{24}{16}$ in. –
52 ft $11\frac{11}{16}$ in. = 18 ft $2\frac{13}{16}$ in.

EXERCISE 11
Pages 100–101

1. $\frac{3}{40}; \frac{1}{5} \times \frac{3}{8} = \frac{3}{40}$

2. $\frac{7}{18}; \frac{7}{12} \times \frac{2}{3} = \frac{14}{36} = \frac{7}{18}$

3. $\frac{3}{4}; \frac{9}{10} \times \frac{5}{6} = \frac{45}{60} = \frac{3}{4}$

4. $\frac{21}{32}$

5. $\frac{4}{25}; \frac{24}{150} = \frac{4}{25}$

6. $\frac{11}{25}; \frac{44}{100} = \frac{11}{25}$

7. $\frac{9}{100}; \frac{3}{8} \times \frac{12}{50} = \frac{36}{400} = \frac{9}{100}$

8. $\frac{21}{40}; \frac{7}{5} \times \frac{3}{8} = \frac{21}{40}$

9. $11\frac{11}{12}; \frac{11}{4} \times \frac{13}{3} = \frac{143}{12} = 11\frac{11}{12}$

10. $3\frac{15}{16}; \frac{21}{8} \times \frac{3}{2} = \frac{63}{16} = 3\frac{15}{16}$

11. $23\frac{3}{5}; \frac{59}{10} \times 4 = \frac{236}{10} = 23\frac{6}{10} = 23\frac{3}{5}$

12. $27\frac{131}{135}; \frac{64}{15} \times \frac{59}{9} = \frac{3,776}{135} = 27\frac{131}{135}$

13. $35\frac{13}{54}; \frac{173}{18} \times \frac{11}{3} = \frac{1,903}{54} = 35\frac{13}{54}$

14. $135\frac{23}{36}; 19 \times \frac{257}{36} = \frac{4,883}{36} = 135\frac{23}{36}$

15. $166\frac{121}{200}; \frac{383}{25} \times \frac{87}{8} = \frac{33,321}{200} = 166\frac{121}{200}$

16. **40 degrees;** $104 - 32 = 72; \frac{5}{9} \times 72 = \frac{360}{9} = 40$

17. $4\frac{1}{2}$ **hours;** $3 \times 1\frac{1}{2} = 3 \times \frac{3}{2} = \frac{9}{2} = 4\frac{1}{2}$

EXERCISE 12
Pages 103–104

1. $\frac{12}{5}$

2. $\frac{1}{3}$

3. $\frac{10}{69}$

4. $\frac{1}{27}$

5. 12

6. 20

7. 28

8. 3

9. $10\frac{1}{2}$

10. $\frac{3}{2}; \frac{9}{16}$

11. $\frac{5}{6} \times \frac{17}{10} = \frac{85}{60} = 1\frac{25}{60} = 1\frac{5}{12}$

12. $\frac{7}{3} \div \frac{4}{9} = \frac{7}{3} \times \frac{9}{4} = \frac{63}{12} = 5\frac{3}{12} = 5\frac{1}{4}$

13. $\frac{7}{4} \div \frac{43}{18} = \frac{7}{4} \times \frac{18}{43} = \frac{126}{172} = \frac{63}{86}$

14. $1\frac{89}{186}; \frac{55}{12} \div \frac{31}{10} = \frac{55}{12} \times \frac{10}{31} = \frac{550}{372} = 1\frac{178}{372} = 1\frac{89}{186}$

15. $2\frac{32}{59}; 6 \div \frac{59}{25} = 6 \times \frac{25}{59} = \frac{150}{59} = 2\frac{32}{59}$

16. $2\frac{23}{200}; \frac{423}{40} \div \frac{5}{1} = \frac{423}{40} \times \frac{1}{5} = \frac{423}{200} = 2\frac{23}{200}$

17. $3\frac{1}{2}$ inches; $21 \times \frac{1}{6} = \frac{21}{6} = 3\frac{3}{6} = 3\frac{1}{2}$

18. **22,000 pounds**; $33,000 \div 1\frac{1}{2} =$

    $33,000 \div \frac{3}{2} = 33,000 \times \frac{2}{3} = \frac{66,000}{3} = 22,000$

FRACTIONS AND MIXED NUMBERS REVIEW
Pages 105–107

1. $\frac{81}{100}$

2. $\frac{59}{10}$

3. $4\frac{1}{12}$

4. sample answer: $\frac{12}{46}, \frac{18}{69}, \frac{24}{92}$

5. $\frac{55}{90}$

6. $\frac{7}{8}$

7. **.68 or 0.68**

8. $4\frac{24}{25}$

9. sample answer: 30

10. $1\frac{7}{12} > 1\frac{9}{16}$

11. $7\frac{1}{2}$ **hours**; $3 \times 2\frac{1}{2} = 3 \times \frac{5}{2} = \frac{15}{2} = 7\frac{1}{2}$

12. $2\frac{5}{8}$ **miles**; $\frac{7}{8} + 1\frac{3}{4} = \frac{7}{8} + \frac{7}{4} = \frac{7}{8} + \frac{14}{8} = \frac{21}{8} = 2\frac{5}{8}$

13. **12**; $4 \div \frac{1}{3} = 4 \times 3 = 12$

14. $\frac{15}{16}; 1\frac{3}{8} - \frac{7}{16} = \frac{11}{8} - \frac{7}{16} = \frac{22}{16} - \frac{7}{16} = \frac{15}{16}$

15. $\frac{12}{25}; \frac{9}{10} \div 1\frac{7}{8} = \frac{9}{10} \div \frac{15}{8} = \frac{9}{10} \times \frac{8}{15} = \frac{72}{150} = \frac{12}{25}$

16. (3)

17. (2)

18. (1)

19. (4)

20. (3)

21. (2)

22. (4)

23. (5)

24. (1)

25. (4)

CHAPTER 4: MEASUREMENT AND GEOMETRY

EXERCISE 1
Pages 110–111

1. pints

2. pounds

3. feet

4. gallons

5. minutes

6. miles

7. days

8. quarts

9. weeks

10. yards

11. **48**; 12 gal × 4 = 48 qt

12. **12**; 84 days ÷ 7 = 12 wk

13. **10**; 30 ft ÷ 3 = 10 yd

14. **10,000**; 5 T × 2,000 = 10,000 lb

15. **48**; 3 lb × 16 = 48 oz

16. **5**; 60 in. ÷ 12 = 5 ft

17. **4**; 240 sec ÷ 60 = 4 min

18. **3**; 6 c ÷ 2 = 3 pt

19. **63,360**; 1 mi × 5,280 = 5,280 ft;
    5,280 ft × 12 = 63,360 ft

20. **5**; 300 min ÷ 60 = 5 hr

21. **108**; 3 yd × 36 = 108 in.

22. **168**; 1 wk × 7 = 7 days;
    7 days × 24 = 168 h

23. **24**; 6 qt × 2 = 12 pt; 12 pt × 2 = 24 c

24. **4**; 8,000 lb ÷ 2,000 = 4 T

25. **80**; 5 lb × 16 = 80 oz

26. **86,400**; 1 day × 24 = 24 h; 24 h × 60 = 1,440
    min; 1,440 min × 60 = 86,400 sec

27. **3**; 15,840 ft ÷ 5,280 = 3 mi

28. **2**; 32 c ÷ 2 = 16 pt; 16 pt ÷ 2 = 8 qt;
    8 qt ÷ 4 = 2 gal

29. **(3) gallon**

30. **(2) second**

EXERCISE 2
Pages 112–113

1. **74 in.**; (6 × 12) + 2 = 72 + 2 = 74

2. **4 ft 6 in.**; 54 in. → 54 ÷ 12 = 4 R6 → 4 ft 6 in.

3. **135 min**; (2 × 60) + 15 = 120 + 15 = 135

4. **5 h 0 min**; 300 ÷ 60 = 5

5. **2 qt 3 c**; 11 c → 11 ÷ 4 = 2 R3 → 2 qt 3 c

6. **1 mi 4,720 ft**; 10,000 ft → 10,000 ÷ 5,280 =
   1 R4,720 → 1 mi 4,720 ft

7. **3 min 20 sec;**
$3\frac{1}{3}$ = 3 min $\left(\frac{1}{3} \times 60\right)$ sec = 3 min 20 sec

8. **52 wk 1 day;** 1 y = 365 days;
365 days ÷ 7 = 52R1 → 52 wk 1 day

9. **3 lb 2 oz;**
50 ÷ 16 = 3 R2 = 3 lb 2 oz

10. **455 sec;**
7 × 60 + 35 = 420 + 35 = 455

11. **Enrique;** Enrique: (6 × 12) + 1 = 73 in.

12. **Sue;** Ria: (8 × 60) + 45 = 525 min

13. **Can A;** Can B: 1 cup = 8 fl oz

14. **4 cups;** 20 c ÷ 2 = 10 pt; 10 pt ÷ 2 = 5 qt;
5 qt ÷ 4 = 1R1 → 1 gal 1 qt = 1 gal 4 c

EXERCISE 3
Pages 115–116

1. **100**
2. **1,000**
3. **10**
4. **1,000**
5. **1,000**
6. **1,000**
7. **1,000**
8. **1,000**
9. **3.2;** 320 cm ÷ 100 = 3.2 m
10. **400;** 40 cm × 10 = 400 mm
11. **400;** 0.4 kL × 1,000 = 400 L
12. **5.5;** 5,500 g ÷ 1,000 = 5.5 kg
13. **600;** 6 m × 100 = 600 cm
14. **8.9;** 89 mm ÷ 10 = 8.9 cm
15. **6,500;** 6.5 L × 1,000 = 6,500 mL
16. **2,000;** 2 km × 1,000 = 2,000 m
17. **342;** 342,000 mg ÷ 1,000 = 342 g
18. **1,400;** 1.4 kL × 1,000 = 1,400 L
19. **10,000;** 10 kg × 1,000 = 10,000 g
20. **0.75;** 750 mL ÷ 1,000 = 0.75 L
21. **5,000;** 5 kg × 1,000 = 5,000 g
22. **6;** 600 cm ÷ 100 = 6 m
23. **7,200;** 7.2 g × 1,000 = 7,200 mg
24. **.24;** 240 m ÷ 1,000 = .24 km
25. **2;** 2,000 L ÷ 1,000 = 2 kL
26. **.512;** 512 mL ÷ 1,000 = .512 L
27. **millimeter, centimeter, meter, kilometer**
28. **kilogram, gram, milligram**
29. **500 mL;** 0.5 L × 1,000 = 500 mL
30. **2.5 L;** 250 mL × 10 = 2,500 mL;
2,500 mL ÷ 1,000 = 2.5 L
31. **70,000 g;** 70 kg × 1,000 = 70,000 g
32. **0.06 g;** 60 mg ÷ 1,000 = 0.06 g

EXERCISE 4
Pages 119–120

1.
2.

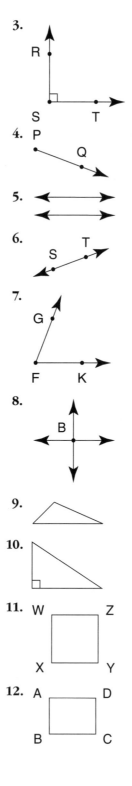

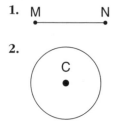

13. 90°
14. circle
15. line
16. right
17. segment
18. parallel
19. angle
20. triangle
21. equal
22. Perpendicular
23. ray

EXERCISE 5
Pages 121–122

1. **3 mm, or 0.3 cm**
2. **9 cm**
3. **13.5 cm**
4. **9 mm, or 0.9 cm**
5. **5.4 cm**
6. **11.7 cm**
7. **km**
8. **m**
9. **cm**
10. **cm; mm**
11. **km**
12. **cm; m**

EXERCISE 6
Pages 122–123

Sample answers are given for 1–14.
1. **Ray TQ, TS, TP, or TR**
2. **Segment PT, TQ, TS, RT, PQ, or RS**
3. **Line RS or PQ**
4. **Right angle RTQ, RTP, PTS, or QTS**
5. **Circle T**
6. **Perpendicular lines RS and PQ**
7. **Square CDEF**
8. **Segments AF and BC, AB and DE**
9. **Triangle CDE**
10. **Segments AE and CF, BD and AB**
11. **Angle FCE, AEC**
12. **Rectangle ABDE**
13. **Segments AB, FC, and ED**
14. **Angles FAB, ABC, and CDE**
15. **T**
16. **F**
17. **T**
18. **F**
19. **T**
20. **F**
21. **F**
22. **F**
23. **T**
24. **T**

EXERCISE 7
Pages 125–126

1. **24 ft;** $P = s + s + s + s; 4 + 8 + 4 + 8 = 24$ ft
2. **96 in.;** $P = s + s + s; 32 + 32 + 32 = 96$ in.
3. **62.8 m;** $C = \pi d; \approx 3.14 \times 20 = 62.8$ m
4. **40 cm;** $P = s + s + s; 8 + 15 + 17 = 40$ cm
5. **44 m;** $C = \pi d; \approx \frac{22}{7} \times (2 \times 7) = 44$ m
6. **48 mm;** $P = s + s + s + s; 12 + 12 + 12 + 12 = 48$ mm
7. **80 yd;** $P = s + s + s + s; 30 + 10 + 30 + 10 = 80$ yd
8. **50 ft;** $P = s + s + s + s + s + s + s + s + s + s; 5 + 5 + 5 + 5 + 5 + 5 + 5 + 5 + 5 + 5 = 50$ ft

9. **2.57 m;** $C = \pi d; \approx 3.14 \times 1 = 3.14$ m; $(3.14 \div 2) + 1 = 2.57$ m
10. **36 in.;** $P = s + s + s + s; 9 + 9 + 9 + 9 = 36$ in.
11. **38 mm;** $P = s + s + s + s; 8 + 11 + 8 + 11 = 38$ mm
12. **45 cm;** $P = s + s + s; 15 + 15 + 15 = 45$ cm
13. **18.84 ft;** $C = \pi d; \approx 3.14 \times (2 \times 3) = 18.84$ ft
14. **120 cm;** $P = s + s + s; 30 + 40 + 50 = 120$ cm
15. **132 mm;** $C = \pi d; \approx \frac{22}{7} \times 42 = 132$ mm
16. **72 m;** $P = s + s + s + s + s + s; 12 + 12 + 12 + 12 + 12 + 12 = 72$ m

EXERCISE 8
Page 127

1. **4 m;** $P = s + s + s + s; 16 = 4 + 4 + 4 + 4$
2. **5 ft;** $P = s + s + s + s; 24 = 7 + 5 + 7 + 5$
3. **9 cm;** $P = s + s + s; 29 = 10 + 10 + 9$
4. **3.5 in.;** $C = \pi d; 22 = \frac{22}{7} \times 7; d = 7; r = 7 \div 2 = 3.5$
5. **(1);** $P = 2s + 2s$; a rectangle must have 2 pairs of equal sides.
6. **(2);** $C = \pi d; 44 = \frac{22}{7} \times (2 \times 7)$

EXERCISE 9
Pages 131–132

1. **154 ft²;** Area $= L \times w; 14 \times 11 = 154$ ft²
2. **900 m²;** Area $= L \times w; 30 \times 30 = 900$ m²
3. **48 cm²;** Area $= \frac{1}{2} b \times h; \frac{1}{2} \times 12 \times 8 = 48$ cm²
4. **154 in.²;** Area $= \pi r^2; \frac{22}{7} \times 7 \times 7 = 154$ in.²
5. **21 yd²;** Area $= L \times w; 7 \times 3 = 21$ yd²
6. **486 cm²;** Area $= \frac{1}{2} b \times h; \frac{1}{2} \times 36 \times 27 = 486$ cm²
7. **81 mm²;** Area $= L \times w; 9 \times 9 = 81$ mm²
8. **42 ft²;** Area $= \frac{1}{2} b \times h; \frac{1}{2} \times 7 \times 12 = 42$ ft²
9. **176.625 cm²;** Area $= \pi r^2; 3.14 \times 7.5 \times 7.5 = 176.625$ cm²
10. **54 mm²;** Area $= L \times w; 9 \times 6 = 54$ mm²
11. **28.26 m²;** Area $= \pi r^2; 3.14 \times 3 \times 3 = 28.26$ m²
12. **15 m²;** Area $= \frac{1}{2} bh; \frac{1}{2} \times 10 \times 3 = 15$ m²
13. **144 in.²;** Area $= L \times w; 12 \times 12 = 144$ in.²
14. **616 yd²;** Area $= \pi r^2; \frac{22}{7} \times 14 \times 14 = 616$ yd²
15. **30 ft²;** Area $= L \times w; 10 \times 3 = 30$ ft²
16. **60 cm²;** Area $= \frac{1}{2} bh; \frac{1}{2} \times 15 \times 8 = 60$ cm²

EXERCISE 10
Page 133

1. **4 m;** $A = L \times w$; $16 = 4 \times 4$
2. **9 ft;** $A = L \times w$; $36 = L \times 4$; $L = 9$
3. **10 cm;** $\frac{1}{2}$bh; $30 = \frac{1}{2} \times 6 \times h$; $= 3 \times h$; $h = 10$
4. **6 in.;** $A = \pi r^2$; $120 = 3.14 \times 6 \times 6 = 113.04$; $3.14 \times 7 \times 7 = 153.86$
5. **(4);** $A = L \times w$; $48 \neq 4 \times 13$; $4 \times 13 = 52$
6. **(2);** $A = \frac{1}{2}$bh; $12 = \frac{1}{2} \times 12 \times 2$

EXERCISE 11
Pages 135–136

1. **160 m³;** Volume $= L \times w \times h$; $4 \times 4 \times 10 = 160$ m³
2. **480 ft³;** Volume $= L \times w \times h$; $12 \times 5 \times 8 = 480$ ft³
3. **216 cm³;** Volume $= L \times w \times h$; $6 \times 6 \times 6 = 216$ cm³
4. **1,331 in.³;** Volume $= L \times w \times h$; $11 \times 11 \times 11 = 1,331$ in.³
5. **56 ft³;** Volume $= L \times w \times h$; $4 \times 2 \times 7 = 56$ ft³
6. **100 m³;** Volume $= L \times w \times h$; $20 \times 5 \times 1 = 100$ m³
7. **8 cm³;** Volume $= L \times w \times h$; $2 \times 2 \times 2 = 8$ cm³
8. **2,744 in.³;** Volume $= L \times w \times h$; $14 \times 14 \times 14 = 2,744$ in.³
9. **3 m, 3 m, 3 m;** Volume $= L \times w \times h$; $27 = 3 \times 3 \times 3$
10. **6 ft;** Volume $= L \times w \times h$; $126 = 3 \times 7 \times h$; $126 = 21h$; $h = 6$; $126 = 3 \times 7 \times 6$
11. **(3);** Volume $= L \times w \times h$; $72 = L \times w \times h$; $9 \times 8 \times 0 = 0$; $0 \neq 72$
12. **(1);** Volume $= L \times w \times h$; $64 = L \times w \times h$; $4 \times 4 \times 4 = 64$

EXERCISE 12
Pages 138–139

1. ***Buran*; 0.6 ft, or 7.2 in.;** $79.2 - 78.6 = 0.6$ ft; 0.6 ft $\times 12 = 7.2$ in.
2. **570,025 ft²;** Area $= 755 \times 755 = 570,025$ ft²
3. **62 m;** $443 - 381 = 62$ m
4. **144 in.³;** Volume $= 12 \times 12 \times 1 = 144$ in.³
5. **160 ft;** $53\frac{1}{3}$ yd $\times 3 = \frac{160}{3}$ yd $\times 3 = 160$ ft
6. **square;**
   Area of circle $\approx 3.14 \times 1 \times 1 = 3.14$ in.²; Area of square $= 2 \times 2 = 4$ in.²

2 in.

2 in.

7. **$1\frac{5}{7}$ oz;** 4 weeks $\times 7 = 28$ days; 3 pounds $\times 16 = 48$ ounces; $48 \div 28 = 1\frac{5}{7}$ oz/day

8. **11 lb 1 oz;** 1-month gain: 8 lb 13 oz − 6 lb 9 oz $=$ 2 lb 4 oz; 8 lb 13 oz + 2 lb 4 oz $=$ 10 lb 17 oz $=$ 11 lb 1 oz
9. **rectangular pan;** Area of 8-in. square pan: $8 \times 8 = 64$ in.²; Area of two 8-in. pans: $64 \times 2 = 128$ in.²; Area of rectangular pan: $13 \times 9 = 117$ in.²; because the base area is less, the brownies will be thicker.
10. **11 loaves;** 5×4 cups $= 20$ cups; $20 \div 1\frac{3}{4} = 11\frac{3}{7}$; Answer must be a whole number.

EXERCISE 13
Pages 141–142

1. **$2,400;** $12/ft $\times 200$ ft $= \$2,400$
2. **24 sections;** 120 ft $\div 5$ ft $= 24$ sections
3. **1,000 ft²;** Area $= 200 \times 5 = 1,000$ ft²
4. **$8\frac{1}{3}$ ft³;** Volume $= 5 \times 5 \times \frac{4}{12} = 8\frac{1}{3}$ ft³
5. **20 yd²;** 12 ft $\div 3 = 4$ yd; 15 ft $\div 3 = 5$ yd; Area $= 4 \times 5 = 20$ yd²
6. **67 ft 4 in.;** Perimeter of room minus opening for door $= 15 + 12 + 15 + 12 - 2$ ft 6 in. $=$ 51 ft 6 in.; Perimeter of door frame (3 sides) $=$ 6 ft 8 in. + 2 ft 6 in. + 6 ft 8 in. $=$ 14 ft 22 in. $=$ 15 ft 10 in.; Total trim needed $=$ 51 ft 6 in. + 15 ft 10 in. $=$ 66 ft 16 in. $=$ 67 ft 4 in.
7. **yes;** Volume of one ice cube $= 3$ cm $\times 4$ cm $\times 3$ cm $= 36$ cm³; Volume of 12 ice cubes $= 12 \times 36$ cm³ $= 432$ cm³; Volume of two trays $= 2 \times 432$ cm³ $= 864$ cm³ $= 864$ mL $= 0.864$ L
8. **500 ft²;** Area of college court: $94 \times 50 = 4,700$ ft²; Area of high school court: $84 \times 50 = 4200$ ft²; Difference $= 4,700 - 4,200 = 500$ ft²
9. **12-in. pizza;** Area of 10-in. pizza $\approx 3.14 \times 5 \times 5 = 78.5$ in.²; $8 \div 78.5 \approx \$.10/in.²$; Area of 12-in. pizza $\approx 3.14 \times 6 \times 6 = 113.04$ in.²; $10.50 \div 113.04 \approx \$.09/in.²$; the 12-in. pizza costs less per square inch.
10. **6.28 in.;** Circumference of 10-in. pizza $\approx 3.14 \times 10 = 31.4$ in.; Circumference of 12-in. pizza $\approx 3.14 \times 12 = 37.68$ in.; Difference $= 37.68 - 31.4 = 6.28$ in.
11. **(3)**
12. **(2)**

MEASUREMENT AND GEOMETRY REVIEW
Pages 143–147

1. **3.7 cm**

2. **16 cups;** 1 gal × 4 = 4 qt; 4 qt × 2 = 8 pt; 8 pt × 2 = 16 c

3. **50 m;** Perimeter = 15 + 10 + 15 + 10 = 50 m

4. **parallel lines**

5. **2,500 g;** 2.5 kg × 1,000 = 2,500 g

6. **16 ft;** 8 ft × 2 = 16 ft

7. **108 m²;** Area = 9 × 12 = 108 m²

8. **circle**

9. **5 lb;** 80 oz ÷ 16 = 5 lb

10. **343 m³;** Volume = 7 × 7 × 7 = 343 m³

11. **18.84 in.;** Circumference ≈ 3.14 × 6 = 18.84 in.

12. **3 m;** 300 cm ÷ 100 = 3 m

13. **5 in.;** 20 in. ÷ 4 sides = 5 in./side

14. **150 cm²;** Area = $\frac{1}{2}$ × 20 × 15 = 150 cm²

15.

16. **50.24 cm²;** Area ≈ 3.14 × 4 × 4 = 50.24 cm²

17. **36 ft³;** Volume = 6 × 2 × 3 = 36 ft³

18. **5 ft 4 in.;** 64 in. ÷ 12 = 5R4 → 5 ft 4 in.

19. (2)

20. (5)

21. (2)

22. (5)

23. (1)

24. (4)

25. (3)

26. (3)

27. (1)

28. (2)

29. (5)

30. (4)

CHAPTER 5: RATIOS, PROPORTIONS, AND PERCENTS

EXERCISE 1
Pages 150–152

1. **6 : 7,** $\frac{6}{7}$

2. **1 to 50,** $\frac{1}{50}$

3. **7 to 3, 7 : 3**

4. **10 to 19, 10 : 19**

5. **13 to 1,** $\frac{13}{1}$

6. **2 : 5,** $\frac{2}{5}$

7. **1 to 3, 1 : 3, or** $\frac{1}{3}$

8. **9 to 1,** $\frac{9}{1}$**, or 9:1;**
2,000 − 200 = 1,800; $\frac{1,800}{200} = \frac{9}{1}$

9. **2 to 9, 2 : 9, or** $\frac{2}{9}$

10. **1 to 2,** $\frac{1}{2}$**, or 1 : 2;**
24 h − 8 h = 16 h; $\frac{8}{16} = \frac{1}{2}$

11. **4 to 1,** $\frac{4}{1}$**, or 4 : 1**

12. **23 to 8, 23 : 8, or** $\frac{23}{8}$**;**
31 days − 23 days = 8 days

13. **61 to 97,** $\frac{61}{97}$ **or 61 : 97;**
$\frac{366}{582} = \frac{366 \div 6}{582 \div 6} = \frac{61}{97}$

14. **4 to 7, 4 : 7, or** $\frac{4}{7}$

15. **19 : 8, 19 to 8, or** $\frac{19}{8}$**;**
$\frac{76}{32} = \frac{76 \div 4}{32 \div 4} = \frac{19}{8}$

16. **2 : 25, 2 to 25, or** $\frac{2}{25}$**;**
$\frac{8}{100} = \frac{8 \div 4}{100 \div 4} = \frac{2}{25}$

17. **1 : 4, 1 to 4 or** $\frac{1}{4}$**;**
$\frac{25}{100} = \frac{25 \div 25}{100 \div 100} = \frac{1}{4}$

18. **4 : 1; 4 to 1 or** $\frac{4}{1}$**;**
$\frac{32}{8} = \frac{32 \div 8}{8 \div 8} = \frac{4}{1}$

19. **67 : 41, 67 to 41, or** $\frac{67}{41}$**;**
76 + 100 + 25 = 201; 32 + 8 + 83 = 123;
$\frac{201}{123} = \frac{201 \div 3}{123 \div 3} = \frac{67}{41}$

20. **100 to 101, 100 : 101, or** $\frac{100}{101}$**;**
76 + 25 = 101

21. **(1)**

22. **(5);** 30 − 3 = 27; $\frac{27}{3} = \frac{9}{1}$; 9 to 1

EXERCISE 2
Pages 153–154

1. **55 words per minute;** $825 \div 15 = 55$
2. **$6.50 per hour;** $\$130 \div 20 = \$6.5$
3. **22.5 miles per gallon;** $135 \div 6 = 22.5$
4. **60 miles per hour;** $210 \div 3.5 = 60$
5. **$.30 per pound;** $\$1.49 \div 5 = \$0.298 \approx \$0.30$
6. **$.10 per pencil;** $\$0.99 \div 10 = \$0.099 \approx \$0.10$
7. **$2.67 per roll;** $\$8 \div 3 \approx \$2.67$
8. **$.10 per egg;** $\$1.09 \div 12 = \$0.0908 \approx \$0.10$
9. **Bill's car;** Consuela's: $330 \div 12 = 27.5$ miles per gallon; Bill's: $300 \div 10 = 30$ miles per gallon
10. **about 0.24 kilometers per minute;** $10 \div 42.5 \approx 0.24$
11. **slower;** $50 \div 6 = 8\frac{1}{3}$ minutes per mile
12. **faster;** $416 \div 5 = 83.2$ words per minute
13. **No;** $\$2.79 \div 15 \approx \$.19$ per ounce; $\$1.99 \div 12 \approx \$.17$ per ounce
14. **12-pack, best; 6-pack, worst;** $\$2.19 \div 6 \approx \$.37$ per can; $\$3.99 \div 12 \approx \$.33$ per can; $\$8.49 \div 24 \approx \$.35$ per can

EXERCISE 3
Pages 156–158

1. **Yes;** $\frac{2}{3} = \frac{10}{15}$; $2 \times 15 = 30$; $3 \times 10 = 30$
2. **No;** $\frac{1}{4}$ and $\frac{2}{9}$; $1 \times 9 = 9$; $4 \times 2 = 8$; $9 \neq 8$
3. **No;** $\frac{16}{3}$ and $\frac{8}{1}$; $16 \times 1 = 16$; $3 \times 8 = 24$; $16 \neq 24$
4. **Yes;** $\frac{5}{5} = \frac{3}{3}$; $5 \times 3 = 15$; $5 \times 3 = 15$
5. **No;** $\frac{3}{4}$ and $\frac{5}{8}$; $3 \times 8 = 24$; $4 \times 5 = 20$; $24 \neq 20$
6. **Yes;** $\frac{50}{20} = \frac{10}{4}$; $50 \times 4 = 200$; $20 \times 10 = 200$
7. **No;** $\frac{1}{2}$ and $\frac{6}{9}$; $1 \times 9 = 9$; $2 \times 6 = 12$; $9 \neq 12$
8. **Yes;** $\frac{8}{3} = \frac{24}{9}$; $8 \times 9 = 72$; $3 \times 24 = 72$

9–16. Sample answers are given.

9. $\frac{1}{9} = \frac{2}{18}$
10. $\frac{25}{20} = \frac{5}{4}$
11. $\frac{12}{13} = \frac{24}{26}$
12. $\frac{6}{3} = \frac{2}{1}$
13. $\frac{13}{1} = \frac{39}{3}$
14. $\frac{17}{3} = \frac{34}{6}$
15. $\frac{5}{11} = \frac{50}{110}$
16. $\frac{10}{3} = \frac{20}{6}$

17. **No;** $\frac{3}{5}$ and $\frac{4}{6}$; $3 \times 6 = 18$; $5 \times 4 = 20$; $18 \neq 20$
18. **No, because the ratios of blue to yellow are not the same;** $\frac{3}{1} \neq \frac{5}{2}$
19. **Yes; yes, they both type at 65 words per minute;** $\frac{650}{10} = \frac{780}{12}$

20. **$2.18;** $\frac{\$1.09}{12 \text{ eggs}} = \frac{\$2.18}{24 \text{ eggs}}$
21. **(2)**
22. **(3)**
23. **(5)**
24. **(4)**

EXERCISE 4
Pages 159–160

1. **130;** $13 \times 10 \div 1 = 130$
2. **500;** $10 \times 150 \div 3 = 500$
3. **36;** $42 \times 6 \div 7 = 36$
4. **16.8;** $7 \times 12 \div 5 = 16.8$
5. **4;** $1 \times 16 \div 4 = 4$
6. **54;** $9 \times 12 \div 2 = 54$
7. **1;** $5 \times 5 \div 25 = 1$
8. **112.5;** $30 \times 15 \div 4 = 112.5$
9. **32.4;** $9 \times 36 \div 10 = 32.4$
10. **1.4;** $7 \times 1 \div 5 = 1.4$
11. **$125;** $\frac{\$100}{8 \text{ lawns}} = \frac{\square}{10 \text{ lawns}}$; $\$100 \times 10 \div 8 = \$125$
12. **3.2 liters;** $\frac{5 \text{ parts juice}}{2 \text{ parts ginger ale}} = \frac{8 \text{ liters juice}}{\square}$; $2 \times 8 \div 5 = 3.2$
13. **125 miles;** $\frac{1 \text{ in.}}{50 \text{ miles}} = \frac{2\frac{1}{2} \text{ in.}}{\square}$; $50 \times 2\frac{1}{2} \div 1 = 125$
14. **384 miles;** $\frac{32 \text{ miles}}{1 \text{ gallon}} = \frac{\square}{12 \text{ gallons}}$; $32 \times 12 \div 1 = 384$
15. **307 calories;** $\frac{\frac{3}{4} \text{ cup}}{230 \text{ calories}} = \frac{1 \text{ cup}}{\square}$; $230 \times 1 \div \frac{3}{4} \approx 307$
16. **$6\frac{7}{8}$ inches by 11 inches;** First try to enlarge to $8\frac{1}{2}$ inches wide: $\frac{1\frac{1}{4}}{2} = \frac{8\frac{1}{2}}{\square}$; $2 \times 8\frac{1}{2} \div 1\frac{1}{4} = 13.6$ inches (too long for 11-inch paper). So, enlarge to 11 inches long instead: $\frac{1\frac{1}{4}}{2} = \frac{\square}{11}$; $1\frac{1}{4} \times 11 \div 2 = 6\frac{7}{8}$ inches.

EXERCISE 5
Pages 164–165

1. $\frac{1}{4}$; **0.25;** $\frac{25}{100} = \frac{25 \div 25}{100 \div 25} = \frac{1}{4}$
2. $\frac{2}{25}$; **0.08;** $\frac{8}{100} = \frac{8 \div 4}{100 \div 4} = \frac{2}{25}$
3. $\frac{1}{10}$; **0.1;** $\frac{10}{100} = \frac{10 \div 10}{100 \div 10} = \frac{1}{10}$
4. $\frac{33}{50}$; **0.66;** $\frac{66}{100} = \frac{66 \div 2}{100 \div 2} = \frac{33}{50}$
5. $\frac{1}{100}$; **0.01**

6. $\frac{9}{10}$; 0.9; $\frac{90}{100} = \frac{90 \div 10}{100 \div 10} = \frac{9}{10}$

7. $\frac{37}{100}$; 0.37

8. $\frac{3}{100}$; 0.03

9. **50%;** $1 \div 2 = 0.5 = 50\%$
10. **60%;** $3 \div 5 = 0.6 = 60\%$
11. **9%**
12. **74%**
13. **10%;** $1 \div 10 = 0.1 = 10\%$
14. **75%;** $3 \div 4 = 0.75 = 75\%$
15. **70%**
16. **16%**
17. **35%;** $7 \div 20 = 0.35 = 35\%$
18. **4%;** $1 \div 25 = 0.04 = 4\%$
19. **2%**

20. **99%**

21. **37.5%;** $3 \div 8 = 0.375 = 37.5\%$

22. **93.75%;** $15 \div 16 = 0.9375 = 93.75\%$

23. $\frac{1}{4}$; $1 \div 4 = 0.25 = 25\% > 20\%$

24. **85%;** $4 \div 5 = 0.8 = 80\% < 85\%$

25. $\frac{1}{2}$; $1 \div 2 = 0.5 = 50\% > 48\%$

26. **0.11;** $0.11 = 11\% > 10\%$

27. **0.6;** $0.6 = 60\% > 55\%$

28. **100%;** $0.01 = 1\% < 100\%$

29. **22%;** $\frac{2}{10} = 20\% < 22\%$

30. **39%;** $.35 = 35\% < 39\%$

31. **.7;** $.7 = 70\% > 42\%$

32. $\frac{3}{5}$; $\frac{3}{5} = 60\% > 58\%$

33. **(3)**

34. **(1)**

EXERCISE 6
Page 167

1. **25%; 0.25**

2. **$33\frac{1}{3}\%$; 0.333 . . .**

3. **50%; 0.5**

4. **$66\frac{2}{3}\%$; 0.666 . . .**

5. **75%; 0.75**

6. $\frac{1}{2}$; **0.5**

7. $\frac{1}{3}$; **0.333 . . .**

8. $\frac{3}{4}$; **0.75**

9. $\frac{1}{4}$; **0.25**

10. $\frac{2}{3}$; **0.666 . . .**

11. $\frac{3}{4}$; **75%**

12. $\frac{2}{3}$; **$66\frac{2}{3}\%$**

13. $\frac{1}{4}$; **25%**

14. $\frac{1}{3}$; **$33\frac{1}{3}\%$**

15. $\frac{1}{2}$; **50%**

EXERCISE 7
Pages 170–171

1. **87;** $0.1 \times 870 = 87$

2. **12;** $\frac{3}{4} \times 16 = 12$

3. **$12;** $0.12 \times \$100 = \$12$

4. **33;** $\frac{1}{3} \times 99 = 33$

5. **851.2;** $0.8 \times 1,064 = 851.2$

6. **$3,000;** $0.05 \times \$60,000 = \$3,000$

7. **23;** $1 \times 23 = 23$

8. **175;** $0.02 \times 8,750 = 175$

9. **47;** $0.47 \times 100 = 47$

10. **$25;** $\frac{1}{2} \times \$50 = \$25$

11. **28,925;** $0.65 \times 44,500$

12. **$8;** $0.01 \times \$800 = \$8$

13. **12;** $\frac{1}{4} \times 48 = 12$

14. **$20.40;** $0.3 \times \$68 = \$20.40$

15. **120;** $\frac{2}{3} \times 180 = 120$

16. **$.98;** $0.98 \times \$1 = \$.98$

17. **$750;** $0.06 \times \$12,500 = \$750$

18. **$1.95;** $0.15 \times \$13.00 = \$1.95$

19. **$18;** $0.4 \times \$45 = \$18$

20. **$60;** $\frac{1}{4} \times \$80 = \$20$; $\$80 - \$20 = \$60$

21. **21;** $0.7 \times 30 = 21$

22. **$5,400;** $0.05 \times \$108,000 = \$5,400$

23. **16 wins, 4 losses;** $0.8 \times 20 = 16$; $20 - 16 = 4$

24. **$3,000;** $0.1 \times \$2,500 = \$250$; $\$250 \times 12 = \$3,000$

25. **20 defective, 980 not defective;** $0.02 \times 1,000 = 20$; $1,000 - 20 = 980$

26. **7%; 42;** $42\% + 51\% = 93\%$; $100\% - 93\% = 7\%$; $0.07 \times 600 = 42$

EXERCISE 8
Pages 173–174

1. $4,000; $10,000 × 0.08 × 5 = $4,000

2. $200; $2,000 × 0.10 × 1 = $200

3. $50; $2,500 × 0.04 × $\frac{6}{12}$ = $50

4. $324,000; $120,000 × 0.09 × 30 = $324,000

5. $150.68; $5,000 × 0.11 × $\frac{100}{365}$ ≈ $150.68

6. $33; $600 × 0.055 × 1 = $33

7. $480; $4,000 × 0.04 × 3 = $480

8. $10,350; $10,000 × 0.035 × 1 = $350;
$10,000 + $350 = $10,350

9. $180,000; $75,000 × 0.08 × 30 = $180,000

10. $1,770; $1,500 × 0.06 × 3 = $270;
$1,500 + $270 = $1,770

11. $1.48; $150 × 0.12 × $\frac{30}{365}$ ≈ $1.48

12. $7492.50; $18,500 × 0.10 = $1,850 down
payment; $18,500 – $1,850 = $16,650 principal;
$16,650 × 0.09 × 5 = $7492.50

EXERCISE 9
Page 177

1. 20; $\frac{\square}{80} = \frac{25}{100}$; 80 × 25 ÷ 100 = 20

2. 4; $\frac{3}{\square} = \frac{75}{100}$; 3 × 100 ÷ 75 = 4

3. 25%; $\frac{11}{44} = \frac{\square}{100}$; 11 × 100 ÷ 44 = 25

4. 1,250; $\frac{200}{\square} = \frac{16}{100}$; 200 × 100 ÷ 16 = 1,250

5. 15; $\frac{\square}{500} = \frac{3}{100}$; 500 × 3 ÷ 100 = 15

6. 50%; $\frac{12}{24} = \frac{\square}{100}$; 12 × 100 ÷ 24 = 50

7. 75%; $\frac{12}{16} = \frac{\square}{100}$; 12 × 100 ÷ 16 = 75

8. 900; $\frac{\square}{1000} = \frac{90}{100}$; 1000 × 90 ÷ 100 = 900

9. 80; $\frac{8}{\square} = \frac{10}{100}$; 8 × 100 ÷ 10 = 80

10. 24; $\frac{6}{\square} = \frac{25}{100}$; 6 × 100 ÷ 25 = 24

11. 9%; $\frac{9}{100} = \frac{\square}{100}$; 9 × 100 ÷ 100 = 9

12. 31; $\frac{\square}{62} = \frac{50}{100}$; 62 × 50 ÷ 100 = 31

13. 700; $\frac{7}{\square} = \frac{1}{100}$; 7 × 100 ÷ 1 = 700

14. 33$\frac{1}{3}$%; $\frac{17}{51} = \frac{\square}{100}$; 17 × 100 ÷ 51 = 33.333 . . .

15. 49; $\frac{\square}{49} = \frac{100}{100}$; 49 × 100 ÷ 100 = 49

16. 40; $\frac{6}{\square} = \frac{15}{100}$; 6 × 100 ÷ 15 = 40

EXERCISE 10
Pages 178–179

1. 21%; $\frac{73 \text{ million}}{340 \text{ million}} = \frac{\square}{100}$;
73 × 100 ÷ 340 ≈ 21

2. 7,440,000 households;
$\frac{\square}{93 \text{ million}} = \frac{8}{100}$;
93 million × 8 ÷ 100 = 7,440,000

3. 112,011 people; $\frac{\square}{215405} = \frac{52}{100}$;
215,405 × 52 ÷ 100 ≈ 112,011

4. 68%; 13,407 + 6,309 = 19,716;
$\frac{13407}{19716} = \frac{\square}{100}$; 13,407 × 100 ÷ 19,716 ≈ 68

5. 24 grams; $\frac{5}{\square} = \frac{21}{100}$; 5 × 100 ÷ 21 ≈ 24

6. $15.00; $3.00; $\frac{12}{\square} = \frac{80}{100}$;
12 × 100 ÷ 80 = 15; $15 – $12 = $3

7. 6 inches; $\frac{\square}{24} = \frac{25}{100}$; 24 × 25 ÷ 100 = 6

8. 64 inches, or 5 ft 4 in.; $\frac{32}{\square} = \frac{50}{100}$;
32 × 100 ÷ 50 = 64

9. 67%; $\frac{16}{24} = \frac{\square}{100}$; 16 × 100 ÷ 24 ≈ 67

10. About 7 hours; $\frac{\square}{24} = \frac{30}{100}$; 24 × 30 ÷ 100 ≈ 7

11. (2); $\frac{5}{8} = \frac{\square}{100}$ = 5 × 100 ÷ 8 = 62.5

12. (1); $\frac{10}{25} = \frac{\square}{100}$ = 10 × 100 ÷ 25 = 40

13. (4); 8 × 100 ÷ 25 = 32; 25% of 80 = 20

RATIOS, PROPORTIONS, AND PERCENTS REVIEW
Pages 180–183

1. **27;** $3 \times 63 \div 7 = 27$
2. **23%**
3. **0.7**
4. **Sample answer:** $\frac{1}{3} = \frac{2}{6}$
5. **$.42;** $5 \div 12 \approx \$.42$
6. **4 to 1;** $\frac{8}{2} = \frac{8 \div 2}{2 \div 2} = \frac{4}{1}$
7. **6 to 7, 6 : 7**
8. **102;** $0.85 \times 120 = 102$
9. **$66\frac{2}{3}\%$;** $2 \div 3 = 0.666\ldots = 66\frac{2}{3}\%$
10. **$\frac{1}{4}$, 0.25**
11. **10%;** $\frac{6}{60} = \frac{\square}{100}$; $6 \times 100 \div 60 = 10$
12. **500 km;** $\frac{1\ cm}{100\ km} = \frac{5\ cm}{\square}$; $100 \times 5 \div 1 = 500$
13. **65 miles per hour;** $130 \div 2 = 65$
14. **$\frac{1}{50}$;** $\frac{2}{100} = \frac{2 \div 2}{100 \div 2} = \frac{1}{50}$
15. **$1.05;** $0.15 \times \$7 = \$1.05$
16. **20;** $\frac{18}{\square} = \frac{90}{100}$; $18 \times 100 \div 90 = 20$
17. **No;** $\frac{2}{5}$ and $\frac{3}{10}$; $2 \times 10 = 20$; $5 \times 3 = 15$; $20 \neq 15$
18. **20%;** $1 \div 5 = 0.2 = 20\%$
19. **$240;** $\$2,000 \times 0.06 \times 2 = \$240$
20. **12;** $\frac{\square}{40} = \frac{30}{100}$; $40 \times 30 \div 100 = 12$
21. **90 women;** $\frac{2}{3} = \frac{60}{\square}$; $3 \times 60 \div 2 = 90$
22. **50%;** $\frac{35}{70} = \frac{\square}{100}$; $35 \times 100 \div 70 = 50$

23. (1)	31. (5)
24. (2)	32. (5)
25. (4)	33. (4)
26. (4)	34. (2)
27. (3)	35. (3)
28. (4)	36. (2)
29. (1)	37. (3)
30. (2)	38. (5)

CHAPTER 6: DATA ANALYSIS AND PROBABILITY

EXERCISE 1
Pages 188–190

1. **43 minutes;** $42 + 41 + 45 + 40 + 46 + 42 + 44 = 300$; $300 \div 7 \approx 43$
2. **42 minutes;** 40, 41, 42, <u>42</u>, 44, 45, 46
3. **42 minutes**
4. **6 minutes;** $46 - 40 = 6$
5. **$105,000;** $85,000; $95,500; $99,900; <u>$105,000</u>; $108,000; $120,000; $124,000
6. **skiing**
7. **18°;** $10 + 12 + 30 + 38 + 22 + 6 + 2 + 0 + 0 + 18 + 22 + 25 + 16 + 33 + 40 + 38 + 32 + 35 + 10 + 8 + 5 + 5 + 9 + 12 + 15 + 21 + 30 + 19 = 513$; $513 \div 28 \approx 18$
8. **2 siblings**
9. **42 years;** $64 - 22 = 42$
10. **$7\frac{1}{2}$;** $5, 6\frac{1}{2}, 7, \underline{7,8}, 8\frac{1}{2}, 9, 10$; $7 + 8 = 15$; $15 \div 2 = 7\frac{1}{2}$
11. **84%;** $75 + 72 + 88 + 90 + 85 + 100 + 77 + 86 = 673$; $673 \div 8 \approx 84$
12. **$40.49;** $\$64.99 - \$24.50 = \$40.49$
13. **$60**
14. **$36,200 average salary; $24,000 median salary; the mean is higher because of the high salary $100,000;** Mean: $\$24,000 + \$15,000 + \$100,000 + \$30,000 + \$12,000 = \$181,000$; $\$181,000 \div 5 = \$36,200$. Median: $12,000; $15,000; <u>$24,000</u>; $30,000; $100,000.
15. **15 days;** 60 is the median, so half the remaining days of March had higher temperatures and half had lower temperatures; $31 - 1 = 30$; $30 \div 2 = 15$ days
16. **65, 66, 68, 69, 72;** The mean is 68, so $68 \times 5 = 340$ is the sum of the five heights. The greatest is 72, so $72 - 7 = 65$ is the lowest. Then $340 - $ (lowest + median + greatest) $= 340 - (65 + 68 + 72) = 340 - 205 = 135$. The two missing heights are 66 and 69: $66 + 69 = 135$.
17. **25 years;** $15 + 10 = 25$
18. **87%;** $80 \times 5 = 400 = $ sum; $400 - (70 + 85 + 78 + 80) = 400 - 313 = 87$

19. (3)	21. (2)
20. (4)	22. (1)

EXERCISE 2
Pages 193–195

1. **8 species**
2. **seal family**
3. **dog/fox family**
4. **35 species**
5. **horse family and pig family**
6. **21 species or about 20 species;** $40 - 19 = 21$ or $40 - 20 = 20$
7. **rabbit family;** $19 \times 2 = 38 \approx 40$
8. **5 times;** $8 \times 5 = 40$ or $40 \div 8 = 5$
9. **2,000 species**
10. **daffodil family**
11. **lily family;** $1,000 + 2,500 = 3,500$
12. **primrose family**
13. **primrose, daffodil, buttercup and iris (tie), carnation and forget-me-not (tie), rose, lily; median is 1,900 species**
14. **2,075 species;** $1,800 + 2,000 + 1,100 + 2,000 + 1,800 + 3,500 + 1,000 + 3,400 = 16,600;$ $16,600 \div 8 = 2,075$
15. **buttercup, carnation, forget-me-not, iris**
16. **21,500 species;** $25,000 - 3,500 = 21,500$

PRE-GED PRACTICE
EXERCISE 3
Pages 195–196

1. **(4)**   5. **(1)**
2. **(2)**   6. **(3)**
3. **(1)**   7. **(2)**
4. **(5)**   8. **(4)**

EXERCISE 4
Pages 198–199

1.
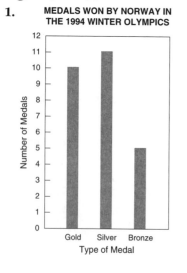

MEDALS WON BY NORWAY IN
THE 1994 WINTER OLYMPICS

2.
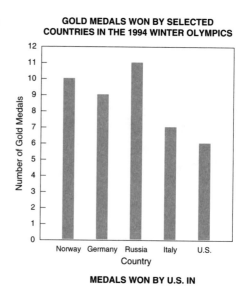

GOLD MEDALS WON BY SELECTED
COUNTRIES IN THE 1994 WINTER OLYMPICS

3.
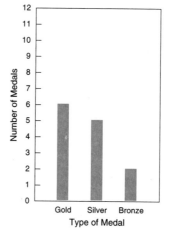

MEDALS WON BY U.S. IN
THE 1994 WINTER OLYMPICS

4.
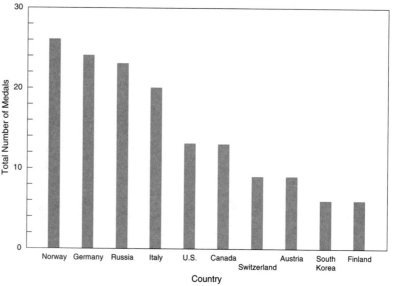

TOTAL NUMBER OF MEDALS WON BY TOP TEN MEDAL WINNERS
IN THE 1994 WINTER OLYMPICS

5. Graphs will vary.

EXERCISE 5
Pages 203–204

1. ≈ 23°F
2. 9:00 P.M.
3. 2:00 P.M., 26°F
4. 7:00 A.M., 8°F
5. 2:00 A.M., 3:00 A.M., 5:00 P.M., 12:00 Midnight
6. 6:00 P.M.
7. 6:00 A.M.
8. 17°F; temperatures listed in order: 8, 10, 11, 11, 12, 13, 14, 14, 14, 15, 15, 16, 18, 18, 18, 18, 19, 21, 21, 23, 24, 25, 25, 26; 16 + 18 = 34; 34 ÷ 2 = 17
9. 18°F; 26 – 8 = 18
10. 9:00 A.M. to 10:00 A.M., 9°F; 19 – 10 = 9
11. 5:00 P.M. to 6:00 P.M., 7°F; 18 – 11 = 7
12. 6°F; 24 – 18 = 6
13. 16°F; 24 – 8 = 16
14. 8°F; 26 – 18 = 8
15. 16°F; 26 – 10 = 16

PRE-GED PRACTICE
EXERCISE 6
Page 205

1. **(4);** The graph does not give the entire history of the fund, so it's possible the price was higher in a year not shown by the graph.
2. **(3);** Since the value of $10,000 increases from $70,000 to $100,000 from 25 years to 30 years, assume that a greater increase than $30,000 will occur but that the increase will be less than $70,000 so $150,000 (an increase of $50,000) is the most logical choice.
3. **(4)**
4. **(1);** decreased 9 times, increased 10 times
5. **(3)**
6. **(5)**

EXERCISE 7
Pages 208–209

1.
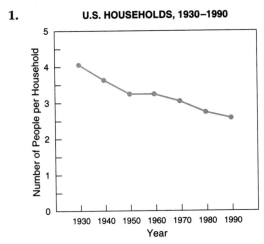

U.S. HOUSEHOLDS, 1930–1990

2.
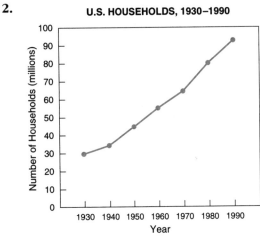

U.S. HOUSEHOLDS, 1930–1990

3.
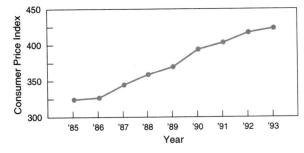

U.S. CONSUMER PRICE INDEX, 1985–1993

4.
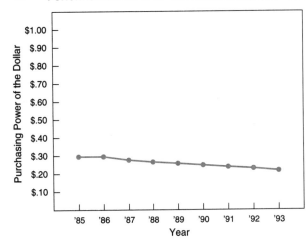

PURCHASING POWER OF THE U.S. DOLLAR, 1985–1993

EXERCISE 8
Pages 212–213

1. **4%**
2. **California**
3. **Alaska**
4. $\frac{1}{10}$
5. **5**
6. **17%;** California + Oregon + Washington = 11% + 4% + 2% = 17%
7. **Oregon**

8. **Alaska, 5,565 miles; California, 839 miles; Hawaii, 762 miles; Oregon, 305 miles; Washington, 152 miles;** $0.73 \times 7{,}623 \approx 5{,}565$; $0.11 \times 7{,}623 \approx 839$; $0.10 \times 7{,}623 \approx 762$; $0.04 \times 7{,}623 \approx 305$; $0.02 \times 7{,}623 \approx 152$

9. **Blacks; 92%**
10. **Whites; 58%**
11. **Females**
12. **Republicans; the graph labeled "All"**

PRE-GED PRACTICE
EXERCISE 9
Page 214

1. **(1)**
2. **(5)**
3. **(2)**; $0.49 \times 10{,}210 \approx 5{,}003$
4. **(5)**
5. **(4)**
6. **(5)**

EXERCISE 10
Pages 217–218

1. **CALIFORNIA VOTERS PROPOSITION 187**

Against 41%

For 59%

2. **POLITICS AS USUAL?**

New era 32%

Not sure 5%

Politics as usual 63%

3. **HOUSE OF REPRESENTATIVES VOTED ON IN 1994**

Democrat 47%

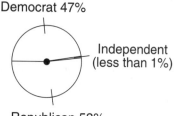

Independent (less than 1%)

Republican 53%

4. **U.S. GULF COASTLINE**

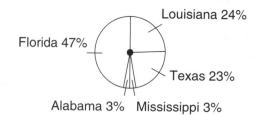

Florida 47%

Louisiana 24%

Texas 23%

Alabama 3%   Mississippi 3%

EXERCISE 11
Pages 220–221

1. $\frac{1}{4}$, **or 0.25, or 25%**; $\frac{2}{8} = \frac{1}{4} = 0.25 = 25\%$

2. $\frac{1}{2}$, **or 0.5, or 50%**; 4 favorable outcomes:
   $10, $10, $50, $100; $\frac{4}{8} = \frac{1}{2} = 0.5 = 50\%$

3. **$50 and $100**

4. **$5**; $50\% = \frac{1}{2} = \frac{4}{8}$, $5 occurs 4 times

5. $\frac{1}{2}$, **or 0.5, or 50%**

6. **1, or 100%**; $\frac{2}{2} = \frac{1}{1} = 1 = 100\%$

7. $\frac{1}{13}$, **or about 0.08, or about 8%**;
   $\frac{4}{52} = \frac{1}{13} \approx 0.08$ or 8%

8. $\frac{1}{6}$, **or about 0.17, or about 17%**

9. **90%**; $100\% - 10\% = 90\%$

10. $\frac{1}{10000}$, **or 0.0001, or 0.01%**

11. $\frac{1}{10}$, **or 0.1, or 10%**

12. $\frac{1}{20}$, **or 0.05, or 5%**; $\frac{5}{100} = \frac{1}{20} = 0.05 = 5\%$

13. $\frac{5}{9}$, **or about 0.56, or about 56%**;
    total $= 10 + 7 + 1 = 18$; $\frac{10}{18} = \frac{5}{9} \approx 0.56$ or 56%

14. **0, or 0%**; $\frac{0}{18} = 0 = 0\%$

PRE-GED PRACTICE
EXERCISE 12
Page 222

1. **(2)**	3. **(4)**	5. **(5)**
2. **(4)**	4. **(1)**	6. **(1)**

EXERCISE 13
Pages 225–227

1. **36 possible outcomes**

2. **11 sums;** the possible sums are 2, 3, 4, 5, 6, 7, 8, 9, 10, 11, and 12.

3. **(3,1), (2,2), and (1,3); $\frac{1}{12}$; $\frac{3}{36} = \frac{1}{12}$**

4. **$\frac{5}{36}$;** 5 favorable outcomes: (6,2), (5,3), (4,4), (3,5), (2,6)

5. **7; 6 favorable outcomes:** (6,1), (5,2), (4,3), (3,4), (2,5), (1,6)

6. **$\frac{1}{6}$;** 6 favorable outcomes: (1,1), (2,2), (3,3), (4,4), (5,5), (6,6); $\frac{6}{36} = \frac{1}{6}$

7. **BBB, BBG, BGB, BGG, GBB, GBG, GGB, GGG**

8. **$\frac{1}{8}$;** 1 favorable outcome: GGG

9. **$\frac{3}{8}$;** 3 favorable outcomes: BGG, GBG, GGB

10. **$\frac{1}{8}$;** 1 favorable outcome: GGB

11. **$\frac{1}{8}$;** 1 favorable outcome: BBB

12. **$\frac{1}{4}$;** 2 favorable outcomes: BBB, GGG; $\frac{2}{8} = \frac{1}{4}$

13. **GBB, BGB, BBG**

14. **$\frac{1}{8}$;** 1 favorable outcome: BGB

15. **(5)**

16. **(4);** 11 favorable outcomes

EXERCISE 14
Pages 229–230

1. **$\frac{11}{51}$, or about 0.22, or about 22%; dependent events;** $\frac{11}{51} \approx 0.22$ or 22%

2. **$\frac{3}{13}$, or about 0.23, or about 23%; independent events;** $\frac{12}{52} = \frac{3}{13} \approx 0.23$ or 23%

3. **$\frac{1}{2}$, or 0.5, or 50%; independent events**

4. **$\frac{1}{2}$, or 0.5, or 50%; independent events**

5. **$\frac{5}{9}$, or about 0.56, or about 56%; dependent events;** $\frac{5}{9} \approx 0.56$ or 56%

6. **$\frac{2}{5}$, or 0.4, or 40%; independent events;** $\frac{4}{10} = \frac{2}{5} = 0.4 = 40\%$

7. **(2)**

8. **(3); the likelihood of it raining tomorrow is greater if it rains today**

DATA ANALYSIS AND PROBABILITY REVIEW
Pages 231–237

1. **36;** 28 + 37 + 19 + 51 + 40 + 31 + 22 + 40 + 63 + 40 + 25 = 396; 396 ÷ 11 = 36

2. **37;** 19, 22, 25, 28, 31, <u>37</u>, 40, 40, 40, 51, 63

3. **40**

4. **44;** 63 − 19 = 44

5. **7 employees**

6. **Ads, Mail, and Editorial**

7.

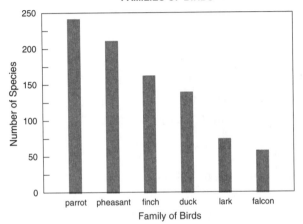

NUMBER OF SPECIES IN SELECTED FAMILIES OF BIRDS

8. **about $25,000**

9. **about 22 years**

10.

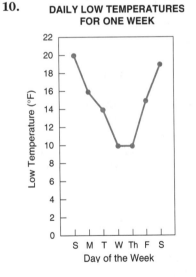

DAILY LOW TEMPERATURES FOR ONE WEEK

11. Food; $10\% \times 2 = 20\%$
12. $800; $0.40 \times \$2,000 = \$800$
13. **COMPONENTS**
     OF BLOOD

Cells 45%

Plasma 55%

14. $\frac{1}{2}$, **or 0.5, or 50%;** 3 favorable outcomes:

1, 3, 5; $\frac{3}{6} = \frac{1}{2} = 0.5 = 50\%$

15. $\frac{1}{8}$, **or 0.125, or 12.5%**

16. BB, BG, GB, GG

17. $\frac{1}{18}$, **or about 0.06, or about 6%;**

$\frac{2}{36} = \frac{1}{18} \approx 0.06$ or 6%

18. $\frac{1}{25}$, **or 0.04, or 4%**

19. (4); 4 out of 5 people at the party are female so write the proportion $\frac{4}{5} = \frac{?}{20}$ and $4 \times 20 \div 5 = 80 \div 5 = 16$

20. (1); (1) area $= 6 \times 9 = 54$; (2) area $= \pi \times 4^2 \approx 3.14 \times 16 \approx 50.24$; (3) area $= 7 \times 7 = 49$;

(4) area $= 5 \times 10 = 50$; (5) area $= \pi \times \frac{7}{2} \times$

$\frac{7}{2} \approx \frac{22}{7} \times \frac{7}{2} \times \frac{7}{2} \approx 38.5$

21. (2); 2 cups in a pint $\times$ 2 pints in a quart $\times$ 4 quarts in a gallon $= 16$ cups in a gallon so 10 gallons contains $16 \times 10 = 160$ cups

22. (3); a coin always has a 50% chance of heads and a 50% chance of tails

23. (5); (1) $\$.69 \div 2 \approx \$.35$; (2) $\$2 \div 5 = \$.40$; (3) $\$.35$; (4) $\$1.50 \div 4 \approx \$.38$; (5) $\$1 \div 3 \approx \$.333$ or $\$.34$

24. (4); (1) $\frac{8}{10} = .80$; $8\% = .08$;

(2) $0.8 = 0.80$; $\frac{4}{5} = 0.80$; $8\% = 0.08$;

(3) $80\% = 0.80$; $\frac{80}{100} = 0.80$;

(4) $\frac{4}{5} = 0.80$; $80\% = 0.80$; $0.8 = 0.80$;

(5) $8\% = 0.08$; $\frac{8}{100} = 0.08$; $0.8 = 0.80$;

25. (2)

26. (2); (1) 5 ft 5 in. + 5 ft 6 in. + 6 ft + 6 ft 2 in. + 5 ft 10 in. $= (5 \times 12) + 5 + (5 \times 12) + 6 + (6 \times 12) + (6 \times 12) + 2 + (5 \times 12) + 10 = 65 + 66 + 72 + 74 + 70 = 347$ in.; 347 in. $\div$ 5 $= 69.4$ or about 69 in.; 69 in. $\div$ 12 $= 5$ R9 or

5 ft 9 in.; (2) 6 ft + 6 ft + 5 ft 8 in. + 5 ft 7 in. + 5 ft 11 in. $= (6 \times 12) + (6 \times 12) + (5 \times 12) + 8 + (5 \times 12) + 7 + (5 \times 12) + 11 = 72 + 72 + 68 + 67 + 71 = 350$ in.; 350 in. $\div$ 5 $= 70$ in.; 70 in. $\div$ 12 $= 5$ R10 or 5 ft 10 in.; (3) 5 ft 4 in. + 5 ft 6 in. + 5 ft 11 in. + 6 ft + 6 ft 1 in. $= (5 \times 12) + 4 + (5 \times 12) + 6 + (5 \times 12) + 11 + (6 \times 12) + (6 \times 12) + 1 = 64 + 66 + 71 + 72 + 73 = 346$ in.; 346 in. $\div$ 5 $= 69.2$ in.; 69.2 in. $\div$ 12 $= 5$ R9.2 or about 5 ft 9 in.; (4) 6 ft 1 in. + 5 ft 9 in. + 5 ft 9 in. + 5 ft 5 in. + 5 ft 10 in. $= (6 \times 12) + 1 + (5 \times 12) + 9 + (5 \times 12) + 9 + (5 \times 12) + 5 + (5 \times 12) + 10 = 73 + 69 + 69 + 65 + 70 = 346$ in.; 346 in. $\div$ 5 $= 69.2$ in.; 69.2 in. $\div$ 12 $= 5$ R9.2 or about 5 ft 9 in.; (5) 6 ft 2 in. + 6 ft + 6 ft + 5 ft 7 in. + 5 ft 8 in. $= (6 \times 12) + 2 + (6 \times 12) + (6 \times 12) + (5 \times 12) + 7 + (5 \times 12) + 8 = 74 + 72 + 72 + 67 + 68 = 353$ in.; 353 in. $\div$ 5 $= 70.6$ in.; 70.6 in. $\div$ 12 $= 5.88$ or about 5 ft 9 in.

27. (5); (1) range: $8 - 0 = 8$; median of 0, 4, 5, 6, 7, 8: $(5 + 6) \div 2 = 5.5$; (2) range: $12 - 4 = 8$; median of 4, 5, 7, 10, 10, 12: $(7 + 10) \div 2 = 8.5$; (3) range: $10 - 2 = 8$; median of 2, 5, 6, 8, 8, 10: $(6 + 8) \div 2 = 7$; (4) range: $10 - 2 = 8$; median of 2, 3, 7, 8, 8, 10: $(7 + 8) \div 2 = 7.5$; (5) range: $9 - 1 = 8$; median of 1, 4, 7, 9, 9, 9: $(7 + 9) \div 2 = 8$

28. (2); 1.8 billion $= 1,800,000,000$; $1,800,000,000 \div 36 = 50,000,000$

29. (1); $52 - 14 = 38$; $3 \div 38 \approx .08$ or about 8 %

30. (4); $48 \times 1\frac{1}{2} = 48 \times \frac{3}{2} = 24 \times 3 = 72$ in.; 72 in. $\div$ 12 $= 6$ ft

31. (5)

32. (3); (1) $.08 \times 2 \times p = .16p$; (2) $.03 \times 8 \times p = .24p$; (3) $.05 \times 5 \times p = .25p$; (4) $.12 \times 1 \times p = .12p$

33. (4)

34. (5); each of $\frac{3}{5}$ and $\frac{4}{7}$ is greater than one-half.

35. (3)

CHAPTER 7: BASIC ALGEBRA CONCEPTS

EXERCISE 1
Pages 242–244

1. 216; $6 \times 6 \times 6 = 216$
2. 81; $9 \times 9 = 81$
3. 10
4. 2,401; $7 \times 7 \times 7 \times 7 = 2,401$
5. 1

6. **1,024;** $4 \times 4 \times 4 \times 4 \times 4 = 1,024$
7. **81;** $3 \times 3 \times 3 \times 3 = 81$
8. **64;** $2 \times 2 \times 2 \times 2 \times 2 \times 2 = 64$
9. **1**
10. **1;** $1 \times 1 \times 1 \times 1 \times 1 \times 1 \times 1 = 1$
11. **343;** $7 \times 7 \times 7 = 343$
12. **0;** $0 \times 0 \times 0 \times 0 \times 0 \times 0 = 0$
13. **5;** $5 \times 5 = 25$
14. **12;** $12 \times 12 = 144$
15. **0;** $0 \times 0 = 0$
16. **1;** $1 \times 1 = 1$
17. **6;** $6 \times 6 = 36$
18. **4;** $4 \times 4 = 16$
19. **8;** $8 \times 8 = 64$
20. **3;** $3 \times 3 = 9$
21.

Number	Square
1	$1^2 = 1$
2	$2^2 = 4$
3	$3^2 = 9$
4	$4^2 = 16$
5	$5^2 = 25$
6	$6^2 = 36$
7	$7^2 = 49$
8	$8^2 = 64$
9	$9^2 = 81$
10	$10^2 = 100$
11	$11^2 = 121$
12	$12^2 = 144$
13	$13^2 = 169$
14	$14^2 = 196$
15	$15^2 = 225$
20	$20^2 = 400$

22.

Number	Square Root
1	$\sqrt{1} = 1$
4	$\sqrt{4} = 2$
9	$\sqrt{9} = 3$
16	$\sqrt{16} = 4$
25	$\sqrt{25} = 5$
36	$\sqrt{36} = 6$
49	$\sqrt{49} = 7$
64	$\sqrt{64} = 8$
81	$\sqrt{81} = 9$
100	$\sqrt{100} = 10$
121	$\sqrt{121} = 11$
144	$\sqrt{144} = 12$
169	$\sqrt{169} = 13$
196	$\sqrt{196} = 14$
225	$\sqrt{225} = 15$
400	$\sqrt{400} = 20$

23. **64 square meters (64m²);** $8 \times 8 = 64$
24. **15 meters;** $\sqrt{225} = 15$
25. **4 and 5;** $\sqrt{16} = 4$, and $\sqrt{25} = 5$, so $\sqrt{20}$ lies between 4 and 5.
26. **12 and 13;** $\sqrt{144} = 12$, and $\sqrt{169} = 13$, so $\sqrt{150}$ lies between 12 and 13.
27. **8;** $\sqrt{60} < \sqrt{64} < \sqrt{70}$, and $\sqrt{64} = 8$

PRE-GED PRACTICE
EXERCISE 2
Page 245

1. **(2)**
2. **(3)**
3. **(5)**
4. **(1)**
5. **(3);** $1 + 2 + 3 = 6; 6^2 = 36$
6. **(2);** $\sqrt{289 - 225} = \sqrt{64} = 8$
7. **(5);** $36 - 25 = 11$
8. **(2);** $\sqrt{49} = 7; \sqrt{64} = 8; 7 + 8 = 15$

EXERCISE 3
Page 248

1. **2;** $(12 + 4) \div (1 + 7) = 16 \div 8 = 2$
2. **21;** $3^2 + 6^2 \div 3 = 9 + 36 \div 3 = 9 + 12 = 21$
3. **19;** $\sqrt{25} + 6 \times 4 - 10 = 5 + 6 \times 4 - 10 = 5 + 24 - 10 = 29 - 10 = 19$
4. **16;** $[(30 - 8) \div 2] + 5 = [22 \div 2] + 5 = 11 + 5 = 16$
5. **4;** $24 \div (1^5 + 5) = 24 \div (1 + 5) = 24 \div 6 = 4$
6. **8;** $100 \div 5 - 3 \times 4 = 20 - 3 \times 4 = 20 - 12 = 8$
7. **5;** $[3 \times (11 - 4)] - 16 = [3 \times 7] - 16 = 21 - 16 = 5$
8. **3;** $(\sqrt{49}) - 1) \div 2 = (7 - 1) \div 2 = 6 \div 2 = 3$
9. **5;** $(2^3 + 3^3) \div 7 = (8 + 27) \div 7 = 35 \div 7 = 5$
10. **7;** $13 + 6 \times 2 \div 4 - 9 = 13 + 12 \div 4 - 9 = 13 + 3 - 9 = 16 - 9 = 7$
11. **18;** $3 \times (10 - 4) \div 9 + 4^2 = 3 \times 6 \div 9 + 4^2 = 3 \times 6 \div 9 + 16 = 18 \div 9 + 16 = 2 + 16 = 18$
12. **14;** $9 \times 8^0 + (6 - 1) = 9 \times 8^0 + 5 = 9 \times 1 + 5 = 9 + 5 = 14$
13. **44;** $60 - [25 - (13 - 4)] = 60 - [25 - 9] = 60 - 16 = 44$
14. **20;** $\sqrt{100} \div 5 + 3 \times 6 = 10 \div 5 + 3 \times 6 = 2 + 3 \times 6 = 2 + 18 = 20$
15. **1;** $(5 + 7) \div (12 - 8) \div 3 = 12 \div 4 \div 3 = 3 \div 3 = 1$
16. **2;** $5 \times 8 \div 2 \times 1 \div 10 = 40 \div 2 \times 1 \div 10 = 20 \times 1 \div 10 = 20 \div 10 = 2$

PRE-GED PRACTICE
EXERCISE 4
Page 249

1. **(3);** (1) 35; (2) 44; (3) 80; (4) 34; (5) 44
2. **(5);** (1) 31; (2) 30; (3) 58; (4) 31; (5) 21
3. **(2);** $14 - 2^3 + 6 \times 2 = 14 - 8 + 6 \times 2 = 14 - 8 + 12 = 6 + 12 = 18$
4. **(1);** $40 + 12 \div 6 = 40 + 2 = 42$; (1) $6 + 4 \times 3 + 12 = 6 + 12 + 12 = 18 + 12 = 30 \neq 42$
5. **(3);** $5 \times (8 - 2) \div 4 = 5 \times 6 \div 4 = 7.5$
6. **(2);** $1 \times 2 \times 3 \times 4 = 24$
7. **(2);** $5 \times 2 + 4 \times 2 = 18$
8. **(5)**

EXERCISE 5
Pages 253–254

1. **yes;** $9 \times 3 = 27$
2. **no;** $10 + 3 \neq 7$
3. **yes;** $24 - 14 = 10$
4. **yes;** $4 \times 8 = 32$
5. **yes;** $\frac{22}{2} = 11$
6. **no;** $\frac{4}{5} \neq 20$
7. $\boldsymbol{y = 7};$ $\frac{5y}{5} = \frac{35}{5}; y = 7$
8. $\boldsymbol{n = 11};$ $n - 1 + 1 = 10 + 1; n = 11$
9. $\boldsymbol{y = 1};$ $y + 20 - 20 = 21 - 20; y = 1$
10. $\boldsymbol{z = 6};$ $\frac{z}{3} \times 3 = 2 \times 3; z = 6$
11. $\boldsymbol{n = 4};$ $\frac{8n}{8} = \frac{32}{8}; n = 4$
12. $\boldsymbol{n = 7};$ $n + 1 - 1 = 8 - 1; n = 7$
13. $\boldsymbol{x = 36};$ $\frac{x}{4} \times 4 = 9 \times 4; x = 36$
14. $\boldsymbol{a = 28};$ $a - 17 + 17 = 11 + 17; a = 28$
15. $\boldsymbol{z = 9};$ $z - 4 + 4 = 5 + 4; z = 9$
16. $\boldsymbol{a = 20};$ $\frac{10a}{10} = \frac{200}{10}; a = 20$
17. $\boldsymbol{y = 32};$ $\frac{y}{2} \times 2 = 16 \times 2; y = 32$
18. $\boldsymbol{x = 10};$ $x + 9 - 9 = 19 - 9; x = 10$
19. $\boldsymbol{a = 34};$ $a + 3 - 3 = 37 - 3; a = 34$
20. $\boldsymbol{z = 6};$ $\frac{9z}{9} = \frac{54}{9}; z = 6$
21. $\boldsymbol{y = 14};$ $y - 8 + 8 = 6 + 8; y = 14$
22. $\boldsymbol{a = 7};$ $\frac{a}{7} \times 7 = 1 \times 7; a = 7$
23. $\boldsymbol{x = 18};$ $x - 15 + 15 = 3 + 15; x = 18$
24. $\boldsymbol{x = 25};$ $\frac{2x}{2} = \frac{50}{2}; x = 25$
25. $\boldsymbol{n = 36};$ $\frac{n}{6} \times 6 = 6 \times 6; n = 36$
26. $\boldsymbol{z = 9};$ $z + 14 - 14 = 23 - 14; z = 9$
27. **(3);** $4 \times 3 = 12$
28. **(4);** $6 - 6 \neq 12$

EXERCISE 6
Pages 257–258

1. **4 items;** $\$28 = n \times \$7; n = 4$
2. **\$2,000;** $\$360 = p \times 0.06 \times 3; p = \$2,000$
3. **15 hits;** $0.300 = \frac{h}{50}; h = 15$
4. **50°F;** $F = 1.8 \times 10 + 32; F = 50$
5. **about 57 miles per hour;** $100 = r \times 1.75; r \approx 57$
6. **\$4,000;** $i = \$10,000 \times 0.08 \times 5 = \$4,000$
7. **\$151.96;** $c = nr; c = 4 \times \$37.99 = \$151.96$
8. **4%;** $i = prt; \$80 = \$1,000 \times r \times 2; r = 0.04 = 4\%$
9. **86°F;** $F = 1.8C + 32; F = 1.8 \times 30 + 32 = 86$
10. **330 miles;** $d = rt; d = 55 \times 6 = 330$
11. **0.300;** $a = \frac{h}{n}; a = \frac{12}{40} = 0.300$
12. **5 hours;** $d = rt; 300 = 60t; t = 5$
13. **about 2 hits;** $a = \frac{h}{n}; 0.380 = \frac{h}{5}; h = 1.9 \approx 2$
14. **\$1.245 per gallon;** $c = nr; \$14.94 = 12r; r = \$1.245$
15. **3 years;** $i = prt; \$750 = \$5,000 \times 0.05 \times t; t = 3$
16. **9°F;** $F = 1.8C + 32; F = 1.8 \times 20 + 32 = 68$ $F = 1.8 \times 15 + 32 = 59; 68 - 59 = 9$

EXERCISE 7
Pages 261–262

1. *J*	9. (2, 1)	17. *C, D, H, K*
2. *H*	10. (−3, −2)	18. *F, G, M, O*
3. *M*	11. (−8, 3)	19. *A, I, J, P*
4. *A*	12. (4, 10)	20. *B, E, L, N*
5. *L*	13. (1, −7)	
6. *C*	14. (5, −8)	
7. *G*	15. (−7, 9)	
8. *B*	16. (−4, −9)	

21–28.

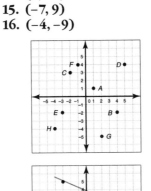

29–30.

PRE-GED PRACTICE
EXERCISE 8
Page 263

1. (4)   2. (2)

EXERCISE 9
Pages 266–268

1. $\frac{1}{2}$; $\dfrac{\text{vertical change}}{\text{horizontal change}} = \dfrac{3}{6} = \dfrac{1}{2}$

2. −1; $\dfrac{\text{vertical change}}{\text{horizontal change}} = \dfrac{-4}{4} = -1$

3. 1; $\dfrac{\text{vertical change}}{\text{horizontal change}} = \dfrac{3}{3} = 1$

4. 4; $\dfrac{\text{vertical change}}{\text{horizontal change}} = \dfrac{4}{1} = 4$

5. 0; $\dfrac{\text{vertical change}}{\text{horizontal change}} = \dfrac{0}{4} = 0$

6. 0; $\dfrac{\text{vertical change}}{\text{horizontal change}} = \dfrac{0}{4} = 0$

7. slope = −2;

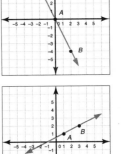

8. slope = $\frac{1}{2}$;

9. slope = 3;

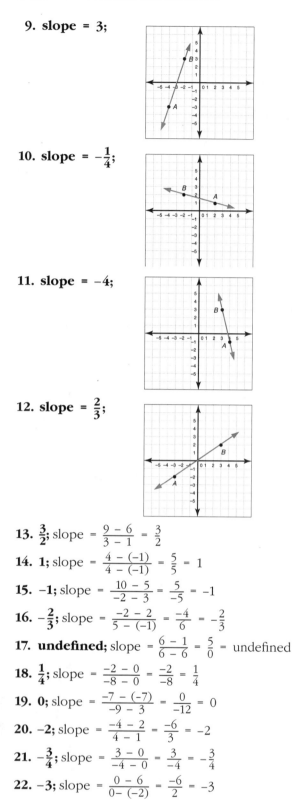

10. slope = $-\frac{1}{4}$;

11. slope = -4;

12. slope = $\frac{2}{3}$;

13. $\frac{3}{2}$; slope = $\frac{9-6}{3-1}$ = $\frac{3}{2}$

14. 1; slope = $\frac{4-(-1)}{4-(-1)}$ = $\frac{5}{5}$ = 1

15. -1; slope = $\frac{10-5}{-2-3}$ = $\frac{5}{-5}$ = -1

16. $-\frac{2}{3}$; slope = $\frac{-2-2}{5-(-1)}$ = $\frac{-4}{6}$ = $-\frac{2}{3}$

17. **undefined**; slope = $\frac{6-1}{6-6}$ = $\frac{5}{0}$ = undefined

18. $\frac{1}{4}$; slope = $\frac{-2-0}{-8-0}$ = $\frac{-2}{-8}$ = $\frac{1}{4}$

19. 0; slope = $\frac{-7-(-7)}{-9-3}$ = $\frac{0}{-12}$ = 0

20. -2; slope = $\frac{-4-2}{4-1}$ = $\frac{-6}{3}$ = -2

21. $-\frac{3}{4}$; slope = $\frac{3-0}{-4-0}$ = $\frac{3}{-4}$ = $-\frac{3}{4}$

22. -3; slope = $\frac{0-6}{0-(-2)}$ = $\frac{-6}{2}$ = -3

**PRE-GED PRACTICE
EXERCISE 10
Page 269**

1. (1)
2. (3)
3. (2)
4. (4)
5. (1)
6. (2)
7. (4)
8. (3)

**BASIC ALGEBRA CONCEPTS REVIEW
Pages 270–275**

1. **5;** $5 \times 5 = 25$
2. **no;** $\frac{3}{8} \neq 24$
3. **$y = 11$;** $y - 7 + 7 = 4 + 7; y = 11$
4. **48.2;** $F = 1.8 \times 9 + 32 = 48.2$
5. **1**
6. **6;** $3^2 + 6 \times 2 - 15 = 9 + 12 - 15 = 6$
7. **$3,750;** $i = prt; 900 = p \times 0.08 \times 3; p = 3,750$
8. **$z = 11$;** $\frac{3z}{3} = \frac{33}{3}; z = 11$
9. **32;** $2 \times 2 \times 2 \times 2 \times 2 = 32$
10. **5 hours;** $d = rt; 250 = 50t; t = 5$
11. **$x = 30$;** $\frac{x}{2} \times 2 = 15 \times 2; x = 30$
12. **27;** $(4 + 5) \times (6 - 3) = 9 \times 3 = 27$
13. **yes;** $4 \times 5 = 20$
14. **8;** $8 \times 8 = 64$
15. **about $.10;** $c = nr; 1.09 = 12 \times r; r \approx .10$
16. **$n = 8$;** $n + 19 - 19 = 27 - 19; n = 8$
17. **-2;** slope = $\frac{8-2}{-2-1}$ = $\frac{6}{-3}$ = -2
18. **R**
19. **(1, –3)**
20. **$\frac{1}{3}$**

21. (5); $10 \div $1.347 \approx 7$

22. (3); $45 \div 2\frac{1}{2} = 45 \div \frac{5}{2} = 45 \times \frac{2}{5} = 9 \times 2 = 18$

23. (2); 4% of $18,000 = .04 \times 18,000 = 720$;
$18,000 + $720 = $18,720; $18,720 \div 12 = $1,560$

24. (3); $100\% - 7\% = 93\%$

25. (4); $6 \times 6 = 36$

26. (2); 30 oz $\div$ 16 = 1 R14 or 1 lb 14 oz;
1 lb 14 oz is close to 2 pounds.

27. (2); $\frac{13}{9} = \frac{?}{36}$; $13 \times 36 \div 9 = 52$ white keys;
36 black keys + 52 white keys = 88 keys
altogether

28. (5); range: $115,000 - $74,000 = $41,000$;
median of $74,000, $85,500, $99,900, $109,000,
and $115,000 is $99,900; mode: none; mean:
$74,000 + $85,500 + $99,900 + $109,000 +
$115,000 = $483,400; $483,400 \div 5 = $96,680$

29. (4); $200^1 = 200$; $5^4 = 625$; $1^{200} = 1$;
$2^{10} = 1,024$; $20^2 = 400$

30. (5); (1) $1.99 + $4.95 + 8($4.99) + 4($2.95) =
$1.99 + $4.95 + $39.92 + $11.80 = 58.66;
(2) $4.95 + $11.80 = 16.75; (4) $58.66 \div 16 \approx
3.67

31. (3); $20 \div $.05 = 400$

32. (5)

33. (4)

34. (2)

35. (3); 8 ft = $8 \times 12 = 96$ in.; (1) $C = \pi \times 2 \times 3 =
6 \times 3.14 = 18.84$; $C = \pi \times 2 \times 8 = 16 \times 3.14 =
50.24$; $18.84 + 50.24 = 69.08$; (2) $C = \pi \times 2 \times
4 = 8 \times 3.14 = 25.12$; $C = \pi \times 2 \times 9 = 18 \times
3.14 = 56.52$; $25.12 + 56.52 = 81.64$; (3) $C = \pi \times
2 \times 5 = 10 \times 3.14 = 31.40$; $C = \pi \times 2 \times 10 =
20 \times 3.14 = 62.80$; $31.40 + 62.80 = 94.20$;
(4) $C = \pi \times 2 \times 6 = 12 \times 3.14 = 37.68$; $C = \pi
\times 2 \times 11 = 22 \times 3.14 = 69.08$; $37.68 + 69.08 =
106.76$; (5) $C = \pi \times 2 \times 7 = 14 \times 3.14 = 43.96$;
$C = \pi \times 2 \times 12 = 24 \times 3.14 = 75.36$; $43.96 +
75.36 = 119.32$

36. (1); (1) probability of 1 out of 4; (2) probability
of 4 out of 52 or 1 out of 13; (3) probability of
$\frac{4}{52} \times \frac{3}{51} = \frac{1}{221}$; (4) probability of 1 out of 36;
(5) probability of 1 out of 6

Glossary

A

angle: a figure made of two rays extending from the same point

area: the amount of surface covered by the figure; measured in square units

B

bar graph: a graph made up of rectangular bars that extend upward or lengthwise; the height of each bar corresponds to one number in the data set; the higher the bar, the greater the number; used to display numerical data given in categories

base: a number used as a factor in a product; in the expression 2^4, 2 is called the base

C

central angle: an angle formed at the center of a circle

circle: a curved flat figure every point of which is the same distance from the center

circle graph: a graph that shows parts of a whole; the circle is the whole, or 100%; the circle is divided into parts, and all the parts add up to 100%; often used to display data given as percents

circumference: the distance around a circle

compatible numbers: numbers used in mental math and estimation; they are close to the original numbers and are used instead of the numbers to make the solution easier or quicker to achieve

coordinate plane: a plane formed by two number lines perpendicular to each other at 0

cross product: in a proportion, the numerator of one ratio multiplied by the denominator of the other ratio

cube: a rectangular solid made up of squares; the length, width, and height of a cube are equal

D

data: information that is collected and analyzed; often, but not always, numerical

decimals: numbers based on a whole being split into ten equal parts one or more times; the U.S. monetary system is based on the decimal system

denominator: the aspect of a fraction that refers to the number of parts in the whole; written on the bottom of the fraction

dependent events: a situation in which the outcome of one event depends on the outcome of the other

diameter: a line segment that crosses the circle through its center from one side to the other

difference: the result of subtraction

E

equation: a statement that two amounts are equal

equivalent fractions: fractions that have the same value

estimate: an approximate answer

exponent: a number that shows how many times the base is used as a factor in a product; in the expression 2^4, 4 is called the exponent

F

formula: an equation with more than one variable; an equation that is always true

fraction: a way of showing parts of a whole; made up of two numbers, the numerator and the denominator

front-end digits: an estimation strategy involving the use of far left digits, or front-end digits

I

improper fraction: a fraction with a numerator equal to or greater than its denominator

independent events: a situation in which the outcome of one event does not depend on the outcome of the other

interest: the money you earn on a savings account or pay on a loan

interest formula: interest = principal × rate × time

inverse operations: operations that undo each other:
1. The inverse of addition is subtraction.
2. The inverse of subtraction is addition.
3. The inverse of multiplication is division.
4. The inverse of division is multiplication.

L

line: a set of points continuing in opposite directions

line graph: graph made up of points that are connected by line segments; often used to display data over a period of time

lowest terms: describes a situation in which the numerator and denominator of a fraction cannot be divided evenly (remainder of zero) by any whole number other than 1

M

mean: the average value of a data set

median: the middle value of a data set listed in order

mental math strategies: finding an answer without writing any numbers

mixed numbers: values between two whole numbers, or the combination of a whole number and a fraction

mode: the item that occurs most often in a data set

N

numerator: the aspect of a fraction that indicates the number of parts; written on the top of the fraction

O

order of operations: the set of rules agreed upon by mathematicians for finding the value of arithmetic expressions:
1. Do operations within parentheses.
2. Do exponents and square roots.
3. Do multiplication and division.
4. Do addition and subtraction.

ordered pair: a pair of coordinates that tell exactly where a point lies in a coordinate plane

origin: the point where the x-axis and y-axis meet on a coordinate plane; its coordinates are (0, 0)

P

parallel lines: lines that run in the same direction and that do not cross or intersect

percent: a means of expressing a number as part of a whole; the word *percent* means "of 100"

perimeter: the distance around a figure such as a triangle, rectangle, or square

perpendicular lines: lines that intersect to form right angles

principal: the amount of money invested or borrowed

probability: the chance of something happening; a measure of how likely it is that something will happen

problem-solving strategies: strategies that include drawing a picture, guessing and checking, and using information from a table

product: the result of multiplication

proportion: an expression made up of two equal ratios

Q

quotient: the result of division

R

radius: the distance from the center to any point on the curve of the circle

range: the difference between the greatest and least items of a data set

rate: an expression that shows a relationship between two quantities measured in different units

ratio: a comparison of two numbers

ray: a set of points continuing in one direction only

rectangle: a four-sided figure with four right angles

rectangular solid: a three-dimensional figure made up of rectangles; commonly called a box

repeating decimal: a decimal number with one or more digits that repeat themselves

right angle: an angle that measures 90°

rounding: a common estimation strategy in which you go up or down to the nearest 0

S

segment: a set of points forming the shortest path between two points

slope formula: a formula for finding the slope: slope = $\frac{y_2 - y_1}{x_2 - x_1}$, where (x_1, y_1) and (x_2, y_2) are the ordered pairs of two points on the line

slope: a measure of how "steep" a line is

solution: the value of the variable that makes the equation a true statement

square: a four-sided figure with four right angles and four equal sides

square root: the number that can be squared to get the original number

sum: the result of addition

T

tree diagram: a diagram that shows all possible outcomes for a probability problem

triangle: a three-sided figure

U

unit price: the price per unit of an item

unit rate: the rate for one unit of a given quantity

V

variable: a letter used to represent an unknown amount

volume: a measure of the space inside a three-dimensional figure; measured in cubic units

W

whole numbers: the numbers beginning with 0, 1, 2, 3, and so on

X

x-axis: the horizontal number line of a coordinate plane

Y

y-axis: the vertical number line on a coordinate plane

Index